MW00339126

THE STORY KEEPER

WEAVING THE THREADS OF TIME AND
MEMORY, A MEMOIR

FRED FELDMAN

ISBN 9789493231047 (ebook)

ISBN 9789493231030 (paperback)

ISBN 9789493231054 (hardcover)

Copyright © Fred Feldman, 2021

Amsterdam Publishers

info@amsterdampublishers.com

For book presentations, questions or comments, please contact the author at: fred.
feldman@gmail.com

Frontcover: Photo of line of refugees (image #43124) obtained with permission from the
United States Holocaust Memorial Museum image courtesy of Dan Lenchner. (image
rotated)

All rights reserved. No part of this publication may be reproduced, distributed, or
transmitted in any form or by any means, including photocopying, recording, or other
electronic or mechanical methods, without the prior written permission of the author,
except in the case of brief quotations embodied in critical reviews and certain other
noncommercial uses permitted by copyright law. For permission requests, write to the
author, addressed "Attention: Permissions," at the address below.

CONTENTS

LIST OF PLATES

Plates in this book and the page number:

I dedicate this book, in love, to my wife Rhoda Irene Feldman, who put up with my obsession for more than 50 years, to discover all I could about from where I came, and who came with me on our own journeys of personal discovery and growth.

Without her, I would never have dared to go on this journey alone.

Only guard yourself and guard your soul carefully, lest you forget the things your eyes saw, and lest these things depart your heart all the days of your life, and you shall make them known to your children, and to your children's children.

...Source: Deuteronomy 4:9

PREFACE

They fled the war machine from countless lands. Deciding to leave was always the hardest part. To stay and hope or to leave family and friends and all that they had known and loved for generations was the impossible question. There had always been strife and war, and life had never been easy for most. But they had been able to adjust and to survive. Was today different?

Life got more difficult day by day and abuse accelerated. Women were the first to suffer, and rape became a weapon of war. Tolerance for racial and religious differences rapidly decayed and old sectarian strife took its place. Those who were friends became enemies. Abusers rose in power and bystanders fearfully turned away their eyes. Hope degenerated, and fear took its place in the old and the young.

In time, the only decision left was to flee, to look for safety, even temporarily, but still to keep the spark of hope alive that tomorrow might be better, that someplace else would bring some measure of safety, and that humanity might prevail.

Thousands, even millions, fled during World War II, leaving all behind. First short steps, leaving their village, their state, their country, hoping beyond hope that they had now reached a place that they might call home again. Hoping that the loved ones they had left behind might have found a way to survive. And always hoping that someday, someday, they might be able to go back to what had once been home and find their loved ones again and return to what had been normal lives.

In the world today, the despair seen in the past is replayed. Even in a world of technological and scientific highs, the despairs of societal and cultural lows are again on display. While millions relax and enjoy their daily life, reading of the tragedies on the other side of the world or seeing them, one by one, live on their televisions, thousands and millions live and die by the barbarism that has engulfed them, that they had done nothing to cause, and that they're helpless to stop.

Yet again, millions are on the run, fleeing their homes, their lands, their families trekking by foot through deserts, fields and forests, climbing hills and mountains to get away, fording rivers and lakes and seas, all the while mourning those they've lost on the way. Every time hoping that they have finally again found a home.

Arab conflict in Africa, unending devastating civil war in Syria, armed struggle in Ukraine with Russia, continued violence in Iraq, Afghanistan, Somalia, the South Sudan and Congo. All created armies of refugees, and we keep seeing pictures of long lines of displaced peoples on roads carrying bags of rags and possessions, pulling their old and carrying their young – desperate for a home and for peace.

Yesterday, the same could be seen. In the 1930s and 1940s the very same conflicts, the battle for power and conquest and the descent into barbarism and, with it, the struggle for survival. The very same question of "Do I stay, or do I leave?" The search for home, for safety, for survival, for a future is paramount today as before. And always and always, even in the depths of despair, there is the effort to keep alive the last spark of hope, the belief that there could be a future for them and for their children.

This is a story ultimately without a time and ultimately without a place. It is a story of families across generations of peace and of war, of homes that become lost and hopes that are kept, and a belief in a future that's better than the present.

While following one family caught in the ravages of war during the Holocaust, it is not a Holocaust story. It is a story that mirrors any of the selfsame families caught in similar circumstances today. While following Jews trapped in a world turned against them, it can easily be mirrored in the sectarian strife and misery of Muslims and Christians attacked in lands where they are "the other" today.

The spark of hope and the belief in a better future drove the family in this story in the past and drives those families today.

Lesbos, Greece. 2016

"Look," she cried. "Straight out there! On the horizon! Do you see it? There's a dinghy bouncing violently up and down on the waves. They're pounding the boat. With my binoculars, I can see people in life jackets holding onto the sides for dear life! The boat's packed solid with people. Oh no! Some of them have been knocked off and gone under! It'll be a miracle if the whole thing doesn't sink."

Over the next hours, they watched as the boat teetered precariously with each wave strike, but slowly it made its way through the turbulent waters toward the shore.

Crammed with refugees fleeing poverty and war in Syria, those on the boat only wanted a chance for themselves and their children to find a place of safety, a home. Seeing the last wave threatening to overturn the boat, with the packed women and children screaming and to keep more from drowning, Talya, along with teammates from IsraAID, plunged into the surf to help pull the boat its last few feet to safety, to help give at least temporary refuge. To help the traumatized children.

Mendel would have been proud.

INTRODUCTION: THE INTERVIEW. PALO ALTO 2002

The past, the present, and the future are inextricably woven together. Like a tapestry with a riot of happy colors in one area, but dim and dark and uncertain in others, with threads that seem to pass tightly and easily from one part to another; but in some places with threads worn and damaged and almost lost. What stories they tell, of times past and times present. One thing is certain: they form the whole and, in many ways, the care with how they're assembled predicts the future and whether the tapestry, the life itself, will survive.

It's 2002 in modern day Palo Alto. An old man and a visitor are seated around an extensive wrought iron table with a glass top. They're looking intently at each other, in conversation, and adjacent to the table there's a movie camera on top of a tripod with camera gear around it. On the table lies a large collection of maps, papers, and pictures. They're just beginning an interview, the camera is rolling, and the old man stares quizzically at the camera gear aimed at him and asks in an old European accent, "What is that?"

"It's a movie camera I brought with me. We're going to do some more taping of your stories, about life before, during, and after the Holocaust. You remember? Like before when I taped you in South Bend? Fourteen years ago."

"How long will we do that?"

"As long as it takes. I'll be here all week. That's all I'm doing this week. I'll be here with you, talking and remembering, like we did before. I have lots of questions and I brought maps and pictures we can look at. Is that okay? We'll rest whenever you get tired."

The old man seems to be getting used to the idea and starts to look at all the paperwork and pictures more than at the camera and all the gear.

Quietly... "OK. I'm not tired. What do you want to know?"

And so, the process starts. The story. Recording times and lives that started years ago on the other side of the world in a little town in Poland, long populated by hard working, religiously observant people living in poor surroundings, but rich with family life and oblivious to the cruel future that fate had in store for them.

PART I

THE PAST

BEFORE THE WAR / A DREAM REMEMBERED

Shmul Mendel Felman / Sokolow Podlaski 1930s

It was a cloudy grey morning in early spring in Sokolow in 1934 with the rain clouds just starting to drizzle and the wind sweeping the rain over the peddlers in the Big Market square. Shmul Mendel was hurrying through the square to go help at the family's store. He was returning from a morning chore and passed by Chaya and her two girls, Freyde and Leah, getting ready to sell their goods.

Mendel's older brother, Fischel, had introduced Mendel to all his friends including Freyde, her best friend Shayndel Pfefferkranz, and others that Mendel had seen from around the town. Freyde was a beauty. Freyde had many friends in town and she and Mendel started taking walks together (**Photo 1**), sharing local gossip or talking about what the latest news was with their families. During one walk around town, Freyde could be seen arm-in-arm with her close friends Yitka Vloss and Elke Rosenstein chatting about their boyfriends. Dressed nattily in their winter coats and rakish hats tilted smartly to one side, they posed in front of one of the town buildings while a street photographer snapped a picture of the three friends (**Photo 2**).

They enjoyed each other's company, even while ominous events were gathering in countries outside Poland of which they were only dimly aware, and which would radically shape their lives. None of them had any inkling of the impending war that would separate them.

Rojza / Sokolow 1930s

Mendel's older sister Rojza was a rebel in the family (**Photo 3**). She knew of changing political activities going on in Germany and, at an early age, became acquainted through her friends with youth movements that were gaining steam in Eastern Europe.

While Mendel and his brother were singularly focused on their home life and helping their parents, Rojza became convinced that conditions for Jews would deteriorate and that she would ultimately have to leave her home to go to Palestine.

One day in July of 1936, Mendel's sister Rojza left home and this time wasn't coming back. She had taken the train and was running away. Mendel went after her to bring her back, but to no avail. Rojza was gone! The circumstances of her leaving, her fate, and the family's fate remained an agonizing unresolved mystery for the next 79 years!

In 1936, Mendel's father passed away, and times became more difficult for his family.

The Interview Continues. Palo Alto 2002

The interviewer says to the old man, "When I interviewed you the first time in South Bend 14 years ago, we covered the time from the early days in Sokolow until the end of World War II. I have those notes and the video recording of that interview, so we don't have to repeat that. We can continue with what happened after that."

But the old man will have none of that. He responds in broken English, "Wait. Wait. There's a lot more to tell you. One of those pictures you show me now. It brings back memories. I know those people. They were wonderful. So many memories!"

It's an old photo he looks at (**Photo 4**) that shows a group of young people, 11 of them, nicely dressed. Though cracked in parts, yellow and faded and with "1938 Sokolow Podlaski" written on the back, it's survived the war and the passages of time. Somehow, it's come into his possession. It has names written on the back in Yiddish and the names have been translated and written in English on the back in spidery handwriting.

He says sorrowfully, "Of the group, only four survived the war." He sighs, "Life in Sokolow became harder and harder during the 1930s, especially after Rojza ran away from home. When the war broke out, everything changed. On September 1st, 1939, Hitler attacked Poland. The German army rapidly overran the country. The week before the Germans came into Sokolow, they bombed the town, killing 500 people."

FLIGHT AND SURVIVAL

Sokolow, September 1939

Mendel was working in the store with his mother when the first bomb fell, not far from the market where Chaya sold her geese and where Freyde and Leah were often found. More bombs fell throughout the city center killing many of the Jews living and working there as German airplanes screamed over the town. In the panic and chaos that followed, Mendel heard that Shayndel's sister was one of the first ones killed as much of the town's center became destroyed.

German airplanes were still visible in the sky, with chaos and devastation around Mendel. His thoughts were frantic. "What happened to my family, my mother, my brothers and sister? Where is Freyde and her family?"

Mendel ran through the smoke and rubble to her house and found Freyde and her family unharmed, but badly shaken. His family had also survived the brutal attack. Over the next days, they learned that Germany had begun the war and that the Polish military had collapsed against the onslaught. Germany and Russia had reached agreement in the Molotov-Ribbentrop Pact that the Vistula River running through Warsaw would be the dividing line between German and Russian territory. It would have left Sokolow in the Russian zone, but the German troops ignored that and marched further, occupying Sokolow by September 11th. The next days were terrible.

There was much debate and consternation among the Jewish families of the town about what to expect and what to do. Maybe it wouldn't be so terrible. After all, this wasn't the first time Sokolow had been occupied. On the other hand, who knew what to really expect as German troops ran all over town harassing anyone they came across, shooting their guns wildly, and terrorizing everyone.

Two weeks after occupying the town, a drunken group of soldiers found Freyde on the street and raped her. She escaped, screaming and crying, running to Mendel's store.

"I can't stay here anymore," she told him, sobbing uncontrollably, while she told him what had happened. "I don't know how, but I'm going to leave and run to the Soviet zone. You decide what you're going to do. I love you, but I can't stay here anymore. We can go together, or I'll go alone as soon as I can, but I'm leaving, no matter what."

Mendel held her, comforting her as much as possible and assured her that if she would leave, he would go with her.

The local German commander soon learned that he had gone deeper into Poland than allowed and pulled his troops out of town with the Red Army coming into Sokolow on September 27th. Over the next two weeks, the Soviets and Germany reached a new agreement that Germany would take back control of Sokolow and Poland as far east as the Bug River, 14 miles east of Sokolow. Before the Red Army retreated from the town to the other side of the Bug River in the beginning of October, they told the occupants that it was their last chance to leave if they didn't want to remain behind when the German army came back.

Mendel told Freyde, "This is our only chance. You and I are leaving now and going to the Soviet side of the Bug. Tell your mother and sister to get ready to go. I'll tell my mother, my sister and brothers and anyone else who listens that we all have to leave."

Mendel ran to prepare his family to leave. Without telling his mother Chinka what had happened to Freyde, he said to her, "You have to pack whatever we can take with us and all of us have to leave. This is our last chance before the Germans come back. The Nazis hate all of us Jews and have already made life in Germany impossible for Jews. There's no knowing what will happen to us if we stay behind. We have to leave now."

His mother Chinka argued with him, "During World War I we have been occupied by the Germans and survived. It was hard, but we made it through. How much harder can it be? Besides, where will we go and how will we live? We don't know anyone on the Soviet side. How will we live from day to day? What will you do? How will we eat? Where will we live? It might be hard, but we should all stay. I've already lost one daughter who ran away and left; I don't want to lose you also. We're not going."

They argued throughout the night, with Mendel unable to convince Chinka. When Freyde came to collect Mendel, she learned that none of his family would go with them.

Chinka said to Freyde, "Don't leave. If you don't leave, Mendel won't leave."

But Freyde said she couldn't stay. "I have to leave!"

Mendel took all his clothes and a bicycle and got ready to go. He helped Freyde pack everything and got a horse and buggy. They went back to say goodbye to his mother who was adamant she wasn't going. He kissed her, and Chinka said to Freyde, "Up to now I've taken care of Mendel. Now it's up to you to take care of him," and with that, Mendel left on his bike while Freyde left on the buggy.

The trauma of leaving his family behind was something Mendel would never forget. Leaving behind his mother Chinka, his sister Surah Rifke, 16 years old, his brother Moishe, 13 years old, and his older brother Fischel, then 28 years old, was painful beyond words. Even worse, Fischel had been mobilized for the Polish army on September 1st but was captured by the Germans and put in prison. Fischel's wife and young son also weren't going to leave and decided to stay behind in Sokolow.

Mendel and Freyde hurried to Freyde's house where her mother Chaya and sister Leah, with many regrets, were also ready to leave with them. Leah's fiancée, Velvul Lopata, concerned about staying behind, had already left before them. With Leah very upset about being separated from him, Mendel looked and soon found Velvul, and Velvul joined the fleeing group.

They left Sokolow in the middle of the day, going east with others who had decided to leave across the Bug River toward the town of Drohiczyn where the Russians already were.

Freyde's mother's older sister, Rosa, was also convinced that it was time to go and frantic on the buggy ready to leave. Her husband, Morris Kaufman, a furrier, came and gave her a pelt to take with her, saying she had to go without him, "It's impossible for me to go, but you have to. Take this, so you'll have something to sell and live off."

Sorrowfully, Rosa said, "It's impossible. I can't go and leave you," got off the buggy and stayed behind. Both of her children, Anna and Srul, were taken off the buggy as well.

A day later, Srul, the older boy of about 12 years old, caught up with Mendel and his party when they were already on the other side of the Bug river. He'd hitched a ride on a truck and came to them and said, "I don't want to stay behind. I want to go, too. I don't want to die." But others chased him to go back home saying, "You can't leave your parents behind and go on alone." He died in the war.

Mendel and Freyde, Chaya, Leah and Velvul stayed in Drohiczyn for a month. During that time, Mendel's boyhood friend, Chayim Kawer, who also left, cycled back to try once again to convince Mendel's mother to leave. However, there was no way to change her mind.

Drohiczyn was a sleepy little place with tiny houses not far from the river, with a church in the middle of the town square, just like many other small towns in Poland. As the war progressed and as Poland was divided between German and Soviet troops and more refugees streamed out of Poland, Mendel and his small group were again faced with a dilemma. Should they continue to stay where they were? They weren't very far from the German army that had re-occupied Sokolow, and they didn't feel safe. There was no work, and they had no idea how they would live from day to day. They needed to find a better and safer place. They moved further toward Bialystok, a larger city that was still in Soviet territory about a hundred kilometers further toward the north. Maybe they could find better choices there.

Late October 1939 they had already arrived in Bialystok, where the two couples, Mendel and Freyde, Leah and Velvul, married in November. Mendel's mother's brother, Aharon Tuvye Schwarzbard, who had also left and made his way to Bialystok and somehow found them, gave the brides away in a simple short ceremony attended by a sparse seven people.

The war was getting worse and worse while they were in Bialystok. Germany was trying to expand its territory day by day. More and more Jewish refugees made their way into the now swollen city from different parts of Poland with everyone fearful and uncertain, struggling with what to do and where to go. Rumors swirled that work could be had deeper into Russia. Again, the dreaded question, should they stay and take a chance, or go? The five of them, with hope that being further removed from the front would be safer, and with the promise from the Russians they might find some place to live and work, Mendel and his party took the fateful decision and left for the Ural Mountains in January 1940, on New Year's night.

Freyde lamented to Mendel, "Only God can know what will happen next. We're going further and further from your mother and family, from all those we've known, and from what has been our home. What's going to become of us?"

Had they really made the right choice?

Out of the Furnace and Deep into Russia

Sokolow Podlaski, Poland to Berezniki, USSR

They were in one of 20 boxcars in a long train of Jews leaving Bialystok, all hoping of going someplace better. What they'd been told was they were going to Berezniki in the Soviet Union where they would be given work and a place to stay. They knew nothing about Berezniki. Berezniki turned out to be thousands of miles away. First from Bialystok to Minsk, Belarus; Minsk to Moscow; Moscow to Nizhniy Novgorod on the Volga River; and finally, to Berezniki in the Ural Mountains.

They stayed on that train for over 18 long days. Along the way, they could exchange a little money on the black market for Russian money. Everyone on the train, refugees all, were starving. Finally, Mendel was able to leave the train long enough to buy some food for everyone in their car to eat and again to get to some hot water. As they traveled, the weather grew colder and colder, plunging to minus 40 degrees, a bone-chilling cold they'd never experienced. To add to their unease, there were Soviet guards everywhere to watch them. Were they going to be prisoners? They were in shock as the train finally reached their destination in Berezniki on January 18th, 1940.

Berezniki turned out to be a terrible place. It was famous for its salt mines, especially for the potash and other chemicals that could be mined and processed to gunpowder, essential for the war efforts. The

Soviets had set up a large munitions factory in the town and needed laborers, essentially slaves, to work the mines and factories that had been set up. Berezniki became awash with refugees and servicemen who'd fled the war zones. Besides the potash that was mined, many toxic chemicals were used for the war effort to produce mustard gas, hydrogen cyanide, and tons of chemicals that went into canisters for the army and air force. The environment was toxic and the climate horrible.

After 18 days on the train, everyone was weary and dirty. They were taken to a large shower room and, with much trepidation, the men and women separated. What was going to happen to them? Would they be reunited again afterward? After standing for some time in the freezing cold, the showers were turned on, and they were all deloused from the time spent on the train. Finally, they were able to find each other again. After all that, they got one free meal.

They were in a different world now. Far from home and family, they looked around at their new surroundings and wondered how they would live there and worried about what they'd be asked to do. At least, they hoped, they'd be given a place to stay. They were asked if they had any skills or specialties that could be put to some use to increase everyone's chances of surviving in that harsh place. Mendel signed up as a carpenter. Velvul said he was a shoemaker. Mendel and Freyde and Chaya were put in one place to live. Unfortunately, Velvul and Leah were separated from the others and sent 30 miles away, beyond the Kama River into the mountains near a factory where they were assigned to make bricks. Freyde and Chaya worried about them all the time. The terrible cold surrounded them constantly, sometimes getting to minus 50 or minus 60 degrees in the mountains. Would they be able to survive this?

Mendel frantically did all he could to communicate with his mother back in Sokolow. Letters sometimes went through, and the news wasn't good. He learned that not long after they had left, the Germans had put in place a six-member *Judenrat* ("Jewish Council"). Even worse, they'd been ordered to provide Jews for slave labor and to collect fines and contributions. About a thousand of Sokolow's Jews were sent to a slave work camp in a nearby village and a forced labor camp was also set up in town. Mendel was desperate and urged his mother to leave any way she could, but the situation for Jews was dire. It was already too late. Mendel was devastated.

In Berezniki, the winter was extreme – the bitter cold was constant. The wind howled, and the snow fell constantly. They'd forgotten what it meant to be warm. The government provided only meager amounts of food so long as people could work. If you didn't work, you couldn't live. The harsh conditions weighed on them daily. It was a constant struggle to get through each day. But if families could stay together, they could hope that life would eventually bring better conditions. It was hope that kept them alive. In February 1940, surviving under the worst conditions, Freyde learned that she was pregnant. As difficult as their life was, Freyde and Mendel were overjoyed at the new life they would be bringing into the world.

With the severity of the winter and the constant need for fuel to keep warm, Mendel's job was changed. He was sent away into the big woods of the Ural Mountains to cut trees, trees 50-60 feet high. Freyde and Chaya were left behind, while Mendel and other men were sent as work crews to bring the timber down. Struggling with the constant snow, the work was made even harder, with snow piles in areas enormously high.

Jobs for the men kept changing, and Mendel, in late March, was brought back to Berezniki to be part of a forced labor gang to build a fence near the town's large chemicals plant. Railroad cars for construction brought in sand, and the men had to move it near the munitions plant where they worked. Mendel was ordered to dig holes for posts for the fence they were working on. Even in March everything was frozen. As he was digging a hole, Mendel saw what looked like hard material at the bottom. Thinking it was ice, he took a pickaxe to dig it out. When he hit it, a blaze of fire erupted and struck his eyes. That was the last thing he saw as he blacked out.

Prison

Mendel awoke, still groggy, and could only see out of one eye. Panic! He'd been taken to the local hospital, and a patch had been put on his injured eye. The doctors finished patching him up and told him to walk home, but as soon as he was home, the Russian police, the NKVD, came after him and arrested him. He was bewildered. Why should he be arrested? What was the charge, and what were they going to do to him? Was this going to be a routine investigation, or was he going to be in serious trouble! As he was being taken to prison, he saw Freyde standing in a food line. She waved to him, knowing nothing of what had happened and assuming, wrongly, that he would be back soon. He waved to her and shouted, "Stay here. I'll be back soon," not knowing that he was going to a dreaded Soviet prison.

In prison, interrogations started immediately. He was told that he had hit an electric cable that ran to the munitions plant and that all power to the plant had been lost when he had severed it.

He was charged as a spy! The chemical plant was crucial to Russia's military efforts, and he was accused of wanting to destroy Russia. He was told that he would go to prison for 30 years or more. It was beyond belief!

Every night, taken out of his cell, he was grilled and often beaten. "How much money did you get for this sabotage? Who told you where the cable was? Who told you to sabotage the plant? Who else was involved?"

Desperately, "I didn't know anything about an electric cable. I didn't know anything was there. I was doing what I was told to do. I was digging a hole for the fence post, and it looked like ice at the bottom. I was just trying to dig it out. I'm not a spy. I'm a refugee from Poland and just trying to help my family live. I just do what you tell me. You tell me I'm a carpenter, I do carpenter's work. You tell me to go to the mountains and cut trees, I cut trees. You tell me to help build a fence, I help build a fence. I am not a spy!"

They screamed back at him, "Mendel, things will go very bad for you if you don't cooperate with us. Sign the papers that you're a spy and you won't stay in prison as long. Otherwise, you'll never get out."

Night after night, month after month, the interrogations and beatings went on, but Mendel was adamant. "I got nothing for this. When I was working, my supervisor was supposed to be there to tell me where to dig, and he wasn't there. He was inside a nice warm hut, warming himself, and not watching us." Mendel learned Russian very fast in that prison being interrogated constantly.

"Just sign the confession that you were doing sabotage and trying to destroy Russia."

"I won't sign. It's not true."

"So, what do you want to say?"

"I wasn't doing any sabotage. I was digging a hole for the post. It looked like there was ice there, and I went to break it up. My supervisor was supposed to be there to tell me what to do, and he wasn't there. I only got paid 5 ruble a day for the job."

"Ok, sign both papers."

But he knew if they wanted to put you in jail, they would throw away the paper that said you did nothing and convict you on the other one.

When Freyde learned Mendel had been imprisoned, she went immediately to the jail asking, "Is Mendel Ephraymovitch here?"

They spit at her, "He's here all right, and he'll be here 30 years from now. He's a spy. He came from Poland, and they sent him to destroy the Soviet Union."

She was adamant, "That's not true. I want to see somebody higher now," she demanded.

They declined her request. "No. You're not seeing anyone else."

She was relentless. Day after day, Freyde went to the police to plead with them for Mendel's release.

Sitting there day and night, crying, they couldn't get rid of her.

They threatened to arrest her also, to which she shouted, "Arrest me! I have nowhere to go. I want to go upstairs and talk to the man in charge."

Finally, she wore them down.

They went to their boss complaining, "There's a woman that comes every day, sitting there all day and all night, crying and won't go away, and she wants to talk to you. What do you want us to do?"

The head of the NKVD was taken aback. "O.K. Let her come up and talk to me."

She came upstairs: a beautiful room with a red carpet. The head of the NKVD, a man named Tellman, looked at her, this woman that his men seemed not to be able to handle.

When Freyde learned his name, she thought he might be secretly Jewish. Maybe she had a chance to get him to do something for Mendel.

He pulled up a chair for her and said, "Sit down. Why are you crying? You're so beautiful. You're so young. You'll find a better husband."

She said, "I don't want anybody else. We dated for four years. We love each other. I'm not going away. I have nowhere to go. I have no one, and I'm pregnant."

Tellman was impressed and also confounded. He said to his men, "Listen, every time she comes and wants to come up to talk to me, let her come up."

She came every day. He was nice to her. He said, "I promise you, when the case comes up to me, I'll let him off free."

But day after day passed, and Mendel remained in prison.

Then the trial started.

Night after night, they would grill him and beat him, holding a gun to his head, telling him he would have to admit he was guilty. But Mendel was like a stone. He refused to admit he was guilty of being a spy.

In jail, there wasn't much he could do. He found a little piece of paper from the meager food they sometimes threw at him. He wrote Freyde a letter, in Yiddish, thinking she would get it, and if someone else saw it they wouldn't be able to read it. He knew she was coming every day. He threw it out of the window writing in Yiddish, "Freyde, *Ich bin nisht schildig* (I'm not guilty). Go see a lawyer."

How could he know that in Russia there was no such thing as seeing a lawyer? He didn't know that there were guards outside the window, who found the paper and took it to the chief.

When Freyde learned the trial started, she went to Tellman and told him again that Mendel was innocent and hadn't known anything about an electric cable.

Tellman told her, "I'll have him out of here the next night."

The NKVD man said, "Tomorrow night, they'll let your husband out at midnight. I want you to come then. I'll let him out in my office."

So, she came. It was a long dark five miles. They didn't let him out. She waited and waited. Midnight, 1 o'clock, 3 o'clock. She fled back home crying. She came home, where her mother was waiting for her. She said, "He didn't come."

Some while later, she heard someone knocking at the window. They had finally let him go. She didn't recognize him: swollen and beaten up. He had a long beard; no shaving for four months. They beat the hell out of him, night after night, grilling him and beating him while threatening him with a gun.

When he was finally let out, Tellman showed him the little piece of paper and said, "See, I got the paper." But Mendel said, "I didn't write anything against Russia."

As it turned out, during the trial other people were called who worked with Mendel, ten people, all laborers like him.

They said, "None of us knew anything about an electric line to the factory." But one man, trying to make himself out as more important and expecting to be rewarded, said, "Yes, he wanted to do it. Yes, he told me he wanted to destroy it, and I tried to talk him out of it."

At the end, they gave the man who was supposed to supervise him a year in jail; until then he hadn't been in prison at all, and Mendel was set free.

Mendel had been in jail from April until August 1940, over four months. After being released, he went back to where he'd been working and was, at least, paid for all the time he was in jail because he wasn't guilty. Life was tough, every day was a challenge, but at least they were away from the Germans and their cruelty.

During all that time, the war expanded with Germany becoming more and more aggressive throughout Europe. Denmark and Norway were attacked in April 1940. Belgium and the Netherlands were attacked and surrendered in May. The war against France opened in May 1940, and Paris fell on June 14th. Germany tried to defeat England also in 1940, but failed, and postponed their invasion of England to spring of 1941 and postponed it again later as the war become ever more complex.

Far from the front lines, Mendel and Freyde again returned to their prior routine of difficult and rigorous lives. Freyde, even while growing bigger with the pregnancy, worked in the fields growing and harvesting crops in the summer. Mendel went back to work as a carpenter, helping construct yet other factories in Berezniki. Yet they knew they were constantly at risk there, if not from the Germans then from the Russians who also had no love for Jews but just needed them for forced labor.

By October 1940, in the middle of war, in the middle of complete uncertainty of what the future would bring and whether any of them would survive but refusing to give up hope, Freyde gave birth to Abraham.

At the end of 1940, having been from home for over a year, Mendel was finally able to get a letter through to his mother informing her of their whereabouts. Chinka wrote back, and somehow, miraculously, the letter found its way to them. With all the destruction and devastation going on in Europe, with all the displaced people everywhere, with all the disruption, how could that letter have gotten through? They read every word with deep trepidation.

She wrote sadly, *"We don't live in the same house anymore. They took away the building. The Germans built a ghetto using two streets around the main synagogue. All of us have to live inside the ghetto. We can still go in and out from the ghetto and we're allowed to buy produce from the Polish farmers whenever we can find any money. Somehow, Fischel was finally released and they let him return to us here in Sokolow. At least, he's back with his wife and baby, but we're trapped. Life is hard, and we can only hope that it won't get worse."*

Life in Berezniki wasn't easy either but, at least, they weren't surrounded by Germans. After Mendel's imprisonment, though, they worried all the time that the Russians might be able to find more arguments against them that could lead to imprisonment – or worse. They desperately wanted to find a way to leave. Leaving, though, wasn't one of the choices that the Russians gave you. Their only interest was to keep their work force, their slaves.

During her pregnancy, Freyde had made friends with a Russian woman who helped her occasionally with laundry and chores. She was willing to get train tickets for them to leave but leaving wasn't easy. Only if you were sick and couldn't work, could a permission to leave be obtained. Mendel and Freyde went to a doctor after his imprisonment, told him that Mendel was sick from the beatings and torture, and asked him to write a letter that he was sick and couldn't be working. Since the trial had gone against them and Mendel had been found innocent, the authorities were embarrassed to still have him around, glad to get rid of him, and finally issued him a permit to leave, a release from their working obligations.

They were able to get tickets to leave by March 1941, although with war all over Europe, they really didn't know where it was safe to go.

Mendel talked to Freyde about their bleak choices. "Leah and Velvul can't leave; they're stuck here. They can't get away. At least they can stay here in Berezniki until the war burns itself out, whenever that will be. They're safe right now. Maybe the war won't come here, and the NKVD will still leave them alone. You and I will leave. We'll take Chaya and Abraham."

Abraham was only five months old, a baby trapped in the vortex of war, completely unaware of the dangers around him. Separated now from Leah and her sister's family, Freyde felt ever more alone in the world. She might never see that family again. And although Berezniki was not potentially the safest haven, it was far from the front lines they heard about and leaving could be a mistake that could cost them all their lives.

Freyde vowed, "I'll go wherever you go, but what will become of us as we wander again!"

Where to go was the immediate problem.

Finding Safe Haven?

They had heard that others who had somehow been able to leave Berezniki went to Orsha near Moscow, a train journey of over 20 hours and 1600 kilometers. So, they headed to Orsha and were able to rent a small apartment. They found many Jews from Poland in the area as well

– even some from Sokolow. In Orsha for several weeks, they still looked where to go for safety and heard reports many Jews had gone farther south to Crimea by the Black Sea, where it was warm and where apparently jobs were to be had. They would also be far from the heart of Russia and the antisemitism they could still see around them.

Berezniki to Crimea, March 1941, 3,200 kilometers

Mendel took a chance. He left Freyde, Chaya and Abraham and went all the way to Crimea. He had found out that he could get there by train. Once there, he would explore the area, find where they could be safe, where there would be a chance for work, and where they could live without the fear of constant harassment or imprisonment. And once finding that, he'd write Freyde and tell her to come, not a small task for her, in the middle of an ongoing and widening war to travel such a distance alone, 1800 kilometers with a baby and an old mother.

He came to a town called Saky in Crimea, next to Sevastopol and found a Jewish kolkhoz, a collective farm where he could work as a carpenter or in the fields and find a place where they could live. He wrote Freyde, *"Take a train and come. I'll wait by the station. Many people here are Jewish. It's a much better place. We can live in peace here."*

How she managed to make that trip, he never knew. Not only was she able to find her way on that long journey, taking different trains, taking Abraham and Chaya with her, she also had managed to send other belongings.

When she got to the station, Mendel wasn't there. There was no telephone. A letter could even take as much as three months. He really didn't know when they'd come. Freyde got off the train and was sitting at the station, not knowing how to reach him. Mendel's supervisor at his new job had somehow been told that Mendel's wife was sitting at the station with her mother and her little boy, and they sent a horse and buggy for her.

She came to the kolkhoz, and they were given a little room where they could live. Finally, life seemed better. Freyde's life seemed to become normal. How wonderful to be able to work, to live in peace, to keep house, even to bake *challah* (Jewish braided bread) for Shabbat. Life was beautiful, not like in the Ural Mountains. Chaya's life became normal, and she became a seamstress making clothes.

Beautiful summer. White flour, buttermilk, Jewish neighbors. So very different from Berezniki. Not all the people in Saky were refugees, but those who had come built up the area. For many refugees, money even came from the U.S. from Jewish relatives to whom they could write. After a while, Freyde and Mendel were even able to get a cow for themselves, and Freyde milked the cow for Abraham's milk. It was good there. Food. Safety. Mendel was working. They were happy. That was until September of 1941.

The War Follows Them / Fleeing Further

Little did they know that the fires of war were getting hotter and that their security and lives would again be on the line. And little did they know that Germany would turn and attack Russia and bring the fighting close to them.

Earlier that year, in April 1941, after Germany secured its hold on the Balkans and then invaded Yugoslavia and Greece, it proceeded to invade the Soviet Union on June 22nd, 1941 violating the pact between the countries. With that, Stalin joined the alliance against Nazi-Germany, but Germany continued to press forward, now into the Soviet Union. In Ukraine, Kiev was already occupied, and, by September 1941, the mass murder of Jews at Babi Yar had already begun. Within a short time, the German army was already in Crimea in Sevastopol and advancing readily. Saky, where Mendel and Freyde were living, wasn't very far away.

The calm and quiet to which Mendel and Freyde had become accustomed was suddenly shattered. Now only 40 miles away from the front lines, they could hear the bombing and shelling. After all their traveling and suffering, was this now going to be their end?

People were mobilized to dig trenches to try and stop the approaching army. Freyde and Mendel were told to return to the kolkhoz and, if they wanted to survive, to take what belongings they could and flee. Along with others, they took a horse and buggy and left, knowing even less than they had before as to where to go and where they might survive. From Saky, the small group of Mendel and Freyde, Abraham and Chaya again set out. Mendel drove the buggy with Chaya and Abraham on top and Freyde walking alongside. Their only choice was to somehow head east and try to stay ahead of the advancing army.

From Saky, they went east 250 kilometers to the city of Kerch, one of the most ancient cities in Crimea and as far east on land as they could go in Crimea. Farther east, they became thunderstruck as they approached the Kerch Strait on the Black Sea. A huge sea lay as a barrier in front of them, and 35 kilometers across the sea lay the western extension of the Caucasus Mountains. Staying behind would keep them too close to what they expected was the advancing front of the army. To be trapped there could spell their doom but going ahead across that expanse of water was also frightening. The war again was suddenly upon them. This time, they had had no prior opportunity to think, to plan that they would have to flee again, to ponder where to go. Each step they took seemed to carry them forward to yet more difficult decisions. To stay or to go was no longer a question as danger swirled around them.

The supervisor from the kolkhoz, who had traveled with them, said, "There are too many people to take care of. Give up what you've taken with you this far, any cattle, horse and buggies. Find a way to cross the Black Sea and, if you make it, take a train on the other side. If you don't keep going, you'll be lost because the war will catch up with you even here."

Little did they know that Kerch would become the site of heavy fighting between the Soviets and the Germans and the city would fall as early as November 1941, a short two months later.

More Unknown Territory – Azerbaijan

With no choices whatsoever, they frantically managed to find someone with a boat and crossed the treacherous strait. Afterwards they learned that the Germans were already occupying most of Crimea behind them. Abandoning the boat, they struggled on. They fled east to a little town called Krimsk and continued even further to a larger town called Krasnodar, about 150 kilometers northeast of the Black Sea they had crossed.

The kolkhoz supervisor's words were prophetic because, as he predicted, units of the German Army occupied Krasnodar between August 12th, 1942 and February 12th, 1943. The city sustained heavy damage in the fighting and Gestapo and mobile SS execution squads, killed thousands of Jews, Communists, and supposed Communist partisans. Shooting, hanging, burning, and even gas vans were used. Mendel and his family learned later that those from the kolkhoz who didn't keep going but stayed with their possessions were lost. German paratroopers caught those who stayed behind, and they were all killed.

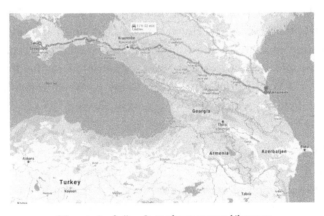

Crimea to Azerbaijan, September 1941, 1,300 kilometers

Mendel and his family abandoned everything they couldn't carry and desperately looked for a train to board to Baku, almost 1,000 kilometers away to get as far away from the war as they could. Even that had problems. It turned out that Baku was a military city and, on board the train, they weren't going to be allowed to enter that city. In fact, its oil fields and refineries were the most crucial factor in the Soviet's war effort. They were forced to disembark at Makhachkala, 300 miles before Baku. Makhachkala is in the north Caucasus region on the Caspian Sea, with very mountainous terrain.

What a strange and diverse Soviet city they saw, very different from everything they had encountered before, with many ethnic groups, mostly Muslim. They were now in what seemed like a completely different world. Hopelessly, their baggage went on to Baku, but they couldn't. They were stuck and could only hope that, at least in this far-flung place, the war wouldn't catch up with them again.

Weary from travel, bone-tired, and finally getting off the train, they found a school where apparently all were refugees, and the only accommodation was for them to sleep on the floor.

One night the Soviet KGB came and looked at their documents. They said, "No good." They wanted to see Mendel's military book. "No good. Come with us to the station. Tomorrow you'll be back."

Many others were also taken. Mendel again was jailed, this time in Makhachkala. He was again accused of being a spy, this time because he didn't have military papers. He was accused of running away and not being willing to serve in the war effort. As it turned out, more than 600,000 people from Azerbaijan were conscripted to the Red Army during World War II from 1941 to 1945. Many perished in far-flung and alien battlefields to which they were sent in Europe, the Caucasus and the Middle East.

Mendel was imprisoned in Makhachkala for three months, again not knowing if he'd ever be released. Finally released, he was sent to the military to see if he was qualified for fighting in the war. He failed their tests. His vision was poor; not good for fighting in the war. Rejected and released. Luckily, this time he was given papers that he was not qualified for military service.

After the three months imprisonment, he was released in February 1942 and managed to find Freyde and Chaya again. Freyde had struggled enormously, fending for herself, her mother, and Abraham, and moving from temporary school to temporary school for lodging. When Mendel asked where Abraham was, Freyde could hardly get the words out. She wept bitterly, and said, "Abraham died."

Devastated, he learned that his little boy had died while he was imprisoned. Beside himself, distraught, he asked Freyde, "How could this be? What happened?"

She could hardly speak. "There was an epidemic of diphtheria among many of the children. Refugee children weren't allowed in hospitals, and they refused to take care of refugees from Poland. If one of them died, all of them died."

Mendel cried, "While I was in jail, I had a dream that he died."

So difficult to get the words out, "We were all sleeping on the floor in the school. There were so many of us that there was no room. One child had a bench he was sleeping on, and he died. When he died, I could at least put Abraham on the bench, so he wouldn't sleep on the cold floor. The second day, he got sick, too. He couldn't breathe, he couldn't sleep, and he was burning up with fever."

She broke down. "I stood in line with 3,000 people to get bread. I carried him with me and got bread. Then I tried to help him by going with him from hospital to hospital. They wouldn't take him."

Mendel wailed in disbelief, "They wouldn't take children; they just let them die?"

The Interview Continues. Palo Alto 2002

The interview has been going for days now. When it started, the whole thing was new to him. He really couldn't relate to it. But as it went back and back into his memories, it was like he awoke and relived it all. It was all around him and he became rejuvenated again. He became completely involved in the process. Remembering all that he'd seen and experienced, all that he'd seen survive, and all that he'd seen die, he cried out in anguish and in anger, "Don't you see all this today? Don't you see the same thing happening to millions of people all over the world and in all countries? Millions of refugees, in lines miles and miles long, packs on their backs, their children in their arms, running like hell, looking for safety, trying to find some place they can call home, even for a little while. Helpless. Dying. Just as it is now; that's how it was then. Many dying. Only a few surviving. Never knowing if you're going to make it, never knowing what would become of us, but never giving up hope. That's how it was for all of us. That's how it is for them."

Now Where Can We Go? March 1942

Even in this far corner of the world, nestled between Iran, Georgia, and Armenia, they got news about the war that had turned into a World War. They knew that Japan had bombed Pearl Harbor and that America had joined the war. They knew that the Soviet Union and Germany had ended their pact and that Russia was now at war with Germany. They knew that Britain was in a deadly conflict that could determine if any there would survive although, at that point, the Luftwaffe hadn't been able to bring them to their knees. They knew that much of Western Europe was under the grip of the Nazis, and they heard horror stories of what was happening to the Jews who were trapped. They feared what might be happening to their own families in Sokolow where all news was impossible. Although they couldn't know it, the ghetto there had been completely closed and there was a death penalty if Jews dared to leave. By summer of 1942, more and more Jews were crowded into that impossibly small space. Workers from Sokolow were being pulled to construct an immense camp at Treblinka, only 21 miles away, and massive fear was spreading through the population as rumors of exterminations began to circulate.

After being imprisoned twice now in his wanderings through vast spaces of the Soviet Union, Mendel agonized over what they should do and where they could go, even if they had any choice. Would their end come to them even in this place?

Their luggage finally came back to them from Baku, but they knew not why. After wandering from one school to another with other displaced persons, they were finally sent away to "Gruzhie" (Georgia). Georgia was a wild mountain country at the intersection of Europe and Asia in the Soviet republic with many mountain villages. They didn't know, but it was a major part of Germany's war strategy to capture major oil fields in the Caucasus Mountains area, especially Baku but also parts of surrounding Georgia that were a major source of oil for the Soviets. The Soviets, on the other hand, desperately needed people to help support the war effort in those mountain areas, and so Mendel and his family were sent there, like it or not. At least they were placed with a local family to house them and help feed them.

First, they were sent to Tiblisi, the capital of Georgia, 500 kilometers away and from there to Chiatura, a mining town rich in manganese and other ores critical to the war effort. It was a terrible place with surrounding steep cliffs, with the mines operated by often drunken miners who had no use for Jews in their midst. Besides, none of them were fit for that work, and the miners didn't want them there anyway.

Amazingly, even in that godforsaken place, they found someone who had come from Sokolow, who had started a store there and who helped them survive for a short time. By late spring, months after Abraham's loss and with Mendel's return, Freyde was again pregnant. Even in that awful place and even with total uncertainty of what their future might be, they had hope that a better future might come to them, and they would not give up.

No matter how hard they looked, they could find no work in Chiatura; no way to make a living and support a growing family. In desperation again, Mendel heard that it was possible to get work around Baku and that it was now permitted to go there. Again, separated from Freyde and Chaya, he left on a 700-kilometer trek with others to scout it out and found that he could get work at a sofroz (agrarian farm) near Baku. Finding work, he sent for Freyde and Chaya to join him and by May 1942, they were back in Azerbaijan, on an agricultural farm (Sofroz Saiear) in a small town south of Baku called Salyan. They never knew why they were permitted to go on.

During the eight months since they had left Makhachkala and wandered throughout Georgia and Azerbaijan, the war had spread widely with millions of troops and civilians captured, maimed, killed.

In Ukraine, from which they had fled, the German army moved rapidly, and Ukraine collapsed in September 1941. In October, in the north, Germany attacked Moscow, not far from where they had been when they had initially fled Bereznicki. Deadly fighting over the winter of 1941-42 killed many, but Moscow didn't fall. Germany shifted its troops across the southern Russian steppes, starting an all-out assault on Stalingrad in August 1942, killing over two million, and lasting until January 1943 when the assault failed. Capturing the valuable oil fields of the Caucasus Mountains, of Iran and of Baku, was a major German objective throughout the war.

While fierce battles consumed vast areas they had left and constantly threatened to follow the family even to the remote corner of Azerbaijan, Mendel and his family continued to hope they might survive the conflagration. They couldn't know the continuing changes of the tides of war; they didn't know what the chances of survival were at any time, but they did know that the battles raged, and the armies continued to move and that, at any time, they might have to flee once more.

In that small village not far from Baku, laboring in the fields to grow and harvest crops under the constant scrutiny of the local Russian forces, they never knew if each day would be their last. From the summer of 1942, they all worked in the fields, Freyde and Chaya growing crops, Mendel operating his tractor to till the soil and later to harvest the wheat that was so essential to feed the Russian armies that kept the Germans at bay. The work was especially hard on the two women. Working in the fields near the Kura River at the end of the summer, the heat and humidity and mosquitoes took their toll, and Freyde became severely ill, infected with malaria. Ultimately confined to bed with chills, high fever, sweating, and delirium and in her third trimester, both she and the baby's life were in danger. Finally, a doctor was found who could relieve the symptoms by giving her injections – injections that almost killed the baby.

In December 1942, significantly recovered, Freyde gave birth to her second son, Ephrayim Yitzhak ("Froim") Feldman. The Russians had arbitrarily changed their family name from Felman to Feldman. The second son was named after Mendel's father who had died prematurely in Sokolow Podlaski before the start of the war. While overjoyed at Freyde's recovery and the birth of their child, Mendel continued to fear what was happening to those left behind in Sokolow. Almost two years had passed since they had heard anything at all. They had traveled across huge distances, had escaped capture from the armies multiple times, knew that things were bad, and they feared the worst. With the war continuing, there were few choices, though. Freyde recovered and went back to work; Chaya became the nursemaid and babysitter, dedicated to making sure that this baby wouldn't suffer the fate of its brother. In the meantime, Mendel was sent throughout Azerbaijan wherever workers were needed.

During that entire time, the fate of the family hung in the balance while the struggle between the Western Allies and the German armies teetered back and forth.

Earlier in that year, in May 1942, the British Royal Air Force carried out a raid on the German city of Cologne with a thousand bombers, for the first-time bringing war home to Germany. For the next three years, Allied air forces systematically bombed industrial plants and cities all over the Reich, reducing much of urban Germany to rubble by 1945.

As it became clearer that Germany was on the run, Mendel agonized about starting to go back. "Freyde, we've been gone from home since September 1939. We've traveled thousands of miles across Russia, from the Ural Mountains to the Caspian Sea. I've been imprisoned twice and lucky to still be alive and free, and with you. We lost our first son and could have lost our own lives many times now. Hopefully, your sister's safe in Berezniki. You have your mother, but I left my mother, brothers, sister, and other close relatives behind, and I don't know if they're still alive. This isn't a place where we can think of living the rest of our lives. Isn't it time to think about trying to go back home?"

"Mendel, you know that I never wanted to leave Sokolow. After I was attacked, I had no choice. It's been so hard with all the running, with the trains, never knowing what was ahead, never knowing if the Germans would catch up with us. With you in prison twice, I never knew if I'd be left alone and how I'd survive. Losing the baby while you were in prison in Makhachkala was terrible. I cried day and night. What could I do, left alone? I almost gave up hope. I know how hard all of this has been on you especially! Always looking for a place for us to go, protecting us, finding us a place to sleep, finding food to keep from starving. And I know how hard it is on you not knowing what's happening to those we left behind, especially as we hear rumors from everywhere about how terrible the Nazis are. If you think we can try to start back, I'll go with you, whenever you think. Wherever you go, that's where I'll go. We made a promise to each other for as long as we live."

By the end of 1944, they decided to go back west. With the German army no longer in Ukraine, the family made their way slowly back. From Baku they returned to Makhachkala, from Makhachkala back to Crimea, and in Crimea they went to Saky where they had been before.

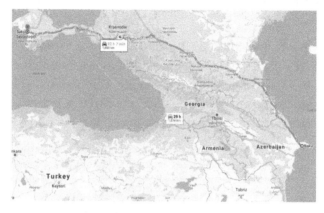

Baku, Azerbaijan to Saky, Crimea, end of 1944

3

DISPLACED PERSONS/A LIFE REBORN

Can We Return? 1944

In Western Europe, one of the largest operations of the war occurred as Allied soldiers landed in France on June 6th, 1944 (D-Day) with bloody battles liberating France by September 1944. Later in September 1944, U.S. troops crossed into Germany while Soviet troops entered Germany from the east. By January 1945, the Soviets started liberating Poland and Hungary, and by mid-February 1945, the Allies firebombed Dresden, Germany. In May 1945, Germany surrendered to both the Western Allies and to the Soviets.

Finding a Way Back Home?

While they weren't home yet and remained in Crimea in 1945, they still hoped that the end of the war would mean that they might be able to return to their families in Poland at some point. In the meantime, they were in familiar space with a place to live. Yisroel Hersch Feldman ("Srul"), Freyde's third son and Froim's new brother, named after Chaya's father, was born in Saky in August 1945, and the family could again hope for a safe future where all the family could be reunited. By March 1946, they finally made plans to return to Poland, despite the efforts of the

Soviets to keep them as forced labor. Because they were still Polish citizens, the government was unable to force them to stay, and Mendel, Freyde and Chaya, Froim and Srul, now a party of five, started the long trip back.

With the war ended, with much of Europe and Asia reduced to ruin, redrawn borders with mass emigrations and unnumbered deaths, many displaced Jews who somehow survived the war, but had been wildly scattered by the winds, were now also trying to find a path home and out of the foreign lands to which they had fled. Agencies were desperately struggling with ways to get them back.

From Saky, the little party of five went by truck to Simferopol where a train of 30 cars had somehow been assembled for the displaced to start to return. From Crimea, the train carried them not to Warsaw, where they could have gone on to Sokolow, but to southwestern Poland. First, they went to Wroclaw, a city of about 200,000 people that had been heavily bombed during the war, then to Wałbrzych 70 kilometers further southwest, and then on to Kamienna Góra, a small town of about 20,000 people circa 100 kilometers from the eastern German border.

It was a long trip of almost 2,000 kilometers. As the train took them across Crimea and through Ukraine and Poland, they were aghast to see devastation and rubble everywhere, and as the train passed through city after city, they were horrified at the destruction that they saw. They passed through Lwow, a city that held as many as 100,000 Jews before the war. The Nazis had built a concentration camp, Janowska, where more than 200,000 were murdered. Other Jews had been sent to Belzec concentration camp further away where upwards of 500,000 were murdered. As they passed not far from Kracow and other displaced Jews were picked up, they learned of the horrors of Auschwitz-Birkenau and the horrors that had been perpetrated on the Jews of Europe.

By the time they arrived in Kamienna Góra, they were shaken to the core and in a total state of shock. The family, at this point, moved entirely on faith, with no idea what they would find or do after they arrived. All they knew was that it was one of the places where the displaced, the homeless, the refugees from the disaster that was the Holocaust were streaming.

Saky, Crimea to Kamienna Góra, Poland, March, 1946, 1,800 kilometers

Kamienna Góra

From all across Europe and Western Asia they came, the remnants of what had been the Jews of Europe before the war. Hidden in attics and basements and barns, masquerading as Poles or Austrians or Germans or Slavs, masquerading as Christians or Muslims, whatever the need or opportunity, they now returned to refugee collection centers to try to find what happened to those left behind. They came bewildered or wary, no longer looking like their former selves, skeletons and injured, many times separated from the humanity that they had maybe known before, now desperately looking for whom they lost, and hopeful they could return to a town and a home that might still exist. Fearful of what might be lost forever, never to be regained, not knowing what "home" could still be for them and any loved ones they still had.

Kamienna Góra was another temporary place for them. Administered by agencies, such as the United Nations Relief and Rehabilitation Administration (UNRRA) or the American Joint Distribution Committee, set up after the war to enable people to return, to collect information on what was left, on who was left, on where they came from, on who they could still be connected to, what could be done with them and where they could go. These collection centers were a lifeline for those trying to recover or build a new life.

The American Joint Distribution Committee (the "Joint") was one of those in Kamienna Góra and other war-torn areas. They collected people and records, temporarily housed them and fed them. They served as a clearing house for records of those who had survived and found their way to other centers. They were a point where connections could be made. They were a center where letters could go out to relatives, to connections in other places such as The United States, Britain, South America, Palestine. Letters that could go where there might be someone who remembered and who could help in relocation, who might provide a transition from "Displaced Person", to "Immigrant", and possibly "Citizen" of a new country and finally a new home.

Mendel and the family registered with the Joint, were given temporary quarters, and started to try to see how to put their life back together. All they knew now was that, with all they had endured and with all that they'd seen on their trip back, they had survived. They still didn't know what happened to Freyde's sister and family or the rest of Mendel's family, but they had survived. There must be a future for them.

The Interview Continues. Palo Alto 2002

We've been at it for days now, telling and retelling what my father remembered from the war and its after-effects. He's now 85 years old, tired and worn from his life experiences, his many travels, and all that he's seen and what he didn't want to see. I'm the interviewer, 59 years old and dedicated to recording my family's history and all it experienced before, during, and after World War II, something I've wanted to do for years. At this encounter, I'm spending a week to expand the story I recorded in 1986 when it left off with the family at the end of the war. I have all my precious documents and pictures with me. They're spread out all around me. While I intend to start where I left off, my father will have none of that. He insists on beginning with the beginning, with the family's histories, with meeting Freyde, and with retelling in even more detail all that they endured during the war and its aftermath. And in the retelling, he's rejuvenated, reliving the details of his life and all that they survived.

Now we're again back in 1946, and he's being asked what happened to him and the family in Kamienna Góra, and he continues the story.

"In 1946, in Poland, I started working. We didn't have anything. We went to the committee that helped refugees, the Bricha. It helped coordinate the largest organized mass migration in the 20th century that brought a quarter of a million Jews from Eastern and Central Europe to the DP camps in Germany, Austria and Italy. We found a man whose name was Yitzhak Bylalef, also from Sokolow. He was the secretary of the committee. He knew Freyde and me, and we had known his children.

"I said to Yitzhak that I had nothing to buy bread, and he gave Freyde 500 zloties. I started working at whatever I could find.

"One time, I see a man come up to our house, because we're Sokolower, and, like all the others, he's looking for people that might know what happened to others that he left behind.

He said, 'I'm from Sokolow. I'm the son of Yitzhak Bylalef.' He was one of two sons; one got killed in the army.

He asked, 'Do you know if my father is alive? Do you know where my father is?'

I said, 'Yeh, just wait in our house.' I went to the office and said, 'Yitzhak, there's a friend at my house, a Sokolower, who wants to see you.'

Yitzhak came to our house and went up to him and said, 'Who are you? Who are you?'

He said, 'Daddy, I'm your son. Don't you know me?'

Freyde started crying at the tragedy that caused father and son to not even know each other. Then they went home together."

They both had changed so much from the war that they couldn't recognize each other anymore, father and son.

"Where were they separated?" I asked my dad.

"During the war. They took him into the army in 1939, and he survived. They were reunited in the town of Kamienna Góra."

He sighed, "So much to remember from that time."

Re-united! 1946

Mendel continued to relive his memory. "Life wasn't easy there. We had no money and the rations we got were barely enough to live on. I asked for work where I could earn a little to keep us going. My experience with farm equipment was valuable. So, they gave me a job as a tractor operator to work the fields."

All the while, the organization tried to come to grips with the massive influx of refugees and their needs.

"Because it was hilly and mountainous all around us, I was sent to another town, Zagan, where I could help on the farms and where I could train others in using tractors for the fields. Freyde stayed behind with you (I was only three years old), and Srul, and your grandmother Chaya while I went on alone. I worked on the farm during the week and returned on Friday nights. I worked there with lots of Polish boys. I taught them the skills I learned while on the run, how to work tractors, how to plow the fields. One time, the Polish boys said to me, 'Jew, what are you doing here? Why don't you go to Palestine?'

"There was another Jewish boy with me that I knew, who'd married a woman from France. I said to him, 'It's antisemitic here too. They'll kill us in the middle of the night.' So, what did I do? We went home, took our clothes, took the train, went back to Kamienna Góra and decided to go to the Bricha to sign up to go to the American zone."

Every day, as soon as they'd wake up, the first thing they'd do is go to the bulletin board of names, of postings they'd made before, looking for those they'd known who might have survived and seen their desperate scribble, looking to see who'd added a note that might be looking for them. And every day, as the list got bigger and bigger, they saw no one that they could recognize, no name that might have survived. They talked to others around them doing exactly the same.

"Have you seen my brother? Have you seen my sister? I'm from Sokolow where my mother stayed behind. Have you heard anything of her? Have you seen anyone from my town? Do you know what happened to it? Were there any survivors? If you see anyone looking for me, remember my name!"

One miraculous day, they heard someone yelling, "Is there a Felman? A Mendel Felman?" They looked around and saw a strange skeleton of a man, young but old.

"Here! I'm Mendel Felman! Who are you? Could I be the one you're looking for? I don't know you."

"My name is Eli. Eli Reich. I'm looking for a Mendel Felman whose wife is named Freyde and who is from Sokolow Podlaski in Poland. Are you him?"

Mendel almost fainted. He grabbed Eli and shouted, "I'm him! I'm him! My name is Mendel. My wife is Freyde. We grew up in Sokolow. We left almost seven years ago when the Germans took the town. My mother wouldn't leave. My brothers and sister stayed behind. Who are you? Where do you come from, and what can you tell me? Do you know what happened to all of them?"

Eli embraced Mendel, and with both crying, Eli told his story. "I grew up in Lemberg, Poland. My parents had ten children. When the war started, Lemberg was taken over by the Russians before the Germans later took it. My parents, brothers and sisters were all killed. The Russians sent me to the Russian army in the Ural Mountains, and later I was sent to work in Berezniki where I met Leah Lopata, Freyde's sister and her husband Velvul. Life there was very hard, but we managed to survive. We stayed in Berezniki until the war was over, and then we started coming back. Leah and Velvul have two daughters now, Belah and Luba. Bela is five years old now; Luba is about a year old. I came here to look for you with Velvul. He's here in the camp today, and Leah and the girls are now in a town called Yahr near the Czech border. Leah told me she had a sister, Freyde and sent Velvul and me to different places to look for her and you. It's a miracle that we found you."

Finally reunited after more than seven years, separated by thousands of miles, never knowing what the war had done to each other, whether either had survived, they came together in joy seeing both had survived. Leah and Velvul were a family of four while Mendel and Freyde and Chaya were a family of five. Now the talk was of what had happened with those they'd left behind.

Mendel could wait no more and said, "I have to go back to Sokolow, to find what happened. It's a two-day travel by bus and train to go to Warsaw, then to Siedlce, then to Sokolow Podlaski. I know it's still dangerous for Jews to travel alone, but I'll steal a Russian uniform and go on. God knows what it's like on the way, to what extent the roads are open, how much destruction there still is. But I have to find out what happened to my family."

"We pooled our money, and I left them all behind and finally set off to find what happened to my family."

Return to Sokolow

It was late spring when Mendel finally arrived in Sokolow. The journey had been long and dangerous, and he'd had to change trains several times, the last leg of the ride being from Siedlce north to Sokolow. The tracks ran north along the same line that eventually took trains to Treblinka. Mendel was weary with travel, not only with the travel from Kamienna Góra, but also with the years of travel, of hiding, and trying to keep his family safe.

It was a cold grey day with weeping clouds shamefully hiding the sun when he arrived. Even with the devastation to the city that the war had brought, with shattered walls and cratered streets, he could still recognize the streets that he'd walked just seven years before, the streets where he and his friends had played, the buildings where his neighbors and relations had lived. Where were they now? What had happened to them? He hoped against hope that they had managed to survive.

Suddenly someone walking on the street seemed to recognize him. "Mendel? So, you survived. There's no one left! There's nothing here for you! It's a shame the Germans didn't get you too!"

He walked away – stunned. After all he'd gone through, after all the war had destroyed, was there still room for hate? He'd grown up here. He'd gone to school here. They'd lived here for generations. It was their home. Why was the world so cruel?

He stayed just a short while. He found out that after he'd left, the Jews had become more and more restricted and finally had been moved into a ghetto made from a small section of the city. The Jews had been emptied of their houses and property taken away. More Jews had been brought into this tight space from nearby cities and not been allowed to leave at all. Hunger and sickness prevailed, and many died. Finally, on Yom Kippur in 1942, on September 22nd, Mendel was sickened to learn that the Germans, with the help of Ukrainians and Poles from the city itself, had ordered the ghetto emptied into the small market where the Jews had once plied their trade. Those who resisted were shot; those who refused to leave the buildings had been murdered in their beds, and the rest rounded up and put in railway cars and sent to the Treblinka Death Camp, a short distance away where they were immediately murdered.

The only trace Mendel could find of the Jews that had once made Sokolow their home was a big hole in the ground, a mass grave a little way from the city. The two cemeteries that had once held their ancestors had been destroyed. Tombstones, "mazevoth" that marked their lives and their deaths and the links to generations past had been pulled and used for paving blocks for roads, buildings, and walls. Nothing was left. His mother, his brothers, his sister, his nieces, nephews, uncles, aunts... all gone with no trace left behind that they had ever lived. He was devastated!

Would he ever be able to find what had happened to Chinka, his mother, that day? Would anyone ever know?

Displaced Persons Camp – Steyer

He fled the city in shock, returned to the trains, retraced his way back to Kamienna Góra to sorrowfully tell his family, all that was left, of what had befallen them. After all the time on the run, after all the time bearing hope on seeing their families again, the news shattered them.

There was no home to return to.

Day after day, they waited to see what would happen to them. They no longer had a link to the past. All they knew, all the family they had left behind, was gone. All the hopes they'd held on their long trek of the last seven years of a return to family and to home were ripped away. The future was impenetrable. Now where could they go? To stay in Sokolow, or even to stay in Poland was now inconceivable. Mendel knew he still had a sister, a link to his past, in Palestine/Israel. If he'd had the chance, he would have gone there also before the war. But what were his chances of that at that moment? Immigration there was now almost an impossible dream. The British closed that door after the war and papers to get there were virtually impossible. Leah and Velvul had the same dilemma. Where could they take their children and what kind of life could they make for themselves? They had barely survived in Berezniki, in Russia. Surviving was all they could think about then; now what could they do? Survival had been the driving force for all them, but now where could they go?

Chaya, Freyde's mother, reminded them that she knew she had brothers and sisters in America who left Europe decades before the war. Maybe that was an opportunity for them. Maybe they could help them get out of Europe? Staying in Kamienna Góra wasn't an answer. It was only a place to find each other and to find choices, but maybe the Joint could help them find a path to a future. Every day the Joint tried to make connections for those survivors who returned to relatives or friends that could be found in other countries. And while they looked for connections for a way to relieve their despair, the Joint found places for the displaced to stay and wait.

With the war's end, however, more and more survivors were flooding the camp. While they were safe in the refugee camp, it wasn't a home, and they didn't know what future was in store for them or where they could go next. The waiting, the uncertainty, added to Mendel and Freyde's concerns for a future. Eventually, Mendel and Freyde and their families were told they would go to a displaced person's (DP) camp. Many were in the process of being set up to deal with the massive remainder from the war, the Jews that were still left alive, those coming out of concentration camps, those returning from far-flung areas of Eastern Europe, even of Asia. Mendel, Freyde and their two sons, and Leah, Velvul with their two daughters, and Chaya would now be sent to a displaced persons camp in Austria while future opportunities might be found.

New travels opened for the party of nine souls and Eli. This time, it wasn't about running away from danger. This time, it was running toward a possible future and maybe even, finally, a home.

They gathered their few belongings and left together, the youngest in baby buggies pushed by the older kids heading to yet new destinations, the youngest happy as only young children can be without understanding the uncertainties still surrounding them. A battered picture survives of that journey (**Photo 5**) showing Srul and Ephrayim dressed in winter garb, heavy scarves around their necks, Srul with a knit cap on his head, Ephrayim with a heavy gray cap, both wearing mittens, Srul in this instance looking forlorn as though he dreads the future that's coming, Ephrayim looking stoically ahead.

Kamienna Góra, Poland to Steyer /DP Camp, Austria May 1946

First, back to Wałbrzych, then by train via a circuitous route to Vienna where they were kept for two to three days, were given shots, food. Vienna was a major transition place. From there, trucks took them to Steyer, Austria to a DP camp near Linz. They arrived in May 1946.

Here was to be their next temporary home for five to six months. It was crowded and primitive with 300 people in one military barrack, with 27 people in their one room together, all with similar uncertain circumstances to themselves (**Photo 6**).

Waiting. Waiting. Looking for the next place.

But, at least here, they were all finally together, Mendel and Freyde and their children, Leah and Velvul with their daughters, and poor Eli who had no one at all except the two families that now made him one of theirs. With the other survivors in that room, all shared the space, ate and slept together, no shower facilities, no toilet. Bare cracked walls with a single bulb on a long skinny wire to light the dim room. But there was hope that the next place might be better.

They were in Steyer for six months, waiting to see what would happen to them next; where the next place might be. Winter set in. Mendel was made a camp policeman to watch the camp at night. Dead tired from all the travel and uncertainty, he'd climb into a camp truck and sleep through the night. A picture survives from that time (**Photo 7**) showing Mendel in a heavy woolen coat, heavy scarf around his neck, a woolen cap on his head, long black boots, snow on the ground, Mendel and six other skinny men standing outside the barracks, the barrack policemen. None of them got any pay, just an opportunity to get bread at the front of the line.

The biggest benefit to them now was that they had help communicating with relatives in America. At least they'd know they were alive, that they had survived the war! The Joint told them that they might, in time, get visas to go to America, but they'd need a sponsor who would certify that they weren't criminals and who would ensure they wouldn't go on the public dole. That would take time.

Going to Israel, Mendel's dream for years, was now an impossible dream, but, at least, the family had one contact in America, one of Chaya's brothers, to whom they could write where there might be a future.

Displaced Persons Camp – Wels

After six months in those over-cramped quarters and with more and more refugees arriving daily, they were finally told that they would have to be moved to another place, a larger facility in Wels, Austria, less than 50 kilometers away.

The Wels facility wasn't a displaced persons camp; it was more like a military garrison and had many barracks to accommodate the large numbers of displaced persons that had come back. It was more highly organized and capable of treating those who returned. Many came back severely ill, many greatly undernourished. Mendel and his family, and the whole group of ten, were put into a single barrack, much better than being in a space occupied by 27 people, but still hard on all of them with no privacy whatsoever. Finally, boards were put up to make separate spaces for them. There was electricity, but if Leah started to cook and Freyde also started, the circuits would break, and no one could cook. Mendel solved it by holding the circuit breaker together by hand so that the electricity stayed on. Overall, it was better than being in Steyer.

Both Mendel and Freyde had suffered during their travels, never having enough to eat, and being severely underweight. Comparing the pictures of them taken as sweethearts before the war in Sokolow, they now hardly resembled their former selves (**Photo 8**). They looked more like scarecrows.

I had contracted tuberculosis on the journey and was extremely underweight. The camp medical directors sent me to a camp called San Gilgal near Linz for sick children to recover. Freyde and Mendel took me there by train, although I strongly resisted going and being separated from them. I didn't want to stay behind, so while I was put in one room for evaluation, Mendel and Freyde went to another room and quietly left, leaving me behind. While I was to remain there recovering for several months, the camp was poorly administered, graft prevailed, and children were hardly fed. On various visits to see their children, parents realized that things weren't going well, removed their children, and complained to the Wels Camp administration, which fired the employees and terminated the camp.

We were safe in Wels, and life for my parents settled down to a routine – taking care of the children, waiting in line for meals, looking for other survivors, looking for how to make life a little better while trying to find a way out.

Mendel said to Freyde, "I can't just sit and wait. I have to do something." He joined a Zionist organization and quickly became a leader. He looked for a job in the camp and other ways to make money to improve their meager existence. They waited and waited. Finally, he and another man were given a job of fixing things around the camp. They fixed roofs because they leaked when it stormed, with water coming into the barracks. They made stoves from bricks so people could cook outside a little. With all that, Mendel got meal cards to get a little more food, but still it was barely enough to get by.

Letters to Palestine / Israel

The most important activity in the camp was again to write letters, to contact loved ones outside of the decimated world of Europe to let them know they survived. To let relatives and friends know who had been lost, what happened to those who had been left behind or who'd been known before the war. It was a heart-breaking anguish to disclose who had perished.

The American Joint Distribution Committee helped in finding addresses to whom to write and to reconnect us with relatives in America or Israel.

Mendel was able to finally get an address and write his sister Rojza, whom he hadn't seen since 1936, 11 years before when she'd run away from home to Palestine/Israel. How much he'd missed her. What excitement it generated!

The letters, written in their native Yiddish, to her and to relatives in the United States, all bore the same incredible news: "I'm alive and in a displaced persons camp in Austria. The Nazis murdered the entire family, our mother and brothers and sister that wouldn't leave Sokolow in 1939 when Freyde and I left. The Jewish community of Sokolow is destroyed. Those who didn't leave were killed in the town or in the Treblinka death camp. In great sorrow, I just can't write you all that I've heard about that or about the millions of other Jews that were slaughtered in the war. During our flight from the war, we were separated from Freyde's sister and husband, but, by some miracle, we found each other after the war, and we're reunited with them and their children now in this camp. Freyde's mother, Chaya, left Sokolow with us and survived. She's well and with us now in this camp. We don't know where we will go from here or what the future will bring, but we continue to have hope that we will yet have a home and a place for our children to grow up in peace and that we may, someday, be together."

In the many letters Mendel exchanged with his sister in 1947, he learned that Rojza had changed her name in Palestine to Shoshana, had married

Rachmil Schwarzbard, a cousin of theirs, in November 1937 in Jerusalem when she was 23 years old. They now also had a son, Ephrayim Yitzhak. Shoshana had named him after their father, just as Mendel and Freyde named their son, me, after his father when neither family had known the other was alive.

Shoshana's son was born in September 1939 in Jerusalem while I had been born in Azerbaijan, both with the same name, both after our grandfather. Years later we would meet under incredibly surprising and emotional circumstances.

Mendel learned that while we were still on our journey, Shoshana had another son, Aharon Tovia, born in Jerusalem in June 1944. I would meet him years later and develop a special bond with him and his family. Only with their help was I able to unravel what happened to their mother when she ran away on that fateful night in 1936.

Shoshana asked Mendel to come live in Israel but getting visas or transit from Europe was very difficult if not impossible. Mendel told her how difficult daily life was in the camp and asked her to send him packages of cigarettes that he might be able to sell to the soldiers around the camp to get some extra money to live on.

Mendel said to Freyde, "I don't have any money and don't know what else I can do. We have almost nothing left that we could sell."

Freyde suggested he could perhaps sell his leather coat.

Selling his coat was desperate with winter approaching, but as he got ready to do that, a large package arrived from Shoshana. The cigarettes he'd asked for came, and now he could sell those to soldiers who were crazy for them.

It worked! Mendel bragged to Freyde, "I sold the cigarettes! The soldiers can't get enough of them. I made a little money on the black market and with the money I got from them, I got a box of cans with tuna fish. I sold those outside the camp."

With time, he had enough money saved to buy himself a bicycle. He put more tuna out to sell, using his bicycle to get around. With the devastation after the war even the Austrians in the town were looking to buy things. After the war there just weren't enough things to go around. He sold to them also, and from the soldiers he got scrip which he sold to someone else and made a little money from that. He sold so many packs of cigarettes, that it was enough to keep the family going. One soldier told him he wanted ten cartons of cigarettes. He got him the cartons and made a little more money. There wasn't much else he could do, and it was one way he could help his family while waiting for a better future.

One time the dreaded Military Police came around. They didn't want black market activity in the camp and wanted to know the whereabouts of the cigarettes and the scrip. Where did Mendel hide the scrip? Anticipating that they were coming, he had taken the cap from the bike's steering wheel and put the scrip inside, the same with the seat. They came, they looked but couldn't find the scrip.

Then he started doing business with chickens. The Austrians loved the chickens, but chickens were more trouble, especially for selling them in the camp to the other Jews. You had to find a butcher (a *shoichet*) to make them kosher. It wasn't easy.

"I'd get the chickens in town, take them to the butcher, then take them to the market to sell for Shabbat. After years of not being able to practice their religion, after years of deprivation, it meant a lot for the Jews in the camp to get a chicken to again practice their religion's traditions."

Besides, the food the camp handed out was strange to them. It included commercial white bread that the people had never seen before. They also were handed out peanut butter and had no idea what to do with that. It was totally foreign to them. At least for dinner, they were given noodles. Not much, just enough to stay alive. Mendel got a lot of customers for the things he was able to obtain and sell.

Freyde also helped, besides taking care of the children. If Mendel had more customers, he'd send them to Freyde. He had her go to a wholesaler near town and buy more cigarettes or sardines with the money they made. They'd pay maybe ten cents for an item and sell it for 30 or 40. Freyde was a good businesswoman with a good head on her shoulders. Besides helping sell things, she was able to make meals for the family in their little space, spaghetti for dinner, chicken for Shabbat. After seven years on the road, running for their lives with no stability, always in danger, and no concept of whether they would survive, it felt like heaven.

Letters to America

Even with life getting better in the camp at Wels, it wasn't enough. We were still displaced persons and desperate to find a place we could finally call home. Freyde and Mendel kept looking and working on that more than anything else they did.

Freyde's mother Chaya knew she had brothers and sisters in America who had left home long ago. Joseph and Bernice (Bryna) had left around 1913 and settled in Indiana. Sarah had left in 1914, and Chaya learned that Sarah lived somewhere around Chicago – not that she knew where Chicago was. Her brother Baruch/Bernard had left early, and she learned he also lived somewhere around Chicago. She knew that she had half brothers and sisters from her father and his first marriage who'd also emigrated long ago to America, but she had no idea how to contact them.

She started with her brother Joseph Rosenbaum, and she was overjoyed that the Joint could help her with his address that was now in a place called South Bend, Indiana. It turned out that he was only a couple hours away from Sarah and Bernard and was in touch with them as well as with Bernice (Bryna) who also happened to live nearby in South Bend.

She tearfully wrote her brother Joseph:

November 1946

Dearest Joseph,

It's been more than 30 years since we've seen each other. I'm so glad that you were lucky to get away long before the horrible war here. Life after you left wasn't easy, but we were able to get along until our father and mother died. I left home also to find a place to live and work in Warsaw, found a man I loved, and married in Warsaw. Misfortune plagued us in the loss of our first children, but we had two daughters, Freyde and Leah, that I love very much. My husband, Avrum unfortunately died young, his business fell apart, and I had to return home to Sokolow. Our father's business had also collapsed. He died, and when I returned home, our mother who was very sick, also died. Life after that was very hard, but we managed. I was able to sell geese in the Large Marketplace, and my daughters helped with everything.

When the war came, Sokolow was bombed and rapidly occupied by the Germans. Life there became impossible. I can't tell you how horrible it was. I escaped to the Russian zone with Freyde and Leah and the men they married, Mendel and Velvul, and we were on the run throughout Russia for almost seven years during which time our families became separated. We've been lucky to survive, especially as we learned of the disaster that befell most of the Jews of Europe who were slaughtered like cattle by the Nazis and even with the help of the antisemites where they lived. You can't believe it where you are, but most didn't survive.

We're now in a displaced persons camp in Austria. By a miracle we found Leah and her family after the war. We're finally together. But all the Jews of Sokolow are gone, and there's no home to go back to. Mendel would go to Israel, but there's no possibility to get there. Thank God that we have our lives, but we have no place to go, and no place that we can call home.

Write me and tell me all about yourself and how my sisters and brothers are in America.

Your loving sister, Chaya

Leah also wrote to tell him of her family and of their plight stuck in the camp with no options in front of them either.

Joseph/Joe wrote back:

My loving sister,

I couldn't imagine what happened to you, and I'm so happy that all of you have survived the war. The stories we hear in the United States about the concentration camps are very hard to believe. How can the Germans have killed six million Jews? How can so many have been killed? Whatever that story is, though, we'll do what we can to help you. With so many displaced people and so many emigrants wanting to come to the United States, the government now has very strict limits on who and how many can come. It will take time to do anything, but we'll do what we can do.

In the meantime, my wife Anna and I are planning to take a trip to Palestine/Israel. We'll try to stop at the camps on the way."

Your loving brother, Joseph

Now the family group of nine worked frantically to make a good impression on their American relatives when they would arrive at their quarters in Wels. They borrowed clothes. They borrowed mismatched dishes and utensils from neighbors. Everyone worked together to make a Shabbat meal of fish, soup, and chicken. Nothing could be spared for this miracle of connecting again and maybe finding a direction where they could go. A future.

1947. A charter flight to Palestine/Israel. Joe and Anna stopped on their way in Linz. They hired a driver and made their way to the camp in Wels. The family awaited their arrival with bated breath. It had been so long since Joe and Chaya had been together; they were so young then, and so much had happened since. Joe was now a successful businessman in America; Chaya had barely survived one tragedy after another. Would they even recognize each other? Would he care? Would they reunite as long-lost relatives, or would he see them as strangers, like people from another planet?

The American visitors were astonished at the rudimentary barracks and the squalor. Chaya had aged more than Joe could believe. Mendel and Freyde, Velvul and Leah still looked emaciated even after the year since they'd returned. Joe and Anna, to the displaced, looked like people from a movie, well dressed, modern, impressive. A picture exists of that meeting taken in the temporary schoolroom that was used for the children, the nicest room on the camp (**Photo 9**). People from two different worlds, the young turned old, the almost dead back to life, the wonders of children conceived in the uncertain hell of running. And the two Americans trying to make sense out of what could never be made sense of.

"Tell me it isn't true. That six million weren't killed, that the newspapers have it wrong. That it didn't happen. It's impossible to believe," Joe said to Mendel.

"It's impossible to tell you in words," Mendel said. "All of our relatives and friends that stayed behind in Sokolow were murdered in Treblinka. I traveled to Sokolow just months ago, and none of them survived. I'll take you to Mauthausen Concentration Camp. It's less than 50 kilometers from here, 20 kilometers east of Linz, and you can see for yourself what can be believed."

At Mauthausen, Joe and Anna saw, still standing, the gas chambers that killed so many and heard stories beyond human understanding of the horrors that were perpetrated there.

Joe gasped, crying, "I didn't want to believe, but seeing this, it's horrible, beyond description. Now I believe. When we're back from the trip, I'll talk to my brother and sisters in America and see what we can do to help you get visas."

Mendel still wanted to go to Israel as his sister had before the war, but with embargoes for emigration to Israel, it was virtually impossible. Joe told him to go to America, that they'd be rich there.

He said, "I see things here in Europe are very cheap. Buy things to bring over." And he gave them a list of things to buy such as gold watches, and earrings. "Bring these to America."

Freyde bought Anna a pair of earrings before she left, but Anna didn't like them. "I can get better things in America," she said.

Joe and Anna stayed two days and left for their trip to Palestine/Israel. In Israel, Joe started a committee for remembering his hometown, Sokolow Podlaski. He had collected $1,000 from others in the U.S. and gave them that to start their memorial organization in Israel. Mendel's sister Shoshana was part of that organization, and Joe had a chance to meet with her and the family she'd started there before he returned to America. His stay was so short that he never had a chance to learn how she'd gotten there from Poland or what her life had been like during the war, a puzzle that remained for decades.

With Joe and Anna gone and with some hope that approval might come for a visa to America, the group settled down as much as they could to life in the camp. The cousins, Ephrayim and Bela, adjusted, as kids do no matter what.

We went exploring around the town and its periphery, happily picking flowers we found in the fields. Srul wandered between the buildings, finding a ball he could play with and be happy. I went to the camp school. I loved to read and would sneak back into the school through a window when school ended so I could read more. The adults did what they could just to make a living while hoping for approval to emigrate, to finally have a place to go.

On the Way to a New Land

After three long years of waiting, papers finally arrived saying that we could come to the United States: Mendel, Freyde, my brother Srul and me, Leah, Velvul, their two girls, and Chaya. Eli's papers didn't come. He had no one who survived, no relatives who could vouch for him, and so we would be tearfully separated possibly never to see each other again. By that time, Eli was like an "uncle" to us and separation for him, for us, and for the rest of the family would be hard. Like other times in our journeys, there were no other happy choices. We could only hope that somehow, we would be reunited later. Eli had no one else.

The journey overseas would be on an American troopship, the *S.S. General Sturgis*, one of many to carry European refugees to new homes around the world. Our ship was scheduled to leave from Bremerhaven, Germany on October 15th, 1949 to carry us to New York. The trip would be long and expensive. By ourselves we could never have raised the money for it. Instead it was paid for and organized by UNRA, the United Nations Relief and Rehabilitation Administration. We were to go overland from Austria to Bremerhaven, from where we would board the ship and then be transported across the Atlantic in what could be turbulent weather.

By train we went first from Wels to Linz.

Wels, Austria to Bremerhaven, Germany, October 1949

Mendel recalled later, "In Linz, I saw this man walking, and I said, I know him! That man walks just like Chiam Kawer, my boyhood friend from Sokolow. We always used to play in the streets together. Impossible! How can it be? Could he, somehow, have survived? Even from the back of him, I know him. He always used to walk just like a duck. No one else walks like that. It has to be him. Freyde didn't believe me. She thought it was impossible, but when the man turned around, it was indeed Chiam!"

They hugged each other and cried. Mendel asked how he managed to survive the war.

Chiam shrugged his shoulders, "I don't know. I just don't know." Miracles!

Again, they had to separate. They both had to go on, not knowing if they'd ever see each other again. How hard was every separation!

In Linz, suddenly, Freyde's mother Chaya took ill. Years of travel and running from place to place had taken a toll, and, at 57 years of age, she had difficulty continuing. However, we were close to finding a place to go, so stopping was out of the question. After everything we'd experienced together, we had to stay together and go on, and we continued to Salzburg, Austria. We'd have to spend two more days in Salzburg waiting for a train to take us on the next leg of our journey. With great trepidation, we finally boarded the train that would take us through Germany – Germany of all places! We would finally arrive in the harbor of Bremerhaven, where a ship would take us to the United States at last, to New York where we thought Joe would meet us. From there, where would we go? We didn't know. Hopefully we'd find a place to finally call home.

What to do to get ready for the long trip? My parents had heard America was cold. Freyde bought a pair of high boots. Mendel bought a feather bed. All they had was packed into a large wooden trunk with the lid hammered shut. They hoped that eventually it would find its way to them wherever they would be in America. Mendel splurged and bought himself a new suit, a blue suit with stripes for whatever might come, in case he needed it. They had managed to save upwards of $600 while in the camps and they spent all but $100 of it that they sewed into the clothes that they were taking to America. Somehow, they were under the impression that "You don't need money in America, but just in case."

From Salzburg we boarded a train that took us to Bremerhaven. From Salzburg through Munich, not far from Dachau, where we learned of the horrors perpetrated there. From Munich, the train passed many small villages and Augsburg, Mettingen, Donauworth, Wurzburg, and finally Frankfurt. Even a year after the end of the war, we were shocked at the destruction, and to see so many bombed out buildings – enormous war damage. And from Frankfurt, on to Bremen, and finally to Bremerhaven, a thousand kilometers in total.

Bremerhaven was a surprise city, different from what we had encountered after the war. Bustling with people – shopkeepers, vendors, hustlers in the streets, immigrants dressed clearly different from everyone else, waiting for a ship to take us all to a new life, hopeful that finally fate would be better.

Mendel and Freyde, on a cool grey October day, wandered through the cobblestoned streets in wonder at what normal life looked like, something none of us children had seen before. On the way to the harbor, a street photographer stationed himself in front of us and snapped our photo and Mendel bought it. A picture still exists of that (**Photo 10**), Mendel and Freyde, me and Srul walking down the street. Me between Mendel and Freyde, holding on to Freyde's coat, Srul holding on to his mother's hand, squinting quizzically at the photographer. Mendel wearing a dark open jacket, thinning hair, skinny from the years of depravation, a small smile finally on his face. Freyde in a long grey winter coat, happy and beautiful, walking now with her family to a better future, her two boys safely with her, holding some luggage to go on the ship.

On the way to boarding the ship, we passed a toy store. We boys had never seen such a thing. Mendel took us inside to look, and I became mesmerized by a small model car. Mendel, seeing me staring hypnotically at it, bought it for me from the small amount of money he had left, a red model MGB with shiny wheels, something for me to treasure forever, and for Srul a toy motorcycle. When I think back on that, it amazes me that he could do that. So little to start with in the new country to which he was bringing us, less than a hundred dollars in his pocket, yet he couldn't hold back from doing something that was important to my brother and me after the years of deprivation.

Ahead of us, the huge ship blasted its horn, impatient for all the refugees to board, to finally get on the way. A long line snaked ahead of us.

We'd never seen a massive vessel such as that, over 500 feet long and, with passengers, over 17,000 tons, capable of carrying over 3,000 human cargo. It had carried much cargo and many troops during the war, had been to Hawaii, France, Singapore, Japan, Calcutta, and Port Said with the troops it carried, seeing much wartime action. Now it was converted to carrying a cargo of hope, displaced person immigrants to America.

It was a mixed human cargo boarding the ship, dressed in whatever they still had, whether their own or from found, cast-off clothing. We boarded with very few pitiful belongings, a small suitcase, bundles of things we still hadn't given up, the last things we'd been able to save to carry us forward.

There were survivors from many places, those who had been forced into labor camps in the east, those who had survived while being forced to work in factories or working on farms, some pitiful few survivors of concentration camps, those who had fled and fled farther and farther east and north, east and south, to the Ural Mountains separating Europe and Asia, to Ukraine and Crimea, to Kazakhstan, Uzbekistan, Turkmenistan, to Turkey, Georgia, to the Caucasus Mountains, to Azerbaijan and eventually including the survivors that had made it to the displaced persons camps, now boarding their ship of hope.

We were horrified that the first thing we encountered was that men and women were separated in the ship, with men settled further back and women bunked forward. Throughout the survivors' journeys, being separated from their families was what they feared most, but now, they realized, that fear could be allayed. Here they were safe.

The ship moved up the river to the sea, and the passengers stood and silently watched the land receding from their view, with Europe fading out of sight, knowing they might never again see the lands, the homes they had come from and hopeful that the ship would bring them to a new home ahead.

The ship was jam-packed with passengers. In the buzz around us we could hear, if not understand, many different languages being spoken, with quite a few refugees speaking in Yiddish, their mother tongue. Although the adults were conversant in Polish and Russian, they were most comfortable in talking to others in Yiddish. For us children, Yiddish was the only language we could really communicate in, although some of us could also understand Russian. For Mendel and Freyde, Leah and Velvul, Chaya, none of us had studied any English in preparation for the next destination. That would remain a barrier to all of us at some point, but not something to worry about then.

The ship moved beyond Bremerhaven into the North Sea, sailed around the United Kingdom and out into the open ocean. The voyage became rough with the ship rolling and pitching in the waves so that many became seasick. For those staying below, the noise and smells and fumes were overpowering. We children, for the most part, preferred being on the open deck, and we spent days watching the ocean waves and seabirds and clouds spinning past. To us it was an interesting and exciting adventure. The adults had a hard time, especially during oncoming winter storms that began in October.

The food we were given was strange to us and hard to get used to. The fruit we now had was something we hadn't gotten in our prior long jour-neys. Apples were treasured. Bananas and oranges were delicacies we had never experienced. The adults, terribly seasick, couldn't eat, but for us children, we relished the new experiences.

The voyage took ten days at sea, and during the last night aboard, rumors buzzed throughout the ship that the next morning we would be arriving in the United States in New York City. The electric excitement kept everyone awake. Sleep was impossible. Early in the morning, long before sunrise, all passengers went on deck in anticipation of the first view of their new land. The night slowly shed its darkness; the October sky gradually lightened in the fog of the brisk grey dawn. And as the ship approached New York harbor, we slowly saw a figure coming out of the mist – the Statue of Liberty that we had heard so much about and dreamed of. Closer and closer we came until, through the mist and our tears, we could see the towering hand stretched out to the sky, carrying a torch that would become a beacon to us for the rest of our lives. And eventually we would be able to read and understand the English inscribed on the plaque inside the base below us:

"Give me your tired, your poor,
Your huddled masses yearning to breathe free,
The wretched refuse of your teeming shore.
Send these, the homeless, tempest-tost to me,
I lift my lamp beside the golden door!"

4

IMMIGRANTS: STREETS PAVED
WITH GOLD

Finding a Way

October 25th, 1949. America! Finally, could this now be the home we were looking for?

It was havoc when the ship docked, with everyone jockeying to get off and hoping to find someone waiting for them. It took hours. Going through the immigration authorities, hoping all papers were in order, fearful that something might be found wrong, hoping that no one would be found sick enough to be denied entry. To have papers stamped. Finally, it was our turn to have our papers checked and to, hopefully, be let in.

The customs inspector examined our group and documents and peered at us.

"What are these papers? What are your names anyway? Shmul? Freyde? Chaya? Ephrayim? Srul? What kind of names are those to come into the country? Those will never work! Here, these will be your names in this country. This is America and you must have American names. Shmul, I see your name is listed as Shmul Mendel? Ok. We won't change it much. You can be Mendel! Freyde? How do you even say that? Never heard of it. From now on you're Frieda. That's a good American name. Chaya?

Chaya? Very confusing; can't even think of what that could be. You're Ida from now on, ok? The two little guys here? You're not going to saddle them with those weird names, are you? They'll get killed on the playground with those. Here, Efrum, you're Fred. We'll keep it simple even. Not Fredrick. Just plain Fred. That's a good American name. No one will bother you with that. And the little guy? Srul? What's that? Can't work. He'll be Irving instead. Just like Irving Berlin. Heard of him? He's the good American guy who wrote *God Bless America* and *White Christmas*. You guys heard of those, right? Can't go wrong with Irving."

Frieda's sister's family did a little better. Leah could stay Leah. Her husband though, Velvul? The inspector couldn't make heads or tails of that. He became Wolf. The older daughter, Belah, was allowed to keep the first letter only of her name. She became Barbara. And her little sister? Same thing. Luba became Loretta.

And with the arrival of the new names and our documents stamped, we breathed a sigh of relief as we were released and ready to become Americans – however that would happen.

Now we were ready to go and find who was waiting for us and where. Where wasn't easy with the huge crush of arrivals who were trying to do the same thing, but finally someone directed us to where arrivals could pass through a gate and be recognized, hopefully, by someone who was waiting for them.

Joe, Ida's brother, had rented a big station wagon and had driven to New York City with his daughter Evelyn's husband, Ted Halasz. Once found, the new immigrants, nine of us, piled into the station wagon with Joe and Ted. Station wagon? What did we know about station wagons? We just followed directions. The few suitcases went on top, and we were finally off to our new city, South Bend, Indiana. Somehow, we knew that Ida had a sister Bryna (Bernice) also in South Bend and that South Bend was not far from Chicago, where Ida had another brother (Bernard) and Sister (Sarah), family she hadn't seen in over 40 years. That was all our group knew about America. We knew it was big; we had heard as others had, that the streets were paved with gold, but didn't know what that meant. Far from it. We'd seen enormous buildings, called skyscrapers – they indeed looked like they scraped the sky. We'd seen huge masses of people on the streets, but also many who looked destitute. We'd seen no sign of streets paved with anything looking like gold. Oh, well. From where we'd been until now, everything looked like we were in heaven.

We drove for hours and hours in the crowded car. Everyone was so tired, we slept against each other. Loretta (Luba), particularly, didn't feel well. She had a fever and red spots appeared on her face. It turned out that she had the measles and all of us were being exposed. It was a good thing that didn't happen earlier or all of us might have been quarantined by immigration and held back.

We finally stopped along the way around midnight for some American food that we didn't recognize (hot dogs!), stayed the night at a small hotel, and continued for hours the next day.

Friday afternoon we arrived in South Bend. It was a city of about 100,000 people, with many stores and houses, neat and quiet. This would eventually become our home. Joe lived on 730 Western Avenue, a busy street. He had a large brick building with a clothing and pawnshop on the main floor and two stories above it, an apartment where he lived and apartments he rented out. To us newcomers he looked very prosperous, and we were amazed at what we saw of the luxury of Joe's home.

Friday night, Anna had arranged a beautiful Shabbat dinner for all, place settings where, astonishingly, everything matched, amid glasses with wine for Kiddush, chicken and potatoes, napkins – a feast! It made our meager efforts to host Joe and Anna, when they had visited in the displaced persons camp, look shabby by comparison. Joe had arranged for a photographer from the local newspaper, The South Bend Tribune, to take a picture (**Photo 11**) to memorialize our arrival and write an article on the new immigrants that they had brought to South Bend.

Mendel, Frieda, Chaya and us boys stayed overnight with Joe and his wife Anna. Leah, Velvul and her girls stayed with someone else in South Bend, not far away. Anna said, "I'm not feeling well. I'm sick. There are so many of you, and we don't have enough room. Tomorrow you'll have to find somewhere else to stay." None of us knew what that meant. Where else could we stay? We were in this country for the first time and, to us, South Bend was a strange new place. Where else could we stay?

Chaya's sister, Bernice (Bryna) Goldberg also met us when we arrived. She was overjoyed to see her sister again after so many years. Bernice's own life in the United States had not been easy since she arrived in 1921; she, herself, had suffered tragedies in her personal life during her years in America and no longer lived with her husband. She had had four children, Irvin, Ruth, Paul, and Bernard, and Ruth had died after just one year.

Bernice said to her sister, "Chaya, I don't have much. I have a small house, and I make a living from selling rags. I have a very small store across the street. It's filled with clothes that I resell that I buy from rummage sales. It's not enough, but I can make a living from that. You and Mendel and Frieda and the boys are more than welcome to stay there until you find someplace else to live. It's not luxurious, but it's warm and dry and a place where you can see what else you can do. Let me help you with this, please."

Tears came to Chaya's eyes. Here was her sister that she'd missed for so long. She could tell by looking at her that she'd had a hard life and didn't have much for herself either. But whatever she had, she was willing to share with them. She hugged and thanked Bernice and told her how grateful she was for letting them stay there. We had been wandering for so long and so far, that any place safe to stay was something to be more than grateful for.

The next morning, we crossed over to her store. During the day, Bernice was there and worked with any customers who might come in. At night, the store closed, the family cooked some meager meals on a cook plate and got ready for sleep on the floor. Two days a week, we went back across the street and had a small lunch at Joe and Anna's. It was never a big lunch, nine people and one loaf of bread, but everything was to be grateful for.

For me, Bernice's store was a marvelous place. In the store, tables everywhere were stacked with all kinds of clothes in all colors. Clothes for men; clothes for women; clothes for kids. More than clothes, discards from families were everywhere. Some games, some books, even a few toys. Lots of things for a boy to explore.

But everything wasn't wonderful. At night, the store got cold. Mice ran around, and cockroaches ventured out when lights went out. If the lights were put on for any reason during the night, the roaches would scatter!

One-night Frieda made a small soup for dinner. Mendel said, "Frieda, you put meat in the soup?"

Frieda looked surprised, "No there's no meat in the soup!"

Mendel looked in the soup. There were cockroaches in the soup. Later, we could laugh at those memories.

One-time Velvul found a big fish market on Western Avenue, a mile away from where we were. He bought bread and herring for all of us to eat. "We loved it. It was the best herring we'd ever had," Mendel remembered.

We were together! No more running. No more being chased by armies. No more being arrested by police. No more being yelled at, abused just for being Jewish.

It was a start.

Finding Work / A Place to Live

Finding a job to make enough money for a place to live wasn't easy. None of us spoke any English. How to find a job when you couldn't speak the language? The people in the Jewish community learned of our plight and came to help.

One of the sponsors of our visa to America besides Joe Rosenbaum was Harold Medow. The Medows had a car showroom but also had a car wash across the street. They hired Mendel to wash cars. Three days after he arrived, he had a job! His job was to take the cars across the street and wash them. Of course, he didn't have a driver's license. He didn't speak or read English, but he knew how to drive. He got paid 90 cents an hour.

He was kept at that job for a month. They couldn't speak with him, but the secretary spoke Polish and he could talk to her. After a month, the secretary came out and told Mendel that he had been fired because he couldn't speak English!

In the meantime, he looked for a place for his family to live, some place other than the rag store with its mice and cockroaches.

They met someone else from the Jewish community by the name of Feingold. He had a store on Chapin Street. Chapin Street was around the corner from Joe and Bernice's stores. It was a tough neighborhood at the time, being the heart of the black neighborhood in the town. Drunks on the street at night with police and ambulances.

Above his store, Feingold had apartments. With his small check from the car wash, Mendel rented an apartment from him on the second floor: 444 ½ Chapin Street. Our first real home in the new world!

We rented it for $40 a month. Our apartment was upstairs, while Feingold's store was downstairs. Mendel and Joe went together to rent it.

Mendel remembered the place and the neighborhood as terrible. I, however, didn't think of it the same way. To me, it was a good place. Big windows in the front where you could look down on the street. Big iron radiators hissing with hot steam; it was never cold, although it was the beginning of winter. We had a kitchen where Frieda finally could make real meals. Two bedrooms, one for Mendel and Frieda and one for Irving and me. A long, narrow staircase leading down to the street where there was always something interesting. We became used to finding an old black man who'd sit on the bottom of the staircase. He was a nice man, and as we started to learn English, we'd sit on the bottom of the stairs with him watching people outside go by, and he would talk with us.

Lots of cars, trucks, and buses going up and down the street. Lots of shops to look in the windows. Down the street was a place that always had music coming out of it. It was a "Cotton Club" with young black people coming in and out and music that fascinated us.

After the first month at the car wash, Mendel needed another job. He talked to Joe to see if he had any ideas. He took him to different job that paid him more, $1 an hour. It was a decent place to work and he found a neighbor who was an immigrant, Mr. Frankel, another new immigrant, also worked there. Mendel still couldn't speak English, but it didn't matter. After a short while, though, they gave him a letter that he took to Joe to read. They had laid him off. The reason, he found out, was because he was Jewish. Joe was incensed. He said, "I'm going over there, and I'm going to sue them," but they never got sued.

Mendel tried again. He went to a junk company that worked with wrecked cars. Owned by someone else in the Jewish community, Rube Silverman. He got paid even less, 85 cents an hour, but it was steady work, and he needed the job.

It wasn't very close to where we lived. The junk company was far south in town. Mendel would take buses in the morning to get there, and he'd work eight hours or more a day. He became good at taking out engines, crankcases and pistons from wrecked cars. The store would resell the parts or the motors he rebuilt. When he worked more than the regular eight hours, he got paid overtime. He was a quick learner and soon knew every part that came with each different car. He could read the books on the cars from the pictures that they contained. By that time, he became the expert in the store so that when someone came in to find a part for their particular car, they'd be sent directly to him. Soon it was common to hear, "Mendel can tell you. He'll find the part for you."

He was treated well there. They recognized he was good and asked him, "Mendel can you make more motors?" Every day he'd do more. They challenged him, "Can you make four or five a day?"

He was young and strong. His years on the run, working on farms and running machinery, had given him that. He could do more indeed. He got so quick that he could take apart up to ten cars a day, and he worked there for about a year when he said to Rube, "Rube, I can't make a living from all this. I make maybe $40 a week, and that's just not enough to pay the rent and pay for food and clothes for the wife and kids."

Rube asked him, "How much money do you want?"

Mendel said, "$1 an hour."

Rube couldn't do that, although when Mendel told Joe about it, Joe said, "You greenhorn, you should have told him $2 an hour." But if Rube wouldn't give $1 an hour, he surely wouldn't have done more.

He looked to see if he could get another job. He talked to another man at the synagogue that they now went to. His name was Sam Brown, who had a brother who was a director at a factory in town, "The Oliver Farm Equipment Company", a leader in producing tractors.

He applied for a job at Oliver's and got hired. It was a union job paying $1.25 an hour and there were a lot of other displaced persons working there – Jews, Ukrainians, others. Mendel quit his job at Rube's and started working at Oliver's. Besides the increase in pay, the other big benefit was that the Oliver factory was also located on Chapin Street, not that far away, just a very short walk or bus ride. It would make his life easier.

At the beginning he got paid by the hour while he learned the production line. He knew all about machines though, and especially about tractors, so that later he was paid by the piece on the production line. It was his job making bases for the plows for the tractors and it didn't take long until he could make 30 to 40 bases for plows in a day. He had more money to take home, and now they could begin to save a little.

Business slowed at Oliver's though, and Mendel got laid off after a year. Almost three years since arriving in America, now 1952, he was again looking for a job. The loss of the job was disheartening, but he always had a good attitude about finding the next job. What he'd learned on the run was to never give up, and it served him well. He saw an advertisement from the railroad looking for men. He applied and could start working there. After a year while working on the railroad, he got a call from Oliver. They wanted him back. So, he worked at both. He worked at the railroad and at Oliver's into 1953, and then he quit Oliver's so he could work for the New York Central Railroad full time.

From arriving as a refugee in 1949, he had found for his family a home, even though it was in the heart of the black ghetto, and while moving from job to job, had been able to provide them with comfort and support. Now he was a railroad man.

Becoming Americans

When we moved into our apartment on Chapin Street in 1949, one of the first orders of business for the family was that I had to go to school. I was over six years old, almost seven that November, and I had to be enrolled.

Their firm perspective was that I had to start to eventually build a future for myself, and I couldn't do that if I didn't go to school. Although I'd always liked school, I didn't want to go now. After all I'd been through until this point, I didn't want to be separated from my family. Besides, I didn't speak English either. Who would I talk to in school? How would the teachers talk to me? And the school wasn't close, either. How was I going to get there? To me, it was way too much hassle. All to no avail, I had to go.

So, on an early crisp autumn morning, I was set off walking with Joe, Frieda, and Mendel to take me to the school. Joe had arranged all. I was going to go to Colfax school, an elementary school that had grades from kindergarten to third grade. It was about a mile away, and they were taking me there on an early Monday morning.

We walked north on Chapin Street, past Western Avenue, past all kinds of shops not yet open in the early morning. We got to a big crossing where there was a traffic light on Washington Street. To our left was a huge stone mansion, which I later came to learn was called the Oliver Mansion having 38 magnificent rooms. It was four stories high and made almost entirely of ornate stone, stone columns on a huge porch and a round portico on the second floor at the front of the home. It was home to the President of the Oliver Corporation where my father would find work several years later. In all our years of wandering, I had never seen anything so large and so grand. I was mesmerized. We turned on LaPorte Avenue and passed a big church on the left. Further down the street were large old houses, starting to deteriorate even then. We went down one side street after another until we emerged on Lincolnway West, the street where Colfax School was situated. There it was a huge red brick building with big windows and big concrete steps on the front leading into it. To me, it looked ominous.

They took me into the building and marched me into the principal's office where Joe explained who we were and introduced him to me. I didn't understand a word. I just plain didn't want to be there. I wanted to go home.

The principal was told that I could only speak Yiddish. What was he going to do with that? In a stroke of brilliance, he took me to a kindergarten teacher in a class that had several children that knew some German who might partly understand my Yiddish. After all, he figured, how different could those be? The kids were to be the translators for us all, and I was left with the teacher and the kids, who just stood looking at each other as though to say, "Well! What do we have here!"

The adults took the opportunity to make their escape. Before I could turn around, they were gone.

Joe, Mendel, and Frieda went home, but when they got there, they discovered that I'd somehow found my way home even before them.

I got a good talking to and was told that they'd take me back tomorrow and, this time, I was going to stay – no running back home! It didn't take any time at all after that until I made my way back and forth to the school every day on my own.

It was more than a little strange for me that I was a seven-year-old in a class with much younger kindergarten children, but they and the teacher made every effort to welcome me and help me learn English. To my surprise, I rapidly came to like the school, the teacher, the principal and my classmates. I learned English almost overnight and soon no longer belonged in kindergarten.

Life settled down to a routine for us immigrants. Our house on Chapin Street, although surrounded by old and dilapidated housing, became our home. Winter settled in, and the heavy South Bend winter snows hit regularly, but the radiators hissed warmth at us. We snuggled in to what soon became our comfortable home, and we could finally feel that we no longer needed to worry about wandering.

It didn't take long before it was agreed that Colfax School was no longer appropriate for me and that I should change schools. Promoted within three months to first grade, I was sent to Washington School. From our apartment on Chapin Street, I could now take the bus from across the street, change to a second bus and be at school without a long walk. Especially in wintertime, with the heavy snows, that was important to the family and me.

I soon became the family's first fluent English speaker, rapidly was taught to write and was soon just like any other child in my class.

In November of our second year in America, a new baby was born, Charlotte (Chinka, named after Mendel's mother who was lost in the Holocaust), the first American in the family. Chubby and pink-cheeked, our family adored her. But even here the family worried about what they'd be able to do to secure a successful future for her, given their modest and meager beginnings.

Reading was my favorite activity. I loved the simple books in school, the Dick and Jane and Spot books with their pictures. I especially loved reading the comic books I found at the corner drug store near our home on Chapin Street, and I was there whenever I could. I was fascinated by the Katzenjammer Kids comics and graduated to Superman and Batman and then any others I could get to. I couldn't afford to buy the comics, but the store came to recognize me and let me read without buying whenever I wanted. Between Washington School in the first grade and those comic books, I rapidly became a skilled and voracious reader. I was Americanized!

My parents also recognized they needed to become Americans, and while living on Chapin Street, they started taking night courses on English for Foreigners at the YWCA. After a long day for Mendel at work, we would be left in the care of Ida, while Frieda and Mendel walked the two miles to class. Ida was never able to go to English class. Instead, she was the family's cushion for the unexpected, the reliable helper, the loving nanny, and the support for the children. For the rest of her life, she was the substitute mother for us, never learning to speak English, only speaking Yiddish.

What a varied group of people Mendel and Frieda encountered in their class, immigrants like themselves from all parts of Europe, speaking Russian, Polish, Slovakian, Hungarian, Italian, French or German, with frequently Yiddish being their common tongue. And the teacher was an American who didn't know any of these languages. Lots of pictures and hand signs were used to communicate. One or another of the students who could speak part of one language, or another, bridged the gap to other students and helped the teacher. It was raucous, exciting, fun and, day-by-day, they began to be able to put words together to sentences and to be able to communicate among themselves and with their teacher whom they all loved. It was gradual and hard work, but they slowly became English speakers even if they spoke with different European accents.

For Mendel and many other men in the class, they were highly motivated to speak and read English. Their first goal always was to learn enough to pass an exam and get an American drivers license, to have a better chance at a job, to earn enough to pay for rent and maybe even to save a little money to someday make a down payment for a house.

By 1951, the family was able to move a short distance away from the ghetto and rent a house. It was a two-story affair, just half a block from Joe's store where they'd spent the first night in America. Directly across the street from that house was a massive gothic church with a towering spire and a school and extensive parking area where they could see church buses unloading their crops of children every morning. Directly adjacent to their house was a small neighborhood store run by two of Bernice's children, Paul and Irvin Goldberg. It was a wonderful place for my brother and me. It had a candy counter where we could stand and look at all the wonders we'd like to buy and where we could sometimes rustle up a coin and walk away with a gumball or chocolate to chew. I loved it there and quickly made friends with Paul and Irvin.

On the other side of our house stood an old apartment building and another immigrant family, the Frankels, occupied the second floor. They had a young son, Johnny. Johnny and I became friends and wandered the neighborhood together, exploring. Loretta and Barbara Lopata, my cousins, lived some distance away from us. We became good friends. They were frequent visitors, and we played children's games together, although the story was that I sometimes taunted them and threw things at them from the second story of their house in jest. It was very different from the past we had all known after the war in Europe when there was no time for play.

Mendel, Frieda and Ida occasionally stopped at Joe's store for brief visits. Joseph was the store's owner-manager, but his son Irving and son-in-law Ted Halasz were also always there working. Sometimes they'd also see Joe's daughter Evelyn, who was married to Ted. Only infrequently would they see Ruth, Irving's wife, in the store. Evelyn was a vivacious "sparkly eyed" girl, always happy and friendly to the visiting relatives. Ruth was a strikingly beautiful young woman who seemed to never age with a wonderful singing voice that could be heard at synagogue or special community affairs.

Very soon after arriving in South Bend, Joe had invited all the immigrants to a dinner to introduce them to the relatives. It was a strange affair for the newly arrived. The "now assimilated Americans" who'd arrived long before the 1920s, looked very different from the "greenhorns" in their midst. The earlier arrivals were all settled and professionals, shopkeepers and storeowners, solid Americans who spoke English without an accent, ate American food, knew American music and dances, and smoked cigarettes incessantly. On the other side were the immigrants with next to nothing. They had no jobs, few possessions, and with customs and traditions that seemed to have vanished in their new country. While they were clearly all relatives, they felt the great differences between them. In their European clothes and their Yiddish language (or Russian or Polish), they had no clue about being American. They and their children just looked bewildered by it all. But they were all family and they were together, and that was what was most important.

Joe did help Mendel and advised him with getting jobs in his early years in the country, but Mendel always felt that he was treated as a "greenhorn." In later years when Mendel worked on the railroad, Mendel felt that he never was much respected by him since he was a laborer, a workman, and not a professional.

While Joe's store was predominantly a clothing store, its main customers were people from the black neighborhood. The store also contained a pawn shop that was regularly plied by those from the surrounding area. I would visit, peer through the cases, and would be entranced by the articles left behind, most of them never being reclaimed but sold later – rings and necklaces and jewelry of all kinds, appliances, radios and binoculars, and cameras.

One of the articles that had been once left behind, a fancy movie camera that recorded moving pictures and even sound, came to be owned by Joe. He took it with him on his many travels, vacations, and world trips. It had accompanied him on his and Anna's trip to Israel when they had stopped to see the family momentarily in the displaced person's camp in Wels, Austria. That expensive 16 mm movie camera was a rare item for someone to own in 1949, but because it was one of the things left behind by someone needing quick cash, it quickly became something that Joe always took along as he documented his special family events or trips or vacations.

Joe used it when he had invited the immigrants to their first dinner, and the film from that dinner is a document of the chasm between the members of the family that had been separated by time and by war: those who had stayed behind and been swallowed up by war and tragedy and those who had been fortunate enough to have left long before those times. None of the immigrants knew or understood that their first encounter with their broad American family was being recorded for posterity. That film was miraculously discovered by accident more than 60 years later when I was engrossed in finally studying my family history.

Living in a house in a peaceful and stable neighborhood was a real luxury but did necessitate some adaptation for all the family members. For starters, the rent was higher and meant more money was needed. Mendel was doing all he could with his work, sometimes working at several jobs at once, working at Oliver's factory in the day and another part-time job at night. Ida, with no capability to speak English and being an older woman, couldn't take a job that paid any significant salary. Even she, however, was able to find part-time work at the local Jewish butcher shop about a mile away where someone was needed to process chickens that were butchered and sold. Ida became a chicken plucker, pulling feathers off chickens so they could be put in display cases for sale. Her fingers red and raw from her work, with chicken feathers still stuck in her hair when she'd walk home at night, she presented a humorous but tender sight to us children when we welcomed her home and plied her with big hugs.

My father couldn't imagine he could ever own an automobile. The thought of expenses associated with that and the complication it would add to their lives made that seem impossible. For the family, getting around meant taking buses or walking. Shopping for groceries was about a half mile away, and Frieda would take a two-wheeled grocery shopping cart with her, and I would help her get her groceries home.

Frieda, too, found a way to help with the family finances. She took in boarders, old men who could no longer live by themselves at home, who were in early stages of mental decline, whose families couldn't find places for them in their own homes or afford extended care or nursing homes. She rented out one of the bedrooms in the house to them, provided them with home-cooked meals, as well as much-needed companionship. While it was critical to her own family's budgetary survival, it was also a lifesaver for both the men as well as their families.

Eli Arrives

When the family had left the Austrian displaced persons camp in October 1949, their friend whom they called "uncle" Eli was unable to obtain a passport to immigrate and join them. He had to stay behind in the camp, and the separation, after finding each other and becoming family, was hard on them all even while they maintained contact through frequent letters.

Not until early 1952, was Eli able to obtain a visa to come to America, to South Bend. He was going to join his "family," the only ones in the whole world with whom he felt he had a connection.

Excitement reigned when we got the letter that he was coming by ship to New York and then by train to South Bend. We were all hardly recognizable to each other when he arrived in South Bend. Mendel and Frieda had been skinny and almost emaciated when he saw them leave Austria, and Irving and I had grown and matured a lot. Charlotte hadn't been born then, and, as a little two-year-old cherub, she was a delight to Eli. Eli himself had changed a great deal. The extra years in the displaced persons camp had aged him, and he was an even slimmer and older version of himself than we had seen in Europe.

Eli was given a bedroom on the second floor of the house on Western Avenue, which grew a little more crowded with his arrival. Mendel and Frieda in one bedroom, Ida, the two boys, Charlotte, the boarder, and Eli filled the house to beyond its reasonable capacity, but what was important was they were all together and safe and the future had prospects for them.

As much as Eli was grateful to his "family," living with boarders was hard on him, especially with the older boarder who lived there now, Mr. Tolchinsky. Mr. Tolchinsky had frequent lapses of memory, tended toward insomnia and periodic bouts of hallucination where he envisioned that people were coming to attack him. As protection, he slept with a brick under his bed.

One morning, Eli sat agitated at breakfast. "I was asleep last night and suddenly woke when I heard Tolchinsky outside the door. I got out of bed to see what was going on and saw Tolchinsky standing with the brick in his hand muttering, 'They're coming to get me.' I'm afraid he'll kill me in my sleep with that brick. You have to do something."

Frieda talked to Tolchinsky's children about finding another home for Tolchinsky, but there was no place else for him to go. His children pleaded with her for their father to stay, and kind-hearted Frieda relented. They took away the brick.

Eli had taken some English classes while waiting in Austria and so was better prepared to find a job. From the local community, he was offered a position in a nearby floor covering and window coverings store. Eli took a job there making window shades and venetian blinds for the kind storeowner, David Moss. Eli worked in that store during the rest of his career and, in later years could be seen driving their truck making deliveries with a sign on the truck that read, "Blind Man Driving This Truck," that always caused heads to turn to see who or what was driving.

As I graduated to higher grades at Washington School, I was able to adapt more and more with the schools' curriculum. Graduating from learning to write block letters, to being able to write script was a major challenge for me, even more so than my other friends there, but I was able to conquer that as well as start to excel in the other school lessons.

The family was rapidly adapting to their American lives and couldn't wait to formally become citizens.

The Thread Called "Remember"

Half a lifetime later, as I think back on those times as new immigrants to what was for all of us a strange new land, I recognize that a transformation had occurred. We no longer dwelled on those chapters of our lives of fleeing from danger, of constantly being on the run, of never knowing whether the book of our lives was at its end or where it would go next. Instead I realized that in our daily lives, our thinking, our awareness, our attitudes had changed. In everything we were doing, we were looking toward new and, what we could dare to hope would be, potentially remarkable futures.

All survivors of a treacherous past, every new immigrant, whether one that lived through the horrors of World War II or the devastation and displacement of other wars, of Korea, of Vietnam, Darfur, Bosnia, Rwanda, Congo, and today Syria, show the same scars. Scars of looking for or remembering those who were lost or couldn't be found, of struggling to find safe places, of finally finding some place to settle and start again. And starting fresh but knowing that their lives will always show them to be different. No matter how much life blesses them, they will always show the singes that marked their searing passage.

So it was with us in those early years in the 1950s. We settled in to find jobs and homes and educate ourselves and become like the ordinary Americans around us. All the while, as we moved forward, the world continued its turbulent changes – the rise of Communism, the McCarthy era, and massive changes in the Middle East. These and others were the big events surrounding our lives, but the everyday events and changes in our personal lives were what encompassed us, making us into typical Americans. Almost. Because no matter how much we took on the appearance of all those around us, there was still that seared beginning that always set us apart.

Even now.

Even now, when I meet someone new and we exchange our first hellos and how are you's and where do you come froms, the difference shows up. My wife will say, "Well, we moved here from Philadelphia, but I was born and grew up in Chicago. I'm a Chicago girl." And when they ask me the same question "and where are you from," and I say, "Well, I grew up in Indiana as a Hoosier, but I was born in Azerbaijan," they inevitably do a double take.

"What?" they say. "Where?" And then the questions begin, and they look at me with different eyes. Growing up; going to college, graduate school: Normal! A career in research? OK. CEO of a biotech start-up? OK, but a little more out of the ordinary. But born in Azerbaijan – and "What's all that about?"

A different universe. But back then, we all had a long way to go.

5

NEW LIVES

A New Neighborhood

With the house on Western Avenue bursting at the seams, with me eleven years old and ready to go to higher elementary classes, with Irving eight and in school, and Charlotte at three soon to be ready for kindergarten, the family began to think about buying a house. Could they hope for a middle-class neighborhood not far from a good school? Through all their efforts, they had somehow saved enough money for a down payment on a house and decided that it was time to move.

Joe advised against it. "You've been in the country for such a short time. You're still greenhorns! Isn't this good enough for you? Remember what you came from. You're not ready to buy a house for yourself!"

Mendel persisted, however, and they looked and looked to see what they could find and what they could afford. Finally, they found a hundred-year-old house in a middle-class neighborhood on Sherman Avenue. Miraculously, it was just three blocks from a school that had grades from kindergarten through Junior High School. What could be better!

It was a ramshackle old house on a corner lot. It boasted a large main floor and three bedrooms and a bathroom upstairs. Even more, it had a large unfinished attic that could be converted separately into a huge livable attic. It had a basement for storage and a one-car garage. The garage looked like it had seen much better days long ago. It was in awful shape at the edge of the lot. No car would ever deign to lower itself to live there! There were no trees on the lot, but trees did line part of the street on the side of the house and there were even some fruit trees in back. The lot had a fenced-in yard with purple lilac bushes inside with glorious fragrances.

The main floor had a front sitting room with built-in white-painted wood shelving, a living room with space for couches and chairs and a fireplace and an adjacent dining room. The main floor also had a reasonable kitchen with room for a small dining table and chairs, and adjacent to the kitchen was a pantry with built-in shelving with plenty of storage space for appliances and groceries, although it had no ducts to heat the room. In the winter, it was always freezing. The house had a gas furnace that kept most of the house warm and, typical of all houses at the time, there was no air conditioning for the hot and humid summers that we'd encounter.

They bought the house for the incredible price of $8,000, which at that time, they considered a small fortune. They made a tiny down payment and took a 30-year mortgage to pay it off. For the life of me, I never understood how they managed to do it.

Not surprisingly, the house wasn't in splendid shape and required considerable work to make it into a home. The exterior of the house was wood siding with faded and peeling paint. The inside of the house also needed painting or wallpapering in every room. The living room and dining room rugs were old, stained, and dirty as were all the rugs in the bedrooms, and the linoleum in the kitchen was yellow with age with scratches and stains.

But it was a big house with plenty of space for all of us, Mendel, Frieda, Ida, me and Irving, Charlotte, Eli, and even our border, Mr. Tolchinsky, who moved with us. It was in a nice middle-class neighborhood with a good nearby school, and we'd fix it up and make it work. Best of all, it was ours! It was in that house that my baby brother Boris was born in 1955, the second American of our family. We never imagined what achievements this latest addition to our family would attain as he grew up, and how important he would become, not only to my parents, but to us all.

After years of wandering, of being displaced persons with an uncertain future, and after years of being "greenhorn" immigrants, we were finally home.

We'd never lived in a neighborhood like that before. It was a quiet place with nice little houses marching up and down both sides of the street. All the houses were neatly separate with manicured lawns and nice bushes and trees on the lots, many having nicely planted flowers on the front. They all had tidy porches where people could sit and watch a quiet rain come down, see what was going on in the street, watch their kids playing on the lawn or even more typically in the street when there wasn't much traffic.

A block away was a small local grocery store where the merchant was an old blind man who tended to his small sales and where people would give him their money, tell him how much they were giving him, and let him figure out what change he should give back. The shop was a place filled with kindness and trust. I loved going there to get a small amount of candy, and the shopkeeper and I would chat enjoying each other's company.

There were no abandoned houses, no big buildings, and no buildings with broken glass in the windows; no signs of anything not peaceful. A block away was a stone church with a modest spire reaching into the sky, and on Sundays the streets were fully parked with cars with their passengers attending services. There was no synagogue nearby or any other sign that there were other Jewish people in that neighborhood.

Next door was a friendly old couple that welcomed us, as did many of the other neighbors down the street. They seemed more to view us as Europeans than as Jews. Halfway down the street was a family, the Kuesperts, with many kids of all ages who welcomed us and who joined us in playing ball in the middle of the road.

But even here, not everyone was kind. We lived on a street corner and on the adjoining street stood a house immediately next door to us with a family that viewed us with suspicion and some degree of malice. They made every effort to be antagonistic, even to the extent of attacking us with shouts of "Dirty Jew! Why don't you go back where you came from! You're not wanted here!" I was shocked. I hadn't experienced that hatred in America before and couldn't understand where it came from or why. We had no place to go back to! Where could we go? There was no way they could understand that. We had no enmity towards them. All we wanted was a quiet place that could be home.

Other neighbors, seeing the abuse Mendel and our family were getting, stepped in to support us, urging us to ignore those neighbors, that they didn't represent the others and repeating that we were welcome. In time, those neighbors were isolated and eventually moved away, and we forgot what they represented. To us, the love and respect our neighbors showed in welcoming us to their community were more than enough to erase the memories of those ignorant people.

A few short blocks away was the new school for me to attend, Muessel School. The school was an enormous two-story red-brick building occupying an entire city block. In the back was a fenced, spacious, black-topped playground for children.

I was ready to start fourth grade, and I entered the school just as any other small American child would. My English by now was natural and without accent, and I looked no different than any other child other than being skinny from the deprivation of my early childhood. Nevertheless, I soon fit in with my peers, and we struggled alike with our lesson plans. I especially loved my English class, taught by a kind elderly woman named Mrs. Molnar. Besides the routine English study that she led, she also spent part of each class reading to us. That was my favorite. What wonderful stories she would read. I especially enjoyed it when each member of the class could participate in the reading. Even the conventional parts of the class, vocabulary and grammar were fascinating to me, and this early class during my growing up left me with a life-long love of English, reading, and writing, and I found, to my surprise, that I could excel in this as I started to do in my other classes.

The Big Friend

Several of my classmates became my friends, and a much bigger young-ster named Lamonte, whom I learned also lived on my block, became my buddy.

When school was over, I would walk the few blocks home, usually alone. Several times I encountered others from my class who were bullies and who started to harass me, not because I was Jewish, but because I was small and because they resented that I was good in school and they weren't. Sometimes, on the way home, they would heckle and tease me and even push me down and start fights. It started to be distressing to go home, not knowing how unpleasant it was going to be.

After much thinking, I arrived at a clever solution. Lamonte and I were close friends now. We'd visit each other at our homes, play games like cowboys and Indians in his back yard, and we'd go exploring together. His father owned a large coal and oil company some miles away, and Lamonte and I would ride our bikes around the neighborhood and even visit his father at work. It was a nice family. We became very close friends. As it turned out, he became the solution to my dilemma. Lamonte was a big guy, and nobody messed with Lamonte!

When school was finished for the day, we started walking home together since Lamonte's house was on the way home for me anyway. We enjoyed each other's company, and nobody bothered me anymore. I had a big friend. Besides, our friendship was mutually beneficial. We'd do home-work together and when Lamonte might get stuck with a problem, we could work it out together. Our friendship lasted a long time, even in later years when Lamonte's family moved miles away to a beautiful house they built adjacent to the river. I would ride my bicycle to visit him, and our friendship continued. I miss him to this day.

Hot Dogs, Salami, Bologna

Mendel and his family had always been serious about their religion. Judaism was important to them. It had been impossible to be tradition-ally observant during their long sojourn in the Soviet Union, much different than traditional Jewish life had been like for Mendel when he

was growing up in Sokolow. There his family had been ritually observant, studied Hebrew, kept kosher, and attended services in the town
Synagogue each Saturday.

Finally, in the United States, our family was able to resume the traditions, at least to the extent that Mendel's job allowed. Frieda now kept a
kosher home. That meant, among other things, using only beef or
chicken that had been humanely butchered by a religious authority,
using no pork products, keeping milk and meat dishes, cookware and
utensils separate and not mixing meat with milk. And always, calling a
halt to the workweek, celebrating another week of survival, celebrating
time together as a family.

Every Friday evening, no matter how hectic or disappointing the week
might have been, no matter the pressures on the family, Frieda would
lovingly get ready for Shabbat. The house would be cleaned to perfection and special foods would mark the occasion. She always made challah. She would pour out some flour, enriching it with fresh yeast, eggs,
and oil with a few tablespoons of sugar to add some sweetness. Letting it
rise, she would knead out the dough on a big wooden board. Finally, the
magic of braiding the loaf. Even a simple three-stranded braid would
have been impressive, though she often made a four- or six-stranded
braid on very special occasions. For major celebrations, like the Jewish
high holidays, she coiled the long-braided loaf into a circle. A simple
brushing-on of egg wash made the loaf shiny and magnificent. She
would pop it in the oven until the aroma of fresh bread made the whole
house sweet smelling. What a wonder to celebrate together peacefully as
a family!

The main course always included chicken soup and dumplings, baked
chicken, potatoes and gravy. These were usually preceded by an appe-
tizer she'd cooked of *gefilte fish*, a special dish made from a poached
mixture of ground boned fish, such as carp, whitefish, or pike. The fresh
fish was typically purchased from the fish market in town or at rare times
even caught by me, fishing on the St. Joseph River not far away.

Mendel came home one day from a long day's work on the railroad,
sweaty and grimy in his overalls from the day's hard work ready for a
nice bath and discovered to his amazement a live carp swimming in the

bathtub, one that I'd caught and brought home and that Frieda made later into gefilte fish.

Even at that time, getting kosher chicken and especially kosher beef was complicated and prohibitively expensive for us.

Getting the chickens was solved locally. Mendel and Frieda found a local farmer, Johnny, who raised and sold chickens and eggs. They were able to get Johnny to bring the eggs regularly and even deliver live chickens to their back yard. Then they had the rabbi of their synagogue meet them and traditionally slaughter the chickens for them. Coming home from school one day, I was horrified to watch this once as some killed chickens briefly ran around the back yard with their heads off! In the basement, Ida and Frieda would pluck the feathers off the killed chickens and process them for freezing in the chest freezer that held their perishable goods. It was always a humorous sight to see my grandmother coming out of the basement with feathers sticking out of her hair.

The family didn't often buy kosher beef. It was just too expensive, but we did get hot dogs and bologna and salami for lunches, either for us kids or for Mendel to take to work for lunches. Even those were too expensive to frequently purchase at the local kosher meat market, but Mendel found a way that worked for him.

He'd go to Chicago.

South Bend was about 90 miles from Chicago, and Chicago had a large Jewish population, with families that had come in earlier immigration waves. Many settled in a near-northside neighborhood. Some of them had come in the same wave of immigration that had brought Mendel and the family to America.

There were several train choices running between South Bend and Chicago. There was a smaller railroad line, the Chicago South Shore and South Bend Railroad with antiquated cars that operated multiple times daily and took about two hours between South Bend and Chicago. The New York Central Railroad also carried passengers and ended in a cavernous terminal in the middle of Chicago. Before he joined the New York Central Railroad, Mendel would travel to Chicago via the South Shore Railroad. Later when he worked for the New York Central, he acquired a railroad pass that allowed him free travel, which he then used.

Unlike South Bend, Chicago had many large establishments that offered kosher meat choices. Mendel would get up early on a Sunday, taking me along with him, and we would bring two large empty suitcases to be filled. Prices in Chicago were much lower than in South Bend, and we could often get almost wholesale prices or significant discounts that allowed Mendel to stretch our meager budgets.

Travel to Chicago was always an adventure for me. I loved the ride, watching spellbound as the train passed through city after city with the countryside speeding past us and the train wheels going clickity-clak clickity-clak. Chicago was amazing to me. Huge skyscrapers in the city center "the loop," that I didn't see back home. Elevated trains circling and screeching not far above me as we walked in the Chicago "Loop." From the train station to the north-side butcher shops, we'd take buses and electrified streetcars with lots of windows and straw seats to get to our destinations. I had no idea how my father knew where to go. I just followed him on faith.

Sundays, the butcher shops were alive with customers of all kinds and speaking languages besides English – Polish, Russian, Hungarian, and often Yiddish. The cases were full of many types of meats, cold cuts, chickens and prepared foods. Chains of hot dogs curled around each other, peered at us waiting to be picked. Sausages and salamis hung on strings from the ceilings emitting tantalizing garlic smells, asking to be eaten. Massive rolls of bologna peered out from the cases asking, "Aren't you going to take us home?"

The shopkeeper, the butcher, and usually many of his relatives, were behind the tall counters, accoutred in thigh-length, high-bib aprons with traces of the last delicacies they'd sliced apparent on them. You couldn't even get them to wait on you unless you took a number and it finally got to be your turn.

"What can I get for you boychik?" they'd ask my father, clearly amused to see the newcomer, the greenhorn, awed by their display.

Mendel chatted with the owner, whom he'd gotten to know from previous visits. The owner knew Mendel's history and knew Mendel was doing what he could to bring his family kosher food that they couldn't afford back in their hometown. Mendel always got a better rate and filled the empty suitcases he'd brought with hot dogs, salamis, bolognas, and even a little bit of corned beef to make sandwiches, as extra special treats. And then it was time to go back home, fully loaded.

We backtracked with dogs following us sniffing hungrily at our haul. We hastily boarded the buses and the trolley with passengers looking around us as we rode, wondering at the tantalizing garlicky odors emanating from somewhere, from our suitcases. Back to the train, back home with enough supply to keep us going until the next time. What an exciting trip it was and how satisfying to come home with the goods. Like coming home, a victor after a long and arduous hunt with the game secured!

Lost, But Found Again

He didn't think he'd ever see him again.

Chiam! Found! Now Hyman Kawer, Mendel's boyhood friend from Sokolow with whom he'd grown up. Mendel thought Chiam was lost forever, but miraculously had found him alive in Linz while, at the same time Mendel and his family was heading toward America. Alive after the war! With somehow other unimaginable stories of how he'd survived and whom he'd lost. And seen in Linz for only a few minutes while each ran to their own hopeful new future. Both unsure whether they would ever see each other again.

Survivors always looked for the ones they lost. In Europe they did so right after the war, but even after, at every new meeting of those who might remember, who might know, who might have heard something, who might have a new shred of hope.

On one of our trips to Chicago, and asking again for those who might have survived, or might have been seen, Mendel learned that Hyman had made his way to America and – by the grace of God – lived in Chicago! Mendel tracked him down and got his address. He found out that operating out of Chicago there was a fellowship, a Sokolower Society, of those with ties back to his ancestral village. Those in Chicago had by 1950 even written a book, a memorial to Sokolow called a *Yisker Book*, a Memorial Book. Chapters in it memorialized how the town had been formed and how the Jewish community had grown. It included its interactions with its Chicago fellows and descriptions and even pictures of the cultural, social, and educational aspects of the town. In addition, it had tributes from American Sokolowers, those who had survived and returned, those who had lived there earlier, as well as those who had never been there, but whose own ancestors had once been from there. I didn't understand, at that time, that such books existed or understood the drive, the longing to find others who came from their past, but it was something that would snare me and become a major driving force in my own life later as well.

Mendel and Frieda wrote to Hyman, learned that he was married to Rose, another survivor with her own difficult story of survival, and that they now had two children in Chicago, a son named Aaron and a daughter named Pam. They also learned that the Sokolower Society was still active and had meetings and events they could attend. They resolved to visit Hyman and his family and attend one of the Sokolower meetings.

Hyman and Rose lived on Ainslie Street in the heart of the vast Jewish neighborhood of Albany Park. It was centered in near-north Chicago around the intersection of Kedzie and Lawrence Streets in a neighborhood that assimilated Jewish immigrants for about four decades. Upwards of 70,000 Jews lived there at its peak. It included those of Polish, Russian, Austrian, Hungarian, Lithuanian, and Rumanian extraction. It had many synagogues; some built at enormous costs, but also tiny neighborhood ones, "stiebels" which were just a room in someone's home. It had dozens of social, economic, and cultural institutions, youth organizations, shops and stores of all kinds, bookstores, delicatessens, butcher shops and fish markets, and bakeries, and restaurants.

And just down the street, unbeknown to me then, at the corner of Ainslie and St Louis around the corner, lived Rhoda, someone who would later play a major role in my own life.

I was fortunate to attend that first reunion of Mendel and Frieda with Hyman and his family. Their apartment was a cramped second floor walk up with an antiquated kitchen and tiny rooms, but warm now with the spirit of camaraderie and fellowship that engulfed them. It was as though the years and the war had never separated them and as though the decades before had vanished. They relived the memories they shared of growing up together and they cried together for the relatives and friends that were no more. Hyman shared with Mendel all he knew about who had survived, who now lived also in surrounding neighborhoods and who could be found in the Sokolower fellowship that was active in Chicago. He relayed who had died after reaching America, and who was buried in the large Jewish cemetery south of Chicago, Waldheim Cemetery.

The day exhausted itself and gradually turned dim as we separated, and Mendel and Frieda and I made our way back to the train station to return home. The stories I'd heard from my family, and the new stories that poured forth from the reunion, emblazoned themselves in my memory and, even at the age of eleven, *formed a spark to ignite a life-long burning to know all that could be known about my past and all that had formed it and to never allow it to be lost or forgotten.* Returning home, at that point, I had no inkling how much of that reunion I would retain and the role that it would play in my later life.

Home – Studies and Baseball

Studying math and science was ok, but social studies was boring. Who could remember all that dry material, and why bother to do so much memorizing of dates? I tolerated those classes but never stood out in them. Music was fun, and I continued to love English. Starting from knowing no English at all when I came to the United States, I absorbed English like a sponge directly from my teachers and loved to read and write.

Social studies, on the other hand, seemed irrelevant to me. Why worry about all this old historical stuff when so much was going on in the world that I became aware of? The cold war was growing hot; Russia, where I was born, appeared to be a menace that could swallow up the whole world. Fear of nuclear war, global annihilation, was rampant in press and in fiction. Bomb shelters were being built everywhere, and I read everything I could now find to try to understand what was going on in the world.

At home, I gradually became a diligent student and, gradually, gradually, a serious student. Irving, on the other hand, three years younger than I, was a happy soul. Studies were ok, but homework was deadly boring. Baseball was what turned him on, and every chance he got, he'd be out with the neighborhood kids, in the street or whatever park they could get to and play baseball.

Irving and I eventually shared the attic bedroom when our grandmother moved out. Irving frequently would dream and sometimes wake up in the middle of the night or even sleepwalk. One night he woke me up from a deep sleep, Irving still asleep but with eyes wide open. "Slide!" he yelled. "Slide home!" Eventually, we both got back to sleep.

Relatives Old and New

Lopatas

On the way home from Muessel School, my brother and I would occasionally stop at our cousin Loretta and Barbara Lopata's house. By 1956, their parents had also moved to our neighborhood and lived in a little house at 1011 Allen Street. It was an old green-framed house sporting a broad porch in front framed with ancient oak trees and a large open grassy lot in back. The two of us would visit, and we and Loretta would play in back. Leah, the girls' mother, our aunt, was the consummate Jewish housekeeper and cook who always enjoyed having us boys visit and always found a sweet treat for us on which to snack. She and her husband, Velvul, renamed Wolf Lopata in English by the customs agent on entering America, never attained wealth or status but always had a friendly home to visit.

Wolf in those years had opened a tiny shoe repair shop on Cushing Avenue near Lincoln Way West street within walking distance of his home. I enjoyed visiting him there, and Wolf could always be seen at his vintage shoe repair machines, patching shoes, or attaching new soles or spit-polishing the shoes until they gleamed with brilliance. It was a task Wolf loved, but hardly enough to make a reasonable living as more modern equipment and cheap imported shoes flooded the market. In time, he regretfully relinquished the shop and joined the city as a utility worker, working on repairing and cleaning city pipes and sewers, a dirtier job, but one that let his family advance and that helped put his children, of whom he was so proud, into careers and through college.

Visits between Irving and me and Loretta became a two-way street with Loretta being a frequent visitor to the Feldman house, as well, where we played board games or chatted on the porch about the future and where fate might take each of us or what we might someday become.

Grandmother Ida

Right between our house and the Lopata house was a tiny house that eventually became my grandmother's home. After years of living with Frieda and Mendel, throughout their travels in the Soviet Union, Berezniki, Crimea, Makhachkala, Baku, the displaced persons camps in Austria, Chapin Street, Western Avenue, and then Sherman Avenue, she finally got her own home. She never could have afforded it on her own, never even dreamed she would have one, but her two daughters, Frieda and Leah, were able to accumulate enough savings to buy it for her as Ida became old. It wasn't the luxurious palace they would have bought for her or even the lavish home they would have liked to afford for her, but it was hers. She had her own bedroom and bathroom, albeit she had to climb stairs for them. She had a kitchen complete with appliances, she had her own living room and even a television set, something she could never have imagined. She never learned to speak English, and none of the television programs were in Yiddish, which was her mother tongue. It didn't stop her from enjoying her programs though, even the daytime soap operas, where she would make up her own script for what she thought was happening on the screen. I was a frequent visitor, constantly amused at the stories my grandmother would concoct to explain what she thought she was seeing on the TV screen.

As Ida got older, her memory declined, and she needed more care and companionship, to the extent that her daughters encouraged her to bring in a lodger to share her home and provide some additional care. Eventually, she declined into mild and then extensive dementia, and her daughters had to place her in a nursing home, something they lamented and grieved over forever.

I never forgot what my grandmother had told me and taught me, as she was my "substitute mother" during our journey when both father and mother had been forced to work in the fields and leave me in her tender care. Only one thing was the constant mantra of her life, "Never do things in spite; always treat others with goodness, with kindness," a lesson that stayed with me throughout my life and something I try to pass on to my own grandchildren.

Aunt Bernice and Uncle Abe

While the family that I was part of continued to be of utmost importance to me, I came to know and appreciate others from my family who had preceded us to the United States. Bernice (Bryna), my grandmother Ida's sister, who had been so kind to us in our first days and weeks in America, was someone who helped us settle down in our first years and assimilate. Mendel and Frieda were constantly struggling with finances, and Bernice helped to show them where they could stretch their scant earnings and still fulfill the family's needs. Bernice, who never had much money either, had a good head for business and bargaining and knew her way around the modern world. She was experienced in finding the necessary short cuts.

Early-on, Bernice introduced Frieda to the world of rummage sales, where Frieda could clothe her entire family with minimal expense. Mendel refused to go, but I was often dragged along on those "shopping expeditions," which I loathed.

"No fun at all," I complained, "to stand around doing nothing and just watch you going through the piles. I'd rather be at the store reading comic books or home reading a library book."

My complaints had little impact on Frieda who was always pleased with the treasures she'd teased out of the piles. It was a very long time before she could stop shopping at rummage sales and go to real stores, where the prices always shocked us.

While Bernice lived a full life as an independent dynamic woman with grown and married sons, her own life had never been easy or free of personal tragedy. She, too, had married young after she had arrived in the United States. She married Abraham Goldberg, a brilliant and enterprising young man who had been born in Russia in 1892 to Chiam and Mary Goldberg, had three brothers and a sister, and had immigrated to the United States in 1903. He married Bernice Rosenbaum (born 1904), in 1923 when he was 30 and Bernice was 19 years old. They had four children, Irvin (born in 1924), Ruth (born in 1926 but only lived less than a year), Paul (born in 1928), and Bernard (born in 1932).

Abe was a brilliant young man, full of ambition and hard working. After marrying Bernice, and in the difficult years of the Depression in America, the two made a living any way they could. They had a small grocery store; they had a second-hand clothing shop. Abe bought an old truck and would haul items to supply their shop. On one of those trips on a cold winter night and on his way back home, his truck pulled up a small hill to cross railroad tracks, when the motor died, and the truck stalled on the tracks. Try as hard as he could, Abe couldn't get the vehicle to start again. An oncoming train struck the old machine with Abe inside, rammed it off the tracks and Abe's head crashed through the roof. His life hung in the balance for weeks. He ultimately survived but was never the same. Long after recuperating and returning home, his brain remained so traumatized that he was never able to return to normal. In time, he left Bernice and their home to wander the city. He found shelter in temporary rooming houses. He survived and ultimately bought an old truck and collected junk or discarded iron scrap that he could salvage and sell.

While affecting his intellect, he always remained a quiet and gentle soul with a kind demeanor. When Mendel and his family finally found a house and moved to Sherman Avenue, Abe would occasionally find his way to our house where he was received with friendship and offered a warm meal. To me, he was always a wonderful person who had a tragic past. He never agreed to stay, but always wandered on. One time, he convinced Mendel to buy a truck to go into the salvage business with him, but Frieda rebelled ("Are you crazy?"), and Mendel returned the truck. Abe eventually passed away in 1969, and I learned that he had been a veteran in World War I and buried with military honors.

Uncle Bernard (Boruch)

My grandmother Ida had another brother who had left Sokolow in 1921 for America and who had settled in Chicago, not far from their other sister, Sarah. Bernard and Ida had corresponded regularly until the war, and he was one of the Chicago relatives who actually visited our family later in South Bend. He was my favorite uncle. On one of his trips to South Bend, he brought me a small camera as a present. I had never had a camera before, was fascinated by it and started snapping photos everywhere, photos of my brothers and sister; photos of my parents and grandmother; photos of every holiday, especially during the Passover Seder, and photos of our everyday life. Many of the pictures of family life that survived came from that camera, and I owe that to him.

Finally! An American Citizen

As the years passed, the family became more and more Americanized. When he was able to get a permanent job on the New York Central Railroad, Mendel in 1955 finally became the proud owner of an American car, a 1947 Dodge sedan. I can still see him in my minds eye in front of the house on Sherman Avenue, the hood of the car raised up, Mendel in his work clothes and railroad hat, working away happily on some maintenance of the engine. It was a used old model, gray on the outside and gray on the inside with the shift lever on the steering wheel and a clutch on the floor. It even had a radio! Mendel and I were thrilled at the luxury of ownership of that car and Mendel was very proud to take his family driving around town in it. How different from the years in Russia!

We had applied for Naturalization papers to become citizens as soon as we became eligible in 1950. By May of 1955, the family attained a life milestone. All of us, dressed in our finest clothes, went to the District Court for the Northern Federal District in South Bend, Indiana and were all sworn in. We were now officially Americans and so very proud! I could no longer be identified as an immigrant, either by speech or by clothing. I looked just like any other youngster in school. I even became a Patrol Boy at my elementary school sporting a sharp crossing guard uniform and "Sam Browne" belt, a singular honor where I was to teach safety and be a role model for it. I'd guard the street corners at the school so that other children could cross the streets safely.

In graduating from eighth grade at Muessel School, I received a number of honors and was proudest of all to receive a special award for citizenship from the Daughters of the American Revolution, an especially singular accomplishment for one that had only a few years before been a Holocaust survivor out of the cauldron of the Second World War and an immigrant to his new home and country.

PART II

BECOMING THE STORY KEEPER

6

CHOICES AND CHANGE

Launched into High School

Propelled by my new status and accomplishments, I entered High School. My new school, Central High School of South Bend, Indiana was now farther than just a few blocks from the house. Walking to school could take more than three quarters of an hour, and many times longer, in the South Bend snows, or I could take a bus part of the way if I was lucky. The school comprised several old brick buildings and was in the "downtown" part of the city. It was central to many neighborhoods and typical of the 1950s centralized schools. It was even then highly racially integrated with a large proportion of students from the city's black neighborhood but with good relationships among us all. It had both excellent academic and vocational programs and opportunities for students to advance in programs that could get them into good colleges or prepare them for jobs directly out of high school. Year after year, the school participated in state contests where it came out on top in both academic as well as in sports competitions. It often won statewide basketball competitions and football games. At the same time, its' students came out on top in math or English competitions. It was an atmosphere that forged student unity and challenged them for excellence whether in academics or in sports.

More than ever before filled with ambition, I entered this new space determined to achieve. While intrinsically not very athletic, I joined the football team as an equipment and water boy and became a part of every game. Scholastically, I joined the school newspaper and became a reporter and then a news editor of the paper. Somehow, I excelled in every class, graduated with a straight A average, became one of the school's three valedictorians and was selected to give the class's commencement speech at my high school graduation. Born in Azerbaijan during a world war when survival itself was a challenge, with no potential for future success or leadership, the opportunities brought to me in America inspired me to strive and to succeed.

My interests became focused in two diverse areas, science and English (i.e. writing). The English and literature teachers inspired me to read and to write; I became increasingly a voracious reader. But I was never certain enough that I could utilize that to lead me to a career. The school's aptitude tests were of no help in guiding me forward at all. They indicated I could go in whatever direction I chose, but where did that guide me? In the '50s, sciences of every kind were making enormous progress and chemistry was leading to new drugs. The role of biology in medicine was starting to be appreciated, although the sciences of cell biology, genetics and genomics, and immunology were still at rudimentary stages.

I loved the school's biology courses but hated the dissection of animals that was part of them. That was an early sign that medical school wasn't a direction for me. And while I excelled academically, college was expensive, my mother was a housewife, my father a railroad laborer, and the prospects of paying for college, any college, were daunting.

Earning money to help my family and me had been a priority even in elementary school. I started delivering newspapers as a delivery boy long before high school. Delivering the Sunday editions was particularly challenging. Dropped to the house at 4 in the morning, the papers needed sorting and packaging, so I could start out on my delivery route by 5 am. The route was spread out in many neighborhoods, and I delivered the papers using my bicycle, even in winter snows. Collecting payments always meant multiple trips to the houses and sometimes being chased by not too friendly dogs, but it gave me spending money that I didn't have to ask for and chances to give back to my family as well.

It also taught me the value of work and the hardships associated with it. In South Bend, stuck in a tough winter snow zone with blizzards hitting off Lake Michigan, winters were particularly difficult with snows accumulating during typical winters to over eight feet high. In the winter, driving in the streets was like driving through tunnels with ice walls surrounding both sides of the street.

I especially came to appreciate my father's hard work on the railroad to support the family. I often saw him leave home on a Sunday night or early Monday morning to go to the train station. He'd be dressed in his work coveralls, his gym bag in his hands, packed to go wherever he was being sent, sometimes locally, sometimes to another city where he'd stay during the week. He would come home tired and dirty, his coveralls covered with grime and grease from working on his machine keeping the tracks straight and clear. Often in the winter, father would come home from a long day's work ready for a night's sleep, when a phone call would tell him he had to go back to the train station to also work the night to shovel the tracks from the blizzard, so trains could get through.

As a young boy in Russia and in Europe, I followed my father wherever we had to go, too young to appreciate that he was leading us from one place of safety to another. In America, I came to appreciate what my father had done and how much, even then, he was working to bring us to a better place.

Being a paperboy didn't bring in much money, only small change, and would never have contributed much toward paying for college. By high school, I was able to get several other jobs. I was hired to work alongside my "Uncle Eli." It was where I was able to work evenings or weekends during high school to earn and save money that might partly help to pay for college. I learned how to make Venetian blinds and shades; I learned to drive the company truck to make deliveries, the truck with a sign on it that read "Blind man driving this truck!" that caused stares of disbelief. I became the company's accountant entering sales in ledgers and learning to keep the store's books. I was able to save money that might help if I could get into a college.

To earn more money, I became a salesclerk as well. I got a part time job on weekends where I became a salesman in the bargain basement of Robertsons, one of the town's large department stores. While it was a cleaner job, I hated the rush of customers when the store's doors opened on a big sale and the women charged down the stairs. They would plow through the tables and goods to pick through and get their bargain treasures. But it was extra money, and everything helped. It also helped me decide on jobs and occupations that I quickly understood I eventually didn't want to do.

In my last year in high school, and with the guidance of counselors, I finally came to believe that I might actually be going to college. Most of my classmates were already applying to state schools such as Indiana University, Purdue University or other state-supported colleges where costs were somewhat manageable. With my small savings, some support from my father, and college loans, I might be able to afford to go. I visited Indiana University and was impressed by its campus but overwhelmed by the size of the classes and the 30,000 students on campus. Unable to imagine that I could afford a better private college, I wasn't planning on applying elsewhere, although encouraged to do so by the school's counselors.

When I learned that admissions staff from the University of Chicago planned to visit South Bend and speak with and interview potential students, I signed up to learn what the University was about, why I should apply there, and how I and my family could ever afford the considerable costs.

The interview I got changed my life. Far from discussing specific curricula, I was told that the purpose of the school was to teach me to think, to question, and to find how to reach answers for myself. Until then, my thinking had focused on specific courses and majors, classes that would lead me to specific professions, training for ultimate jobs. The mission of the University to teach me to think, no matter where I went or what I chose to do, intrigued and fascinated me. I was attracted now to learn, to encounter ways of thinking, to broaden my horizons and not just to find a track to a job but to gain skills that would stay with me and carry me, job or not, throughout life.

But the University of Chicago was expensive, and I didn't know if I could really find the resources to accomplish that. I applied anyway on the slim chance that a path might somehow appear.

Graduation from high school brought with it a four-year partial scholarship from the Elks Club leadership who were impressed by the challenges that I had overcome, the successes they could see, and a future they could envision. The University also offered me a four-year scholarship that bridged the costs that father and I would pay. Unbelievable!

Mendel was thrilled. A son of his, a son of a railroad worker, would not only attend college, but go to one of the most prestigious schools in the country. That was a goal he had never imagined while trekking across thousands of miles during the war, while only looking for a home, a place where we might survive.

College and Beyond

After my high school graduation in June 1962, my parents drove me to Chicago to see what a University looked like and where I would spend the next four years. They were awed by the campus, massive gothic stone buildings, home to scientists and authors alike, lawyers and businessmen, Nobel prize winners, mathematicians, astronomers, architects of renown. It was a national leader in higher education and research, an institution of scholars unafraid to cross boundaries, share ideas, and ask difficult questions. It was a place where the modern nuclear age began when Nobel Prize winner Enrico Fermi and his colleagues conducted the first controlled, self-sustaining nuclear chain reaction on December 2nd, 1942, on the University's campus.

The son of parents from Sokolow Podlaski, Poland, unexpected survivors of the Holocaust and plain ordinary people who survived against formidable odds and eked out a meager living would go to the school that had fostered these unimaginable giants.

The world was a complex place when I came to Chicago in September 1962 to start college.

And as in Dickens's, *The Tale of Two Cities*, it was the best of times, it was the worst of times, it was the age of wisdom, it was the age of foolishness.

The U.S. earlier had broken diplomatic relations in Cuba and anti-Castro exiles had already been killed at the abortive Bay of Pigs invasion. The Cold War was in full swing and East Germany in 1961 had already erected the Berlin Wall between East and West Berlin to halt the flood of refugees seeking freedom in the West. The USSR had detonated a 50-megaton hydrogen bomb in the largest man-made explosion in history. There were already 2,000 U.S. military advisers in South Vietnam with fierce debate about the next steps to halt the advance of Soviet and Chinese ambitions in the world.

John Fitzgerald Kennedy was President of the U.S. having beaten Richard Nixon in 1960, and the space race was accelerating with John Glenn being the first U.S. astronaut to circle the earth in orbit.

Dropping me off to college was an emotional event for my parents and me. For Frieda, her oldest son would now be leaving home. With all the heartache she had experienced in her life, with all the wandering, with the loss of her first son during the war, with only change being a constant, she cried. For Mendel, it was a time also of mixed emotions, pride at my accomplishments, sadness that I would be away. For me, I felt trepidation at the challenges ahead, melancholy at leaving my parents, brothers Irving and Boris, sister Charlotte. and Grandmother Ida, excitement at the opportunities ahead.

I would live on campus at one of the large dormitories, castle-like Burton Judson Court ("BJ") with vaulted ceilings, arched walkways, vines of ivy climbing the limestone, wood detailing in the rooms, and a tower, where notables such as astronomer Carl Sagan, Senator Bernie Sanders, literary critic George Steiner, and noted oncologist Otis Brawley had once also resided. I managed to get a single room in Dodd House, one of the smaller houses. BJ was on the south end of the campus that stretched from 53rd Street on the north to 60th Street on the south. The "Midway" a broad stretch of green parkway separated the campus north of the dorms. The Midway was a popular place to walk, play ball, or picnic in the summer. Burton Judson was immediately adjacent to the University's Law School and the dormitories housed undergraduate students as well as the Law students in separate houses. All the students mixed in the dormitory dining hall and generally sat together with their housemates. I was awed.

For the first time, I met students in the house from all over the country, big schools and small, from New York City and from small towns in Iowa and all from the top of their classes, almost all valedictorians of the schools from which they came.

Before college even officially began, and independent of their high school courses and grades, students were administered "entrance exams" to determine their proficiency across a wide range of subjects. It determined where they had already gained sufficient mastery, where they might still have deficiencies and what courses they needed to still fulfill the school's general course requirements. Exams were administered in English, in mathematics, in history, in languages, in sociology, in humanities. If the students passed the specific exams, they no longer needed to take those courses. If they passed enough of those exams, they could potentially skip a year or more of college courses and proceed directly to courses in declared majors. If they didn't do well in some, they would be required to take remedial courses to catch up.

It was a challenging environment for me. I did well in the English exam, passed out of a requirement to take a language, having taken 4 years of German in high school. But history and sociology and the humanities were areas to which I had only very limited prior exposure. Especially sitting in a large hall to take exams in music and general humanities, I felt very unqualified and found I had little to no knowledge of the questions that were asked. Those exams established my curriculum for the first two years.

It was kind of an old-fashioned concept, but the school seated the students alphabetically during the entrance exams. I found myself seated in front of a student by the name of Rhoda Irene Feldman. Back in my dormitory, I checked out the students in my 1962 entering class in the class book and looked up Rhoda Feldman. All I could tell from the class book was that she came from Chicago. I learned later that her family had originally lived in an apartment building on the corner of St. Louis and Ainslie Streets, only a few blocks from where my father's boyhood friend Hyman Kawer lived. She was a pretty girl with dark brown hair, a wonderful smile, and gleaming eyes, and I decided I wanted to get to know her.

On completion of the entrance exams and before the official start of school, the University gave the students a break by taking them for rest and recreation for a weekend in Wisconsin. At Lake Geneva, Wisconsin they could unwind from their testing ordeal, start to get to know their schoolmates, and enjoy relaxing or walking around the lake.

It didn't take me long to find Rhoda, although she was accompanied by her dorm-mate. We introduced ourselves and the three of us took a stroll around the lake, although I would have preferred that it was just Rhoda and me. Later, after a group dinner that night and at a dance that the school had in the camp's lodge, I watched Rhoda enjoying the music and dance. Her sparkling eyes and vivacious manner attracted me, and I asked if I could dance with her. For me, as bashful as I was, it was very unlike me to chance that with any girl. It was the beginning of an enduring friendship.

The weekend was short, and the students were transported back to the school to begin college schedules.

One of the first courses I attended was a class in humanities. Humanities! What was that about? Was that something I really needed? I didn't have a clue. After all, my interest and intent was to major in science. Biophysics was what I had in mind, and my first days in Humanities 101 were a blur.

The instructor in humanities, a very large black man by the name of Dr. Moses, also seated the students alphabetically, and it seemed that fate had seated Rhoda directly behind me again. As the school year progressed, I found that I loved the studies in Humanities. I'd always loved music, and I established a new understanding and appreciation for it, especially for classical music. My friendship with Rhoda also grew, and we frequently spent time together on weekends going out or listening to music at my dorm. Rhoda's roommate, Mary, also became friends with the two of us and gave Rhoda her nickname of "Ronnie" which stuck with Rhoda long after college, such that all her friends called her by that name.

While my liberal arts studies were going well, I found that studies with higher math, with calculus, were more difficult than I expected. It turned out that math wasn't my thing, and I changed my major from biophysics to biochemistry. But the chemistry classes I took that year were far different from the simple chemistry I'd had in high school and competition with an entire class of valedictorians was much more rigorous than the competition I'd had before. Even with a class made up entirely of such high achievers, the university graded on a curve and I found that, contrary to getting all A's in high school and being at the top of my class, I was now in the middle of the class. The university was on a quarter system lasting only 10 weeks, which meant exams came frequently; midterms came after only five weeks and finals five weeks later. Readings for courses were huge and testing very frequent, and I found it was all I could do to keep up.

By the end of the year, I finished with B's and C's, and it was all I could do to keep my scholarship. In the second year, my biochemistry major required me to take Organic Chemistry, a requirement not only for my major but also a requirement for every pre-med student in my class. Competition was fierce, and no student helped another; if anything, one student undermined another to get higher on the grading curve. It was one of the courses that determined which pre-med student would survive and still be able to get into a medical school on graduating from college. Many didn't survive.

I struggled through my courses, but did so poorly in Organic Chemistry that, at the end of the year, I lost much of my university scholarship. Disastrous! Going home for the summer, I grappled with what to tell my parents and what to do. Without the scholarship, how could I afford to continue at the university and how could I deal with the disappointment my parents would have in my failure? I went home feeling disconsolate.

Sitting around the kitchen table with my mother and father, I said to them, "It's really been hard at the university, and I've had a terrible year. I just got my grades, and I didn't do well. The university is taking most of my scholarship away. I'm not going to be able to afford to go back there in September, and I'm going to look to apply back to a state school for the next year, probably to Indiana University. I'll work during the summer and be able to save enough money to go there. I'm just really sorry to disappoint you."

Mendel said, "You've never disappointed us. We know that you tried as hard as you could. It's a very hard school with only top students. It's not surprising that it was harder for you. But you're not going to drop out of the University of Chicago and go to Indiana University. You need to go to a top school, and I'll find a way that you can go back there."

I was amazed at my father. Here was a man who had only gone to the third grade in school, who had never finished elementary school, much less high school or college. Yet he understood the importance of education and stubbornly refused to settle for less than the best. Here was a man who was a laborer, who came home from work grubby and tired and who struggled to make a living yet refused to believe that he couldn't find a way. And here was a man who would do anything to find a way to make sure his children would get everything they deserved.

"But how?" I said. "It's so expensive. I can't make up enough money to go there without that scholarship. You already work so hard, and you don't make enough money either to make up the rest. I can't go back."

"I'll find a way. I'll work more hours; I'll work more overtime. We'll get the University to give us more loans, but you're going back." With all that we've gone through, with all that you've already accomplished, you deserve a good school. You're going back. Spend the summer getting ready for the courses you'll take when you go back so it won't be so hard for you then, but we'll find a way."

We hugged each other and cried together, but it was decided. I was going back.

This night and this discussion were something I remembered for the rest of my life.

Numerous discussions with the University followed. Somehow, Mendel increased his contributions, and the University increased their loans, so I could go back.

Mendel worked harder than ever to help keep me at the University.

America was very different from the challenges Mendel had faced keeping his family safe in Europe during the war, but life wasn't easy for him here either. He worked outside all the time in every kind of weather, and the work wasn't easy. In the summer, he'd be out in the blazing hot sun. He was very proud that he had become a master at running his enormous tamping machine that made the tracks run true and straight. There was no air conditioning on his machine and hardly a cover to protect him from the sun. And it wasn't always working on the machine either. There was a lot of manual labor he had to do on the tracks also. In the winter, with massive snowstorms in the area, with bitter cold, he was charged with keeping the tracks clear and open so that trains could keep to their regular schedule. His constant mantra to his children was, "I want you to study so that you can make something out of yourselves, so you can get good jobs. I don't want you working on the railroad like me."

He never seemed to comprehend how much his children thought of him. They knew how hard he worked to keep the family afloat and give them every chance in life.

The summer of 1964 was so complicated.

I managed to find a job working at the University of Notre Dame during the day in a biophysics laboratory for a Japanese professor. The laboratory was part of the University's Germ-Free Specialty Laboratory run by Professor Morris Pollard, an acquaintance of ours from the synagogue to which we belonged.

During the evenings, I did advance readings of the courses I would take. I also decided to re-take the Organic Chemistry course and I reviewed and studied what comprised a whole year of that course in the summer. When I returned and took that course again later that year, my grades for it were at the top of the class, and I got A's for each course.

Weekends were special. My relationship with Ronnie had deepened over the time at the University, and we grew to love each other. After the first year during the summer when I traveled by train to Chicago, I proposed to Ronnie at her parent's house. We were officially engaged. We would marry two years later.

Rhoda's mother was against the engagement. After all, my parents were immigrants with no social status at all, and I was also an immigrant. Her perspective on immigrants was completely negative. In her mind, what would I ever amount to?

My mother was also against the engagement. When I told her about it, she said to me, "Are you crazy? You're too young. You have too much to do. You have to study. It's not time to think about getting married."

Every weekend traveling to Chicago during summers, Ronnie and I would wander holding hands around the Chicago loop, sitting on park benches, listening to concerts in Grant Park, wandering in the museums, enjoying each other's company, finding it harder and harder to part as the weekend ended.

Periodically, Rhoda traveled to South Bend, and my brothers and sister loved her. Boris, the youngest, was enraptured. She was like a big sister to him. Mendel and even Frieda and Rhoda's parents, came to recognize the bond between us, recognized that the two of us would succeed together, and approved of our plans.

While I had summer jobs to supplement my college funds, so did Rhoda. She had her own scholarship and school loans, had excelled in her studies and was able to pay for her schooling with little help from her parents.

While working in the laboratory at Notre Dame during the summer of 1964, I was told that I had suddenly gotten an urgent call. When I called home, my mother was hysterical.

"You have to come home right away. I got a telephone call. A train at work hit Mendel. I don't know if he's alive or dead!"

I rode my bike every day to Notre Dame. I ran to it and raced home as fast as I could. I'd driven Mendel to the train station that week because he had to work out of town between South Bend and Chicago, and Mendel's car was now parked at home. When I got home my mother was sobbing. She gave me a telephone number of someone from the railroad who had called. Managing to reach him, I found out that my father had been operating his machine on the main tracks outside of Gary, Indiana. Somehow a train that should have been shunted to another track had hit his machine. Mendel was in the hospital, and the spokesman didn't know how he was.

I got my mother in the car, and we rushed to the hospital in Gary at a speed exceeding 90 miles per hour. Never had I driven so fast and, all the while, I was hoping that a police car would stop us and escort us at top speed to the hospital. Mendel was alive!

He was unconscious but he would make it. We learned later that someone had erred in switching the track and, as the train approached his machine at high speed, my father had jumped off at the last second, saving his life while his machine was destroyed. He was in the hospital for days, badly banged up but eventually was able to return home and recover. My mother was never the same.

Whenever my father worked out of the town, she worried. When he was late coming home, when the roads were covered with snow and he was driving, when the highways were covered with ice, she worried. He got hell when he got home because he hadn't called to tell her he was going to be late. She would have worried in any case.

They had survived so much! He had been imprisoned and could have been killed many times during the war. But in peacetime in America, her wartime experiences had worn her down so much that she always worried happiness would again be taken away from her.

Time eventually returned their lives to normal. Father kept working on the railroad, mother always worried.

I worked during summers and went back to the University to study. My relationship with Ronnie got ever stronger. When we were separated, we wrote each other love letters and couldn't wait to be together again.

By our fourth year in college, we were anticipating getting married and starting to think about our future after graduation.

In our last year, we decided we would get married in June of 1966 upon graduating from college. Our mothers, meantime, had warmed to the idea but had gotten out of control in their planning, expecting to invite hundreds of people. Neither family could afford a large and expensive wedding. My father, still a laborer on the New York Central System railroad, was already in debt from the college expenses. Rhoda's stepfather Nathan had a low-paying desk job for Commonwealth Edison Electric in Chicago, had a long history of heart trouble and was also in no shape to pay for a large wedding. Rhoda and I scarcely were able to pay our college expenses, and we discussed the dilemma. "We have to do something. They're going crazy with wedding planning and neither can afford what they're doing. By the time June comes around, they'll have invited 300 people and they'll be in debt for the rest of their lives. We can't let that happen."

We called our parents together in November and said to them, "We're not going to wait until summer to get married. We're going to get married next month in Chicago, between college quarters. We're going to get married on December 26th of this year. Stop planning for a big wedding."

The parents were horrified. "How can you do this? You're still in school. How will you finish? Are you doing this because you're pregnant? (Our son David wasn't born until 12 years later!)

Somehow reason prevailed. The extensive planning was cut short and the wedding was planned for December 26th, 1965.

As we got closer to that date, we searched for an apartment in neighborhoods near the university, not an easy task since the university was surrounded by decrepit housing. In any case, both of us had part-time jobs at the university and couldn't afford much. Rhoda worked in a laboratory as a research assistant. I worked at the University of Chicago Billings Hospital in a microbiology laboratory testing samples obtained from the hospital's emergency room.

Eventually we were able to rent an apartment a mile south of the University. It was a tiny efficiency apartment with badly leaking windows, a kitchen, a bathroom, and a living room with a sofa bed. It was half a block from the Illinois Central railroad tracks going north, and every time the train passed, the windows rattled and the building shook. But it was only $25 a week, which was the most we could afford.

We rented it at the beginning of December and started preparing for our wedding. An expensive wedding gown was out of the question. Rhoda had begun work very early over the summer on a Christian Dior wedding dress pattern. By the end of summer, the satin under-dress and the lace over-dress were both basted. She hired a local seamstress to complete the dress and make three bridesmaids dresses from material she supplied. As time grew near, the seamstress reported that all was going well. Then she said she'd been ill but was feeling better and would certainly finish. Finally, just three days before the wedding, she showed up at the dorm with the basted dresses and the pile of uncut cloth and said, "I just don't have time to do this. Find someone else."

The bridal headdress shared the same fate as the bridesmaids' dresses. Material was returned uncut. I worked the night before the wedding putting the headdress and veil together. Amazingly the bridesmaids' mothers turned the returned material into gowns. The next day, we took all we had and went to the wedding on the north side of Chicago in a blizzard.

The wedding brought our relatives together, although I knew few of Rhoda's relatives and Rhoda knew few of mine, and none really knew of our simple beginnings. Pictures were taken, dancing held. My parents, Mendel and Frieda, fashionably dressed in formal garb, no longer green-horns, looked every bit like proud Americans, nervous but beaming to take their son to the marriage canopy. Nathan and June, Rhoda's parents proud to accompany their first daughter down the aisle. My brother Irving, 20 years old, tall and skinny, looked somewhat uneasy in these elegant surroundings. Charlotte, my sister, a beautiful 15-year-old young lady appeared regal as she walked in the bridal party. And Boris, my younger brother, ten years old, dressed nattily with his favorite bowtie, loved the party, taking over the musician's drums during the dancing and thoroughly enjoying himself. But to me, it was a total blur. My legs shook as I walked down the aisle, but now we were finally married.

There was no honeymoon. There was no money for that, and we still had to finish school. We had a week to enjoy each other's company before going back to school and back to work.

Both of us decided that we wanted to continue our education and aimed for advanced graduate degrees. Both of us came from homes where money was never available for any extras, where no one from my family had ever gone to college much less graduate school, and the pathway to do that wasn't at all clear. We started applying to graduate schools with biochemistry departments in our last college year, but few departments wanted to take two people who were husband and wife for their students. No prospects for graduate school looked promising.

We were invited to interview at a biochemistry department at the University of Wisconsin, but once there were told by the professor, "I just wanted to see what two students from the University of Chicago looked like that would come here together. We don't have room for the two of you, but if we invite you, you could choose which one would come." We left angry at the affront. There was no way one would come at the expense of the other.

Still, we hadn't been accepted to any graduate schools and were totally uncertain of our future together. We were, at least, together and, while that brought us much comfort, at the same time the world was going crazy.

By the end of 1965, 190,000 American troops were in Vietnam and the war wasn't going well. By April 1966, there were 250,000 US troops in Vietnam, a number which grew to more than 385,000 by the end of 1966, and more than 500,000 by 1968. In 1969 the inevitable happened. A military draft lottery was established for conscripting men to the military, and I wound up with a low number in the lottery, being very much at risk.

On top of war issues, civil rights demonstrations were also heating up. More than 2,600 demonstrators had been arrested in Selma, Alabama and marches and confrontations escalated in 1966 and beyond. It made it hard to just concentrate on our classes.

Going back to our classes in January 1966 now meant a daily commute to the campus from our tiny apartment in South Chicago. We could either go by train using the Illinois Central commuter line that ran near our apartment or use the old VW Beetle that was a wedding present from Mendel and Frieda. Taking the car meant having to find a parking place on campus, not an easy task. Taking the train meant trudging in the snow a half-mile from the train stop on the perimeter of the campus.

The apartment we rented was but a place for us to be together. It was a minimal shelter in all respects. From the time of our marriage in December and through the winter, we became the only white residents in the neighborhood, and we witnessed the decline of all city services around us. The winter streets were only plowed of snow infrequently, garbage was sporadically collected, and selections in grocery stores nearby became increasingly slim. Parking overnight was a significant problem. We could occasionally park on the street near the apartment, but more than once, we awoke to find that the old Volkswagen Bug had been pushed from a legitimate parking space to an illegal one and sometimes in front of a fire hydrant. Besides the apartment being our home, it was also home to armies of cockroaches that brazenly ran across every room. Their breeding grounds were inside the kitchen cabinets and under sinks, and even after several extermination assaults, the bugs were always able to re-establish their residence. It was not unusual, if Rhoda or I had to turn the lights on in the kitchen going to the bathroom at night, that we witnessed armies of roaches scurrying across the floor and walls to bolt for their hideouts.

One unusual morning we had a particularly rude awakening. While Rhoda was still in bed and I was shaving in the bathroom, the ceiling above our sofa bed collapsed into the room and directly onto where I had been sleeping only minutes before. The room was repaired while we were in classes that day, but our skepticism heightened as to how long we could continue to live there.

Spring came and with it a letter from Purdue University. The letter came as a telegram from the Purdue University Biochemistry Department, one of the graduate schools to which we'd applied. Both of us had been accepted to their graduate program! The message said, "We don't want to send letters to you separately and have one of you find out before the other that you've been accepted and be disappointed, so we're sending one telegram to you both. Congratulations!" I never forgot the humanity of that letter.

By June 1966, we had completed all our college requirements, were ready to graduate, ready to leave our first home, and ready to move up to a better place in West Lafayette, Indiana where we'd secured a kinder apartment.

Graduation day was a milestone in both our families' lives. No one in Mendel and Frieda's family could have envisioned that their son would be a college graduate nor be bold enough to continue toward a graduate degree, even a doctorate, for heaven's sake. Rhoda's parents had always hoped she'd work toward a secretarial job, never envisioning that she could be a college graduate and puzzled by why she'd go on to graduate school and what she'd do with a graduate degree. Wasn't being a secretary a secure and good enough job? Even so, the pride showed in both families' faces as they saw Rhoda and me in graduation caps and gowns. We marched with our classmates in magnificent Rockefeller Chapel on the University of Chicago campus, still alphabetically one behind the other, but now with a merged family name, me as well as Rhoda Irene Feldman Feldman. Now we were ready for the next stage in a graduate career that none of us could have ever envisioned.

Over the years, Mendel had moved the family so many times from temporary place to temporary place, each time hoping that it was the last place and that he'd find a safe and secure home. For me, my college graduation was the beginning of moving from place to place with the hope that Ronnie and I could build a future together and even with the possibility of some kind of advanced academic career.

And so, we piled our few belongings into our VW with some spilling over into Mendel and Frieda's car as they helped us make our first move to graduate school, Purdue University in West Lafayette, Indiana. This really became our first home, and we would spend the next four years there together.

It was an unusual department and an unusual class that we were a part of. That year, the department had decided that the future potential for biochemistry was bright with an explosion of discoveries in the sciences. They had hired a new and young phalanx of professors, young graduates from other biochemistry departments across the country in a wide variety of specialties. These new professors would guide us and our class to achieve a breadth of knowledge that we could apply in future academic or applied industry pursuits.

Both Rhoda and I succeeded in our research and programs, although Rhoda had to work considerably harder to keep her boss happy. Both of us selected unique and individual research proposals. These had to be presented and defended to the professors for us to pass their preliminary examinations and proceed beyond master's level work to continue into doctoral programs. While Rhoda had excelled beyond me in both college work and graduate studies, I was astonished to see that I excelled in every one of my graduate studies, even advanced organic chemistry, the simple version of which had been such a nemesis for me in college. Many of our fellow students had graduated from colleges that concentrated in the sciences and many had already had significant advanced science courses. We found, however, that our liberal arts courses served us especially well. Learning to ask the right questions and search for the best answers turned out to be advantageous, in addition to giving us a lifetime of enjoyment in learning beyond the sciences that we were mastering. We revelled and grew in our studies and our understandings of where our knowledge would lead us.

Four years of graduate study passed quickly and we both received our PhDs in 1970. My doctoral thesis and publications were in the area of protein chemistry. My interest in advanced biochemistry research led me to consider further research in areas of cell biology and other biochemistry disciplines. I became convinced that detailed knowledge in biochemistry was a key to approaching understanding across a wide field of biological sciences and medicine. I applied for postdoctoral research studies with a renowned biochemistry professor, Dr. Henry Mahler, in the Chemistry Department of Indiana University. I was offered a position in post-doctoral research with a salary of $2400 a year. It seemed a gigantic amount to me then. It wasn't enough, though, for Rhoda and me to rent a more modern apartment or to even consider starting to raise a family, now five years after our marriage.

On graduation, and yet again with help from Mendel and Frieda in moving, we relocated to Bloomington, Indiana. Not quite what my parents experienced in their moves early in their lives, but ours weren't stable for a long time either.

Rhoda had several more months of work to finish up her thesis, and she stayed behind at Purdue to finish her work before joining me at Indiana University. I began my research in trying to understand how different portions of a cell interact when it has different DNA from separate parts of the cell.

I studied a model system of yeast where mitochondrial organelles have their own genetic system and interact with the cell's nuclear DNA to synthesize and control molecules made up from both. Who could have ever imagined that a boy born during the war in Azerbaijan would ever have an opportunity like that or even know what it meant? My parents, certainly, were awed at the opportunity even while blanking out on the research details I told them about.

Rhoda came to Indiana University without a job and began a local job hunt at the University. She was attracted to research in the biology department by a young professor, Dr. Milton Taylor. He was studying human genetics in mammalian cell systems and offered her a job as a postdoctoral researcher, nothing like the secretarial job her parents had initially envisioned for her.

Both Rhoda and I worked independently on our programs, often coming home long after dark, often returning after dinner back to our labs, and both having success in our research and publishing papers. Neither our families nor we could ever have anticipated that we could have progressed so far from our simple beginnings.

While continuing to advance our research at the University, we continued to stay connected with our families at home, Rhoda with her family in Chicago, me with my family in South Bend. Both families were a four-hour drive away, and Rhoda and I visited them as frequently as we could to maintain family ties.

Even so, time hadn't waited for us while we were finishing school and much had happened at home. Charlotte, my sister, the first in the family to have been born in America, had gone to college, the University of Wisconsin in 1969 and graduated in 1973, moved to Chicago and gotten her first job in journalism. In 1971, my brother Irving got married and moved to Ottawa, Canada. In 1973, Boris, my youngest brother, started college at Yale University, graduated in 1977 and went on to law school where he headed the prestigious Yale Law Journal. Joseph Rosenbaum, my uncle who had signed Mendel and Frieda's visa documents to come to the United States, passed away in 1974. I was saddened that I'd never had much of a chance to know him or learn how he had transitioned from being a young man from a small Polish town to a successful American or, even more, how he had dealt with the separation of his family back in Poland. How much I had to learn about our past!

During all that time, Rhoda and I became authentic researchers, but postdoctoral research wasn't an end in itself. Ultimately, we had to consider what our futures would bring. Our commitment to the programs slowed down our starting a family. For me, I anticipated the completion of my research grant and started looking for a job. After all that extensive study, I wanted finally to be doing something to use what I'd gained. I anticipated working at a university where I could teach, obtain research grants and do fundamental research and train advanced students also to do research. And to fulfill this expectation, I started applying for jobs.

I wrote hundreds of application letters to universities over the course of two years with few responses. Some universities responded in my second year of searching, and I received requests to visit and to present my research progress in lectures while looking for a job with them. I presented lectures wide afield: at Auburn University in Alabama, at the University of Cincinnati, at St. Johns University in Newfoundland. I applied for a position at the University of Maine. None were ideal, and the realization set in that, even if I had a job at those or similar universities, the potential for obtaining substantial research funding for doing advanced research was slim and unrealistic.

To expand my search opportunities, I attended nationwide science conferences that had job fairs and search services and, for the first time, saw that industry looked for people like me with advanced science experience. I soon realized that my vision of a professorial career in academia was not where I wanted to go. I saw my research professor, after 30 years of superb research and publications and service on top national science committees break down when his grants neared ending. And I saw the never-ending restart of research with new students that enter the graduate system that had to be trained. I saw a system that was constantly in a mode of restarting. I wanted to be involved in doing something productive.

I began to consider a career in industry instead. There I could use the skills and knowledge obtained in pursuing basic research for medical benefits, for development of treatments or drugs in areas of high medical need.

Finally, after two years of desperately searching, and almost convinced that I'd never get a job, I received three job offers. One was as an assistant professor at the University of Mississippi School of Medicine teaching medical students while doing research. A second was a position as an assistant professor at Mayo Clinic also doing research and teaching. The third was a position in industry at Armour Pharmaceutical Company in Kankakee, Illinois doing no teaching but working to apply my biochemistry skills to the development of drugs as a Senior Development Scientist. Mississippi was not where we wanted to be, and I didn't want to spend my life teaching medical students. Mayo Clinic had a wonderful reputation for research and medicine, but with "only" a PhD and no MD, I would, in some respects, always be somewhat of a second-class citizen.

Armour Pharmaceutical Company was an intriguing choice. The laboratories in which I would work didn't look like a company; they looked like giant biochemistry laboratories with major resources to conduct applied research. And the objective of using my background to do things that would help people with significant medical problems was highly attractive. Besides it was within driving distance of both my and Rhoda's families, and after discussion with Rhoda, I took the job in September 1974, and we bought our first home in Park Forest, Illinois.

7

THE BRIDGE OF GENERATIONS

David Born (1977)

Finally! After living in one temporary apartment after another, we finally had a place we could call home! Long past being an immigrant to America and Holocaust survivor, long past the travels and travails of Eastern Europe, and long past the long road of education and looking to start a job and a life, I settled down with Rhoda to begin our own family and a new life. Work at the pharmaceutical company was easier than I ever expected it to be. So much easier working on problem solving and developing improvements to drugs than arcane and risky research that might fail or only lead to publications in dusty tomes in libraries. Progress came early, and promotions followed.

Starting a family was much harder than anticipated and, with a great deal of medical help, our son, David, finally arrived in December 1977. But work got increasingly more complicated as goals and targets became more ambitious and harder to reach. As my responsibilities and success in the company grew, travel also increased and attendance at important conferences, domestic and international, now also added to my responsibilities. It got harder and harder for me to devote enough time to family. But even so, and with a child in tow, we spent more time traveling to Chicago and to South Bend to keep family ties tight, and exploration of my family's history had to be put on hold, especially with all the changes we encountered.

Family Ties

My sister Charlotte had married David Jacobs in 1975, and they, too, began their professional education, training, and job searches. They also started moving around, going first to Carbondale, Illinois followed by Springfield where David received his MD, on to Pittsburg, then New York City for advanced studies and to NIH for a fellowship with world-renown Dr. Anthony Fauci. Through all that, Charlotte advanced her career in journalism. Ultimately David Jacobs started his practice in Washington, D.C., and Charlotte went on to become a Congressional legislative assistant. Frieda couldn't believe it. A daughter of hers working in the halls of Congress!

My baby brother Boris graduated Yale Law School with honors, clerked in New York City for Federal Judge Abraham Sofaer, and then worked as an associate at Arnold and Porter law firm in Washington, D.C. Mendel couldn't believe it. A son of his, graduated with high honors from Yale, a lawyer. Boris bought him a Yale cap that Mendel, from that point on, was never seen without.

Nathan, Rhoda's stepfather, who had been suffering from heart problems for a long time, eventually passed away in June 1979. Rhoda's mother's health declined significantly afterwards, and she was in and out of hospitals and spent long periods of time in our home.

Ida (Chaya) Altman, my grandmother, who had traveled with the family from Sokolow Podlaski throughout Russia and Azerbaijan, gradually developed Alzheimer's disease. She died February 3rd, 1981.

My First Trip to Israel. July 8, 1979

One day in spring of 1979, Rhoda, our son David and I visited Mendel and Frieda in South Bend for a weekend. I had some exciting news to tell my father. "I just learned that my company is sending me to Israel this summer to attend meetings at a conference of The World Federation of

Hemophilia. I'll be going the beginning of July and will be there for a week. It will be my first chance to visit Israel!"

Mendel was thrilled. "We have relatives there. My sister Shoshana and her children live not far from Tel Aviv. You should spend time with them and get to know them. That will be wonderful."

"I don't know them at all," I countered.

"You've shown me some pictures of them, but that's all I know about them. I won't have time to visit them. I'll get to Israel in time to register for my conference, and the meetings will start the next morning. I'll be in meetings all day every day for five days. I won't have time to meet them, much less spend time with them."

"You won't even see my sister that survived and that I didn't see since 1936?"

Mendel looked very disappointed, but let it drop. Again, it seemed I had to choose between work and exploring my family history. Even then, no time for both.

Saturday night, July 7th I flew to Israel on El Al, the Israeli airline. It was an overnight flight, but it was abuzz with conversation and excitement. It seemed like no one was going to get any sleep, and it was a long flight. Somewhere near morning, numerous *Chassidim* (a strictly orthodox Jewish sect) arose dressed in their traditional garb with black hats, black jackets and white shirts, donned their *taleisim* (prayer shawls) and began their morning prayers shaking vigorously back and forth as they prayed.

Breakfast was served shortly before the plane started its descent, and I could begin to see the outline of Israel below us as the plane left the cloudless blue sky above the placid Mediterranean Sea.

I was more than surprised at my own feelings of excitement to be arriving for the first time in Israel. I was a firm supporter of Israel, especially knowing how important it was as a haven for Jews after the Holocaust, but my own emotions at stepping off the plane onto the ground, onto the land of Israel amazed me. I was here on business, yet my emotions overtook me. So many of my ancestors could never make it here. So many died trying, and here I was, just a short 14-hour flight from the United States.

By this time, I was already a knowledgeable international traveler. I expertly negotiated my way through security, picked up my luggage, and made my way to the exit and hailed a cab to take me to my hotel in Tel Aviv. Weary from the trip and arriving late on Sunday afternoon, I quickly registered and made my way to my room. Five minutes after putting my luggage down, I got a telephone call.

"Fred, it's me, Ephrayim Yitzhak, your Israeli cousin. Welcome to Israel! My mother and father, my brother and sister, we're all here in the lobby! We came to see you. We're coming up to your room. It's wonderful that you're here."

I was astonished! I had no idea that these people knew I was coming or knew when I arrived. My father must have told them even though I didn't think I'd have any time to visit with them. I didn't know these people. What was I going to do with them?

A knock on the door! They were here. I opened the door and they rushed in, hugging me and crying. I was amazed! I was crying too! Here was the sister of my father who left Poland 43 years ago in 1936 and made her way to Israel. She had survived. She'd reached Israel and married. Here was her husband, Rachmil, and her children, born in Israel. I looked at their oldest son, Ephrayim Yitzhak, just as I was Ephrayim Yitzhak, both named after our grandfather who had died young in Poland, the victim of Polish antisemitism. He was I, also born in a strange land, a land different from that of his ancestors. He was born in Israel; I was born in Azerbaijan, but we were the same. We hugged each other and cried. How could I ever have expected these emotions!

I ordered food to be brought to the room and we spoke for hours. They didn't speak English, and I didn't speak Hebrew. Through their broken English and my broken Yiddish, we communicated. We spoke of family, we spoke of history, and of our connections to each other. All of us could feel the love between us. I was overwhelmed.

They left at midnight. What an amazing experience! Tomorrow I'd have to go to my all-day meetings, but they'd meet with me again.

Each day, I woke at 6 a.m. to get ready for my meetings. Meetings, endless meetings each and every day. At 5 pm I'd finish and head for the lobby. They were there to meet me every single day. They took me to their apartments, to Shoshana and Rachmils, to Ephrayim and his wife Tamar's. Dinners, amazing dinners with endless food and conversations at each of their homes until midnight and then back to the hotel. I hardly got any sleep, but it was wonderful.

Wednesday the conference meetings were suspended while participants were piled into buses to act as tourists and be shown the country. Tel Aviv was wonderful, just like any other modern city, but adjusting to the desert outside the city and to Arab villages that the bus went through was a culture shock. The diversity of the population, ultra-Orthodox Jews in 18th-century garb, fur hats and long flowing coats in 100-degree heat, Arabs in *kafiyyeh*, traditional Arab headdresses, long flowing cotton robes, all seemed totally foreign to me. And sand and desert everywhere. It was a country I thought I could never get accustomed to.

One of the stops in Tel Aviv was at the Museum of the Diaspora, "*Bet Hatfutsot*." As we entered, the first thing I could see in the two-story foyer was an enormous iron cage suspended and stretching to the ceiling and filling the room. Iron bars resembling a prison, barbed wire above and around me. The other conference participants went on leaving me alone there.

It was a shock to stand there, to feel what those in the Holocaust death camps must have felt as they saw they were imprisoned and would maybe never, ever, leave. It chilled me to be there.

I left and climbed a large dark staircase to the second floor and entered a hall of faces. Hundreds of faces stared at me, Jews from around the world. Jews of every nationality and age. Young. Old. Black hair, brown hair, blond, red. Bearded and clean-shaven. Men and women and boys and girls. These were the survivors in the world who hadn't been destroyed in the Holocaust and had been dispersed, had survived, and flourished. How I felt attached to them! I was stunned.

A second room. Filled with wooden replicas of synagogues from what used to be the Jewish world. Synagogues burned and destroyed during WWII and sometimes with the hapless Jews still inside them. Styles of construction of all types. Simple wooden structures from tiny villages; ornate and massive buildings from large cities with major Jewish populations. The synagogues gone; the people gone. Only models left to remember them. What an impact it had on me to know more about that world that I'd lost.

Another room. Jewish music, Klezmer and Yiddish lullabies, wedding songs and dirges, hymns and chants, old Yiddish songs and modern Israeli ballads. I could listen to selections in small listening chambers, and I could purchase some selections to bring home – never to forget. Surrounded by the history, the culture, the music, the faces that I'd seen there, I knew that I'd be changed forever. Deep inside me, I knew then that I had to pursue every thread that connected me to them and to my own history.

Nearing the end of the trip, nearing the melancholy time to separate from those I now knew and had come to love, I was asked, "When will we see you again? When can we meet your wife and your son?"

"I don't know," I said. "I can't know when I'll be back, but I know that I will. I didn't know any of you when I came, but now I do, and I'll never be able to forget. We'll write. We'll send pictures, and I'll come back when I can."

My father was right. Meeting them was something not to be missed, not to be taken lightly and not to be forgotten.

I returned home on July 19th, 1979, changed beyond anything I could have anticipated. But true to my word, I visited them again on another business trip in 1984 and times after that.

My work increased in intensity in the years that followed, responsibilities grew and with it much more travel, Stockholm in June 1983; Rio de Janeiro in August 1984; Milan in June 1986; Madrid in May 1988; Athens in October 1992; and Mexico City in April 1994. Travel and work were taking over my life.

Jewish Genealogy – A Beginning

But while pressures of work and responsibility grew, a spark had been reawakened that wouldn't be quenched in my commitment to learn my family's story. Over the years, I had sat with my mother and father, with my grandmother Ida (Chaya) listening and asking questions about their family history. I'd jotted down notes and dates and stories, copied old photos that had somehow survived their travels. After seeing the history of my people from my first trip to Israel, from my experience with relatives I'd never known, I increasingly began to explore what I could learn in earnest.

The scraps of paper that detailed every facet of my family's life became precious. And Rhoda and David also learned, bit-by-bit, the gripping history they were a part of.

Within our own community in Park Forest and with our friends, we formed a nascent genealogy society. From this point on, the accumulation of family history and stories and the compilation of a rudimentary family tree and family stories began seriously. It was impossible to put off any longer exploring the history and the stories of which I'd only had an inkling before.

Rhoda's Family

Rhoda's beginnings were very different. She was born an American in Chicago to June Schwartz and Charles Tasler, but the marriage didn't last long. Her father abandoned them when she was just four years old. With no financial resources, her mother struggled to raise Rhoda and her sister Donna until June remarried to Nathan Feldman. Rhoda's step-father provided a home for them until Rhoda left for college and later married me. But family history for Rhoda was less compelling and not until very much later in life did Rhoda begin her own family explorations.

For a long time, I had known that my family was different from all the others of my friends that I'd encountered in schools as I went through life. We had seen things and had been in places around the world that few had.

By the time I had a family of my own, I'd already heard the stories from my family many times and written down bits of history. I thought I knew most of what there was to know about that life. I used that to compile my first family tree that showed David, me and Rhoda, then our parents, and their grandparents. I knew names and places and dates, at least those that I'd gotten from my father, who seemed to have a razor-sharp memory. I even had names of some great grandparents, although no additional information about them. And with that, I thought I could be done. I knew what there was and believed there might be nothing more to find.

The Transfer of History – 1986

One day in November of 1986, I borrowed a video camera and headed to South Bend to begin to interview my parents and formally record their family history. What I believed would be a two-hour venture turned into an all-day program with everyone clustered around Frieda's dining room. Rhoda became the "camera man," while nine-year-old David ran around the room periodically stopping to listen little by little to the transfer of history.

I said to Mendel and Frieda, "So here's where we're going to start. We're going to fill out a one-page ancestry chart with the information that you've given me over the years, and then we'll fill out whatever we know about each relative. That shouldn't take long. Then I have questions about your history in Europe and where you went during the war. A big map is taped on the wall, and we'll track your journey. We should be able to do all that in a couple of hours."

Filling in the chart started by putting down David's name. David liked that a lot. Then followed Rhoda and me as parents, and we proceeded to follow my ancestry. Mendel's history came first. I said, "We start by putting in your name. I'll fill that in: Mendel Feldman."

Mendel, "No. That's not right."

I couldn't believe what I was hearing. "What do you mean that's not right? That's your name. That's what we've always called you. I know your Hebrew name also: Menachem Mendel ben Ephrayim Yitzhak. (Mendel, son of Ephrayim Yitzhak) Right? Is that what you mean?"

"No. My name is Shmul. Shmul Mendel."

Shocked, I asked my dad, "Where did that come from? I never heard that before. You mean your first name is Shmul? Samuel?"

"Yes."

"Well, why are you called 'Menachem Mendel' when you get called to the Torah?"

"That's how they do. I don't know."

I was totally flabbergasted with how his interview started and astonished that I didn't even know my father's first name. This was going to be interesting and not at all what I expected.

"OK. We'll put that down and go ahead."

And so, we continued. Tracing back Mendel's mother and father, born in Sokolow Podlaski, Poland and their parents also born in Sokolow Podlaski, Poland. But for Mendel's grandparents, I only had their names and a few dates.

Frieda's memory was much more lacking in details than Mendel's. She had her mother Ida's name, originally Chaya, and a few dates and a little information on her father. Mendel, though, could fill in more information on Frieda's grandfather, Ida's father, Yisroel Hersch Rosenbaum. Mendel knew that he'd been married twice, had many children from both wives and that Frieda's mother Ida was born from the second wife, Bayla Ruchel. He didn't know the name or any details of Yisroel Hersch's first wife.

Besides the specific genealogy information, Mendel could relate much about all their lives and, as the day wore on, he painted a vivid portrait of the lives of their ancestors and their village before the war.

Hours had already elapsed by the time we got to the start of World War II, and with this, everyone was close around the table and enraptured, not only with the story, but also with the process that was underway.

Frieda could hardly speak through her tears as she told how a German had attacked her in the first days of occupation of their village, and how she'd told Mendel that they had to leave. Mendel traced their path into the Soviet Union and how they moved ever further away from all that they'd known. With the story of their time in Berezniki, Russia in the Ural Mountains and Mendel's arrest by the Russian NKVD, Frieda broke down, remembering the terrible times they'd gone through, never knowing if Mendel would return to her and if they'd ever be together again and survive.

Again and again they fled, seeking more secure refuge until they found temporary sanctuary in Azerbaijan. Suddenly, in Makhachkala, Mendel was arrested the second time on their journey and jailed. When Mendel was finally released from prison, he found that their first son Avram had died.

As the story progressed, back and forth to the map on the wall we went, incredulous at the vast distances they traversed, amazed that hope could survive while they were so beleaguered.

But one fact especially intrigued me, and I kept coming back to it quizzing Mendel. "Your sister Rojza (Shoshana) left Poland before the war. How and why did she leave and what happened to her?"

Mendel's Story – Meeting Shoshana 1968

Mendel unrolled his story. "Shoshana ran away from home in 1936. She was a Zionist, so wanted to go to Israel, but our parents refused to let her go. So, she ran away. When my mother found out, she sent me after her to get her home. I went to Warsaw but didn't find her there and came back home. I told my mother that she was gone. Later I found out that she got to Israel, married a cousin Rachmil Schwarzbard, and raised a family. I saw her when we finally made our trip to Israel in 1968."

There was so much more that I wanted to know about Mendel's sister and her early departure to Israel, but Mendel went on to relate his reunion with his sister on their trip to Israel in 1968.

"We visited them for a short time while when we were in Israel on a tour. I took two days off from the tour schedule to visit her. I met her and her children, Ephrayim, Aharon, and Bat Ami. Ephrayim met me at the airport and took us to our hotel, which was terrible. We had found out that Frieda's friend Shayndel had also survived the war, in Russia, and had made her way to Israel. Ephrayim helped us find her and to spend time with our friend Shayndel from the Sokolow *havurah* (youth group).

"I remembered Rachmil when he and his family were in Sokolow. While we were in Israel, Rachmil and I played chess and talked. Rachmil remembered everything.

"Shayndel came to our hotel and said I should come and stay with her since it was a terrible hotel. We went to her house in Lud and stayed about a week before we went to stay with Shoshana. We saw Shoshana for several days. Ephrayim took us."

I wanted to know much more than just facts. "Tell me about what it was like when you first saw Shoshana. You hadn't seen your sister for 32 years. So much had happened in the meantime: The war, her immigration to Israel, your travels. What was it like to see her again?"

Mendel responded with what they were doing in Israel. "We met, had dinner, stayed some days, and then we had to go on tours."

During so many years, Mendel had been able to lead his family everywhere during the war, in danger, across thousands of miles. Now 32 years later and finally reunited with his sister, he couldn't do it anymore. The enormous heat, the stress of hours of air travel, the time zone differences, the time pressures of the tours they were supposed to be on, the tiny apartment that they were in with Shoshana – all this overwhelmed him.

"Were you close to your sister?"

"Yes."

They were signed up with a group. The group went on tours, and Mendel felt they had to go. They had to see Israel, and they had already missed much of the tours. Besides, my brother Irving, who was on leave from the army, was also in Israel, and they kept looking for Irving.

But things seemed to be missing. There was so much more to learn about the story of Mendel's sister. Many questions still weren't answered, questions that couldn't be answered then, questions that, ultimately, I couldn't find answers to for many years and that drove me to understand that ultimate reunion of brother and sister.

As darkness fell around Rhoda, David and me, the saga of Mendel and Frieda leaving their village, their home and their families, of their countless escapes and wanderings, the conclusion of the war, their return to Poland, and their ultimate confinement in displaced persons' camps in Austria came to an end. The rest of their story and finally their entry into America had to wait for other interviews.

What had started as a short trip, to review some known family history, expecting to spend just a few hours, had surprised us all, taken all day, and bonded us together even more. It sealed my interest in knowing more about the past and the forces that had kept our family together and that had enabled them to survive.

Time and the Family

In the years that followed and the changes to the family that accompanied them, nothing could dampen that interest.

My brother Boris married Robin Cooper in 1986. They eventually settled in Palo Alto, California where Boris began his career with the high-tech law firm Wilson Sonsini.

Rhoda's mother June suffered from chronic illnesses, lived for some time with us in Park Forest, but eventually succumbed to kidney disease and passed away in 1988.

Mendel and Frieda had raised their children in the rambling old three-story home on Sherman Avenue in South Bend and had regretfully moved to a smaller ranch home as their children one-by-one left home for college and careers. After Mendel had a heart attack in 1981 and retired from the NY Central Railroad, they put their home up for sale and finally, in 1991, they left that home to live in a condominium in Rockville, MD not far from my sister Charlotte and her husband David Jacobs.

Life in Park Forest, Illinois continued as usual for my family and for me with work and travel, and for Rhoda working as an Assistant Research

Professor at Pritzker Hospital at the University of Chicago. David went to Junior High School in nearby Richton Park, Illinois where the educational opportunities began to look limiting. After 17 years our family decided to leave Park Forest and bought a house in Frankfort, Illinois where David started High School in 1991.

That house was in a densely populated oak forest with a burbling little creek at the back of the house. David got a spacious bedroom with an adjacent play space. We loved the location, but the school had disadvantages. While advanced in studies, the school had no other Jewish children, which didn't matter much to us until David encountered some harassment about being Jewish from some nasty children. It was a shock to us that there could still be such ignorance. We had a meeting with their parents, after which the harassment ceased, and David enjoyed his experiences at school after that.

Over the following years and with more moves, as I advanced in my professional career, travel increased sharply, both domestic and international. I became a leading world authority in hemophilia treatment. My research led to the development and registration of advanced therapeutics, and my expertise in manufacturing technology made me an expert in the field. Over the next years, my travels to World Federation of Hemophilia meetings took me around the globe, even to Japan and Australia. I became recognized as a major industry contributor to the field.

8

ISRAEL / FAMILY MYSTERIES

Israel 1992. Picture of Fischel, Wife, and Baby

Even with all the major distractions of my job, the interest in my family's story never waned, and I was able to visit Israel several times more. Each time, no matter what the schedule or program, I diverted to visit my Israeli family and every time returned to visit the Museum of the Diaspora for which I developed a strong affinity. In visiting my father's sister Shoshana and her husband Rachmil in 1992, I told Shoshana about my deepening interest in our family history and my interviews of my parents of their life in Poland before the war.

Shoshana brought out a small photo of two people and a baby. "Have you seen this before?" she asked.

"No, I've never seen this picture. I don't think my father had it. But I think the man is Fischel, my father's older brother. Is that right? Is the woman his wife?"

"Yes, that's Fischel, and that's his wife and their baby. They were married in 1938."

Mystery of Shoshana's Leaving

I sensed that this meeting was an opportunity not to be missed, to learn more about Shoshana's departure from Poland that I couldn't discover any other way.

"Shoshana, I'd like to know more about when you left Poland and came to Israel. When I interviewed my father, he told me that you believed a great deal in Zionism and that you ran away from home in 1936 to go to Palestine. He said that his mother sent him after you and that he went to Warsaw to find you, but to no avail. Can you tell me any more about that?"

I was shocked when she said, "That's not true. That's not what happened. I did run away from home. I was involved a great deal with Zionism, because I believed that Jews in Europe were in great danger, and that we all had to go to Palestine. My mother didn't believe it and wouldn't listen to me. Finally, I did run away from home to go to Palestine. What's not true is that when Mendel got to Warsaw, he did find me! He tried to convince me to come back home, but I couldn't. I convinced him that I had to go on to Palestine and to tell our mother that he didn't find me, and that's what he did. From there, I went on and that's how I got to Palestine."

I was stunned at the discrepancy between what I'd heard when I interviewed my parents in 1986 and what Shoshana told me. The mystery of Shoshana's leaving home left a deep hole in my understanding and a commitment to one day understand it. Even when I could interview my father again years later, I failed to understand what had really happened. No understanding of that could come until I returned to Israel many years later, years after my father had passed away, years after Shoshana had passed away.

At the end of this visit to Israel in May 1992, Ephrayim asked me, "Well, when are you finally going to bring your family to visit us. When are we going to be able to meet your wife and your son? My parents will die before they ever get a chance to meet them."

I replied, "I would love for you all to meet my family, and I'll speak to my wife and see when we might be able to come."

It didn't take long after returning home before I said to Rhoda, "We have to take a trip to Israel."

She said, "Are you crazy? I don't know anyone in Israel. Why would we go?"

"We have family there: My father's sister and all her family. I've visited them now three times, and they're wonderful. They want to see you and David. My cousin Ephrayim said his parents would love to see you and David. You have to go. I want you and David to meet my family."

"I'm not going. It's a long way. I don't know anyone in Israel. I don't speak Hebrew and they probably don't speak English. Besides it would be very expensive."

The conversation ended, but I wasn't going to give up. As weeks went by, I learned that there were trips over the summer for families to visit Israel with children who were going to have a Bar or Bat Mitzvah. "Bar Mitzvah tours" they were called, and these were scheduled through synagogues, with airfare and hotels included. The child got to go free. I tried again.

"David had his Bar Mitzvah in our synagogue here, and it was wonderful. He loves our synagogue and practically did the whole service by himself. It was amazing, and it was amazing for all our American family to come to celebrate that with us. But we have family in Israel as well. They couldn't come, and they want to see us also. More and more I understand that one of the most important things for me is for us to be close with our families, to know each other and have a strong connection with our common histories. There are Bar Mitzvah tours that we'd still qualify for. We could go with another synagogue, and David could have a repeat Bar Mitzvah on Mount Masada. It would be a tremendous experience for him; we'd get to tour Israel, and we could meet with our Israeli family. They have special all-inclusive fares, and, besides, David would get to go for free."

"Our synagogue doesn't have such a tour planned for this year, but I'll look into it and see if there's a different one that we could go on," she relented.

We found a synagogue north of Chicago that had an Israel Bar Mitzvah tour scheduled, and I was elated that they had room for us. We decided we were going, and for the first time ever, I decided to keep a diary on my trip. My hope for the trip was to span the generations, to connect those who had survived and migrated to the west to those who had survived and migrated to the east. To connect generations and families that time had separated.

I wanted to go, especially after my last visit with Ephrayim, although I had some reservations. Could I really be gone two weeks from work? I'd been traveling for work so much already that year! What about my job responsibilities? There were so many pressures at work already.

However, finally, I felt we, as a family, had to go. This was an important time for all of us. David had three more years of high school before him, then college. It was time for us as a family to share in something big and important. Something to remember for all our lives.

9

DIARY, AUGUST 1992. FAMILY REUNION

Spanning Time and Generations – My Diary

Monday. A big limo picked us up at 6 am; we got up before 5! We had finished packing past midnight, but everything is finally ready. Everyone's excited, even me, and I travel so much that it has lost most of its excitement. But this time is different.

The flight left about two hours late. We'll really be tired by the time this flight's over. The plane is packed with seats all cramped together, impossible to sleep; hard to rest; anxious to get there. Are we as a family really going to Israel?

Tuesday. We finally arrived the next day at 11 am. We're here in Israel – together. It's going to be more than a tour. It's going to be an emotional experience, although I don't think any of us actually believe that at this point. We find the tour bus and our tour guide, Zvika Krupik. Nice name. He's a nice enough fellow, about my age, easygoing but with a rugged humor. He jokes a lot. Will he be able to add significance to the trip, or will it be only a tour?

Zvika knows we're tired but tells us we must see some important things before we can go to the hotel and takes us to see the Rappaport sculpture, "Scrolls of Fire". He shows us pieces of Jewish history in it: Abraham, the giving of the scrolls/tablets to Moses, the growth of the Jewish people, their captivity into Babylon, the continued cycle of growth and enslavement – dispersion/Diaspora, until the emergence of the state of Israel and the ingathering of exiles.

Zvika is a Zionist, and he talks like a man with a heart and a vision. I like him already.

As we take our first steps to go into Jerusalem, Zvika has us say a blessing.

Still before going into Jerusalem, our bus takes an old road to the city, so we can see what Israel had to deal with in 1948 with virtually no infrastructure and surrounded by hostility. My father's sister, Shoshana, had already been here since 1948. What had her life been like at that time?

We stop at a forest and buy a young sapling for David to plant. We dedicate this to the memory of Rhoda's parents, June and Nate Feldman. I feel like crying again just to think of it. Rhoda's father would have been proud, and her mother would have been happy. It's a reminder that this trip is not just about connecting us to my history and to my family, but also to Rhoda's.

Coming into Israel this time feels different than before. It feels natural, almost like coming home.

We check into the hotel on one of the hills overlooking beautiful Jerusalem and then take a taxi into the city. We decided to look at replacing our wedding rings. After 27 years, they don't fit anymore. Lots of things don't fit anymore. We find some beautiful rings after looking around and have them custom made for delivery in three days time, to the hotel – a good start for a fresh start for a great trip. Even Rhoda seems excited to be here, buying lots of presents for others. What better way to spend money than to bring other people good memories and make others happy? Isn't that how we make ourselves happy?

We walk around some more, have a nice dinner, and go back to the hotel exhausted.

Wednesday. We don't have to meet at the bus until 3:30, but we get up at 6:30 am to get ready and have a typical Israeli breakfast – humongous. Our first stop on this day's tour is Hebrew University for an opening welcome speech from the Vice Chancellor. Is this what I wanted to do? Really?

The university is impressive. We're taken to a small lecture room where the chancellor, a middle-aged man with a British accent, gives a speech. And what a talk! Fascinating and inspiring! He talks about the role of the university in the life of Israel, growing a society from the top down – programs for teaching and integrating immigrants from all over the world – building an educated, motivated society, building programs for teaching children and their teachers. Building major world-class research programs. How different is the world these immigrants, these survivors from WWII have created, sharing their knowledge with the world. And the chancellor doesn't talk from notes. He talks from the heart instead! By the time we go, I wish he was my teacher.

What a good way to start our visit! I think even our son David was impressed. I asked him and got, "I thought it was interesting!"

Back to the bus to see a model of the old city in the Holy Lands Hotel. Who wants to see a model, when the real thing's here? Why aren't we just going there? The model's huge. Laid out to scale on small hills, just like Jerusalem.

Zvika walks us around it, shows us an aerial view of the city, and gives us a lecture on how it developed: the Muslim quarters, the Armenian quarter, the Christian quarter, the Jewish quarter. He gives us an overview of the history of the country from the first settlement of King David through the Crusades. It's a reminder to me of the many destructions and displacements of peoples throughout history, WWII just being one of the worst, one of the latest.

Our guide knows a lot of history. Fascinating! I'm enjoying it all. I have to have more faith in these people. They're really good. Day three, and I'm already glad we came.

Back in the bus. Zvika takes us into the Old City through Zion Gate. We go into the Jewish Quarter. We visit the rebuilt synagogues of Rabbi

Yochanen Ben Zahai with four interconnected synagogues. The oldest of the synagogues are 400 years old and are below ground level because the Muslims didn't want any Jewish or Christian buildings to be higher than theirs. They're beautiful and each one is different.

We continue with Zvika pointing out archeological details as we walk. The excavations done between 1969 and 1981 turned up the "Cardo," dating from the late Byzantine period, from 6th century AD. This was a wide street (73 feet wide) running through the heart of the city. Six centuries later, the Crusaders adapted part of the Cardo (by now much narrower) as a sort of medieval shopping mall. Now there are modern shops all along the street. Some small excavations near the street and the old souk show parts of Old Testament fortifications and the First Wall of the Second Temple.

We continue with Zvika telling us more history and reach the Western Wall of the Temple. So much activity there, with people in all kind of garb, Chassidim dressed in black, wearing different hats, ear locks, beards, little kids that look identical to them. Also soldiers with automatic rifles, tourists, Arabs, nuns – all kinds of people. The sun is hot and bright. And there is the Western Wall – ancient, big, with the Old City surrounding it – old buildings everywhere and beyond and up the hill you can see the Dome of the Rock. What an exciting place to be. How could I not see that before?

Rhoda went to the women's side. David and I went up the narrow, left lane to the men's side. We went up to the Wall and touched it. Old. Filled with many little notes; slips of paper in each crack, containing appeals and wishes. Men and boys praying at the wall in all kinds of fervor – passionate and intense.

What do you do here, besides look around? How and what do you pray?

David wandered to look around on his own while I walked over to a Chassidic bookstall. They helped me put on *tefillin* (phylacteries: a set of small black leather boxes containing scrolls of parchment inscribed with biblical verses). I didn't ask and they didn't ask. I wanted some slips of paper to write on. I got inspired. They gave me some paper, and I wrote three notes – one for our health and happiness, one for my parents, and for the wife of a friend with cancer. I stuffed the notes in some cracks in the wall and said the prayers.

David was off saying some prayers on his own at the wall. I suggested he should get some tefillin as well, but he turned me down, said it was OK. He told me later that a Chasid had asked him for some money. David told him he didn't have any money, and the Chasid told him to give him his camera! Unusual people! Nothing ventured, nothing gained, I guess.

When leaving, David told me it was an inspiring place. Rhoda said it was very interesting. I can't say I really felt God there, but you could sense an electricity, excitement, expectation. It really is a special place.

Back on the bus, Zvika took us to a cemetery, a rather strange stop for a tour. Another of Zvika's apparent quirks? He didn't say a word, but led us on foot through a strange, vast, beautiful cemetery to a particular site and lined us up at some well cared-for gravesites, manicured, with flowers on top, and Hebrew inscriptions on the headstones. After everyone was silent, he told us we were in a corner of the cemetery reserved for young people aged 19, 20, 21 – soldiers who died in action. So many gravestones! He said that every family lived with the burden of knowing one of their sons could die in battle and how difficult it was on the family, knowing they had to send their sons to defend the country, but knowing also that many didn't come back.

He said that, in Israel, it was considered a privilege, an honor, to serve and there was competition to be accepted and serve in a front position. When a young man was turned down, his parents would pull strings to get him in. Yet they know the chances he might never return, but what were the choices? Here, and in many other parts of the world, difficult choices to be made between living normal lives and defending their freedoms.

We stood in silence, in thought, deeply affected. No one said a word as we went back to the bus. While driving back, we all thought about that last stop.

Today we had to attend the Bar Mitzvah rehearsal. After all, that was what the trip was supposed to be about. We met the rabbi, a round little man with a beard, a real character, a little general. He gave each kid a chance to start to read his lines, let them read a couple of seconds to get a feel for the kid, then cut them off and moved on to the next kid. Just like that he got through 25 kids in two minutes! He assigned them each an English reading part, then told them to practice, "not to screw up!" Then he dismissed them. I sure wouldn't want him as a teacher or rabbi!

Thursday. We got up at 2:30 am. Yes, 2:30 am! Are we crazy or what?! Stumbled around washing, brushing teeth, showering. At 3:30 am we were on the bus in the dark, heading for Masada. I think David thinks it's all sort of crazy. Does he know what it means, what it's for? Does Rhoda? Will this tighten the bonds to each of us, to our history?

In the dark, leaving Jerusalem, you can see giant shadows of mountains vaguely looming outside. The excitement gathers. No one sleeps. We get to Masada around 5 am. Still dark. We climb and reach a plateau where we can see a cable car with a line going up into the darkness. We pile in and, as we go up, the sky starts to lighten. We see the cliffs darkly in front of us. David and I hold our *talesim* (prayer shawls) and cameras as we go up.

On top, we go in the dark over the rocks to a six-foot rock-enclosed space – a rock wall surrounding an empty area with rock benches carved in the sides going up – what was once an old synagogue. This is the old mountain refuge of Bar Kochba and his band, the small group of rebels who revolted at the Roman occupation of the Second Temple in Jerusalem. When the Romans no longer allowed the rites of circumcision, the "Brit Milah," when they prevented them from praying as Jews, when they defiled the Temple, they revolted. They were hopelessly outnumbered and beaten back. The Romans sacked Jerusalem, burned their Temple to the ground and burned the city.

The small surviving band of rebels escaped to this mountain stronghold, some 300 of them, where they took it over from a small garrison of Romans. They held it for some three years. Rome sent an army to destroy them – three divisions that camped at the base of the mountain but couldn't take it. Finally, they built a great earthen ramp, using Jewish slaves in front to prevent attacks downward. Bar Kochba knew that, because of that, he was beaten, and the end was near. He gathered his people and said to them, "Will you stand by and see your children slaughtered and your wives abused and killed? It is better to die as free men than to live as slaves." It reminded me of the motto of our current home state of New Hampshire, "Live free or die," or of the rallying cry centuries later of the French Revolution. For ages, this has been the ultimate decision to be made, whether ages past or in tyrannies to follow, live as slaves in unjust regimes or rebel and demand freedom.

They committed suicide on top of the mountain leaving their supplies of food and water untouched, so the Romans would know they were not driven to die by want but by desire for freedom.

Zvika and the Rabbi told this story as the dawn came over the mountain. The boys and girls sat on one side, parents on the other, with a *bima* (a prayer table) in the front. Each child wore a *tallis*, a prayer shawl. David put on his own, and I wore mine. Each child read his or her portion in English, and then the Torah reading began.

What a life moment to stand on this mountain, in the footsteps of those brave people, continuing our traditions today – a moment to treasure and never forget, a moment for pride, a connection to the history of our people.

David was called to the Torah – David Fischel Moshe ben Ephrayim Yitzhak – three generations in memory: myself, Ephrayim Yitzhak son of Mendel, Fischel and Moshe, my father's brothers murdered at Treblinka death camp, and David. I strongly feel the connections to all those who came before us, but for my son and my wife that passion may have seemed curious. Here, in the immensity of this space and its direct connection to our history and our people, all of us could feel how much we were a part of something bigger.

Hard to keep from crying. We are proud, happy and sad. Proud of our son and his accomplishments, happy to be with him at this moment, sad at the memory of those lost who couldn't be here with us. This moment alone was worth the entire trip.

What a wonderful feeling among all these strangers up here. Crying, laughing, feeling like a big family. The Rabbi gave a sermon on completion of the service. A wonderful, from-the-heart talk addressed to the kids. Telling them where they fit into the chain of history. Impressing on each of us, children and parents alike, the importance of knowing where we came from and what we stand for. What a keen insightful mind. I could have listened to him forever.

We go down the cable car. Zvika is going to take us to the Flour Cave. The bus drives into the desert – desert cliffs and mountains all around. No sign of water anywhere. We stop out in nowhere. Why? Shimmering heat. Zvika is going to take us on a hike, he says, to the Flour Cave. Many decline to get out, including David and Rhoda. Zvika insists they can do it. And most go on. Hot. Hot. Sun beating down. We start into a shallow path, inclining down, a wadi, an empty creek bed. As we continue, the sides get higher until we're in a ravine. High walls, soft chalky rock rubs off on you.

The path winds and winds. Shadows are black or white, no grays. Zvika says that when the rains come, you have to get out of the roaring flash floods that suddenly come. Then you need to run up the slopes. Life is like that also sometimes when you only have a choice to respond imme- diately when the tide turns against you and there's no time to think about other choices, only to act.

As we wind around some bends, we see sporadic army patrols: two or three guys wearing full gear with automatic rifles walking in the heat. We also see groups of Israeli army women, young girls, walking, sitting in the shade under cliffs listening to lectures, learning desert survival. What beautiful kids they all are: black hair, skinny, vivacious and all carrying automatic rifles. What a contrast they make, so young, so alive, carrying guns that kill. Is it real? Does life need to be like that anywhere, for anyone?

Even with the baking heat, it really isn't a bad walk. We come to a slope and the path goes through caves that wind upwards. Eventually the path leads up hills and ladders and finally up and out. Our little group looks at one another, red-faced, covered with flour-like chalk, we're a comical sight, but we all made it. Hurrah! It's a life-lesson in miniature.

We pile into the bus, stop for a brief dunk in the Dead Sea, have lunch, and drive back exhausted, falling asleep. Nap time!

That evening, we're scheduled for a gala banquet at the Jerusalem Hilton. Hundreds of people there with the kids sitting together. Lots of food, music, fun, singing, and, in the background, slides of Operation Moses bringing home the Ethiopian Jewish immigrants, families reunited, smiles, tears, hugging. Also slides of Operation Exodus, Russian Jews returning. Faces of all kinds from throughout the Diaspora returning to their ancestral homeland. So many internal problems for a country to deal with yet spending vast resources on rescuing people. If only countries had been willing to do this during World War II! If only they were willing to do this now, in our time.

The gala finishes with a certificate presentation. Each child goes forward to light yet one more candle, for light, for peace, for hope! All these shining hopeful young faces. I'm proud to be part of it all; the hope for the future. And to conclude the event, a huge cake in the shape of a Torah with each child's name inscribed in it, in English and Hebrew. To be written in the book of life. We stand in line, David and me, to get his cake, his name to bring back for us. We hug. I think we're both close to tears.

Friday. We're up early again but feeling refreshed. We start with Eshkol Heights where Zvika tells us about Project Renewal – rebuilding of old neighborhoods, renovating buildings, putting in cultural centers for families, for the children, to keep people together.

Our guide takes us to Yad Vashem (The World Holocaust Remembrance Center). While we wait to go in for the Memorial Service, Zvika talks to the kids and us about what happened in the concentration camps and how the world must never let it happen again. How we must be strong; how everywhere all of us must stand together, one for the other. He talks about the silence of the world that allowed the Holocaust to happen.

We go in for the *Kaddish*, the Memorial Service. An immense dim stark room, balconies around the perimeter for people to stand and, in front, surrounded by railing are plaques commemorating the concentration camps where so many perished. Auschwitz, Dachau, Buchenwald, Bergen-Belsen, Treblinka where Fischel and Moishe and my father's mother and others perished. Maybe this will help David understand my passion in studying our history and the Holocaust.

The children were told to dress in all white, in memoriam, and separated from us, so very symbolic! As we wait inside, silent, thinking, the children are led in, quiet, solemn. They are led one by one, two by two to stand behind the markers for each camp. Silent witnesses to remember forever what happened there. Kaddish. Silence. I can barely keep from crying remembering all those souls – children, parents, grandparents who never had a chance to live out their lives, for whom we have to live, to keep their memories forever. Something never to forget.

The ceremony over, we re-unite to go through the museum. We separate to wander alone through the words, the wounds, and the horrible pictures. Beyond comprehension. I've seen this so many times now, read so much, yet each time it's painful. I wind my way to the top floor and get forms to fill out for those who perished, to make sure their names are registered, not forgotten. I vow to let no name be forgotten.

As I wander up and down the halls, I periodically see David, serious, pale, looking at the unbelievable sights. He knows about the Holocaust, but here it's real. Here you know without a doubt what happened. Here you see history run through you, and you can wonder and scream inside: how could the world let this happen? I think David understands me better now.

I saw something this time I hadn't seen before, the Memorial to the Children Who Perished, the most tragic of all – the children who never understood at all why they were singled out, persecuted, and murdered. Children who never had a chance to grow up, get married, have any chance of happiness. We walk through the dark, then come in a room filled with stars, points of light to infinity, with whispers of Jewish children names, Yankele, Roisele, Suralle, Fischele... all gone! Almost a whole world disappeared with them, children and people who must live on through us and through our deeds.

We go back to the bus, but we've lost David, somehow. We look back and forth, with some panic in this stark environment, but eventually, we find each other again and leave.

Later that day, we're getting ready to return to the Western Wall for *Kaballah Shabbat* (evening prayers). Rhoda doesn't feel well and stays behind, so David and I go with the group to the Wall. People are coming from all directions to be together Friday night at the Wall. Chassidim of all sects, black hats, fur hats, black suits, suits with trousers tucked in leggings, kids running around everywhere, regular kids, kids with long curly hair with ear locks (*peyes*), clones of their fathers, girls in modern dress, girls with very modest dress and kerchiefs, a riot of differences. All pray at places along the wall, in disunity, in almost cacophony, but here it's ok. Songs come from one part; chanting and shaking back and forth from another, hands reaching out to touch the wall.

I don't just want to watch. I want to be part of it, and so does David. The women from our group went off with Zvika to help them find a place to light Shabbat candles. David and I go to the Wall and take some prayer books at one of the stands. They have Hebrew on all the pages, no English at all. I haven't seen one of these in years, not since my grand-mother died, not since I was growing up. We find the afternoon prayers in the book, and David and I stand at the Wall to pray together. We don't really feel part of this though. A group forms around us and the little table near us, more conservative-looking Jews, not Chassidim. One of them starts to pray and we start to respond.

Now we have our own *minyan* (quorum) around us. None of us know each other, but we feel like we do. We're part of that family. We pray together, out loud, chanting; it feels wonderful. While we pray, other groups spring up. They chant aloud also, pages behind where we are, voices together or apart, all praying, comfortable together. And maybe that's the most important part of this experience, that praying together or apart, the same or different, we're all comfortable with each other and feel like we all belong.

Many of the songs our "group" does are familiar. Surprisingly they do them with the melodies we use, that our Rabbi taught us. How wonder-ful. From our town in Illinois to Jerusalem.

Your senses expand standing here. Especially wonderful, David and I, father and son, standing together, in peace, praying together, him helping me in places to keep the place, me helping him. It was a peace-ful, wonderful moment.

Saturday. We go on a tour of the Old City and start at the City of David Museum. It's in an old tower-like structure, renovated and modernized on the inside, and it contains the history of Jerusalem.

Zvika comments that during many times in the Diaspora, those who left and found themselves in foreign lands were gradually assimilated, found the new life attractive, sometimes easier, and when opportunity arose to return, decided to stay. And so, Jews, as the "other," became spread throughout many lands of the earth, many retaining their beliefs and traditions, but many also being absorbed and sometimes accepted into the culture of the new lands where they lived. But as later history showed, as times changed and pressures on societies grew, even those who were accepted often became rejected, despised, and thrown out, persecuted or worse. How painfully similar to what we see in the world today.

We continued and toured other parts of the Old City, concluding with wandering through the Arab quarter. What a contrast! The marketplace and stalls are full of vendors, colors all around, exotic smells, music, and noise.

The Dome of the Rock looked beautiful on the outside. We tried to get in, but it was closed to tourists for prayer at that hour. The inside is a place of prayer to commemorate the rock from where they say Mohammed descended to heaven. The rock is also said to be the same used by Abraham, whom Muslims also revere, when he was going to sacrifice Isaac. How can two peoples with such history in common not live together in peace or not be able to reconcile their differences?

In the afternoon, when we returned to the hotel, my cousin Ephrayim and his wife Tamar Schwarzbard and their son Alon came to visit us. I remembered my last visit with them when Ephrayim had said to me, "You've been here twice, but you've hardly seen anything. We haven't met your wife or son; they haven't seen my mother Shoshana or father Rachmil, and they're getting old. We want to see them. Life is for family."

I thought about that a lot over the summer. He was right. It was nice to sit and talk together. We talked about a lot of things, but about a couple of things extensively. One was about my job and the heavy work and travel schedule versus Ephrayim's decision to limit his job and spend time with his family. We talked about "the road not taken" and the impossibility of never knowing if the choices you made were the right ones or if you would have been happier if you had made a different choice in life.

How many times have families throughout our 3,000-year history of wandering and uprooting our families and lives, much more so than we have, sat around a table, like we in Jerusalem and talked about the same questions!

Who's right? Is there one answer? No way to ever tell. The asking sometimes provides as much satisfaction as if there is only one answer. How wonderful to be able to sit like this with family and ponder life's questions. I really felt a strong sense of family, lifelong attachments, even though we'd only seen each other three times over eight to ten years. Rhoda and David didn't say that much during this, David especially did a lot of serious listening. Ephrayim was right when he told me we had to come.

The other thing we talked about at length was Alon's interest in a career. He's in the army now and has some time to take a decision, but he's a serious young man. He's Ephrayim and Tamar's younger son, lean, sharp, tanned, beautiful. Ephrayim wants him to capitalize on his electronic and computer skills learned with the army and stay with it, maybe with the army, maybe with a bank. He sees security there.

Alon wants to study more – accounting, more computer courses, looking for something different, looking further to the future; the father looking one way, wanting easy security for his son, the son not interested in the short term and security, willing to take chances with the future. How often has that debate gone on in the world?

David again listened seriously. What a wonderful opportunity to see loving families and reunited generations working together on common problems, unanswerable questions! Our families were separated by a vast world, yet truly connected.

After Ephrayim and his family left, dinner was in the hotel since it was Shabbat evening and also the holiday of *Tisha B'Av* (commemoration of the destruction of the Temple). How ironic and how fitting for us to be in Jerusalem, reunited on this very date!

Dinner was mostly gone. We went a little late, and most choices were gone. We looked around and saw many irate Americans. The poor waiters – it wasn't their fault. The hotel was being cheap. The waiters were doing the best they could. I felt like being angry at them also but took a good look at who our waiter was. His English wasn't good. He didn't look happy either, but he kept polite with everyone.

His name was Alex and, talking with him, I realized he was a Russian immigrant, trying to earn a living. And as I looked around, I realized a lot of the waiters and busboys were immigrants. Many were clearly having a hard time that night. No choices, unhappy customers, but trying as hard as they could. When I saw this, the food didn't much matter anymore. I said to David, "You know, Alex is a Russian Jew." He looked hard, and he got quiet too.

What a wonderful thing. Even the international hotel where we were staying was hiring these people. I don't know if they deserve the praise or if, somehow, they got a special deal for some tourist leverage with them, but I didn't care. It's amazing how patient you can be when you see a good cause.

I felt so good that when I left, I asked for the manager and told him what a wonderful thing the hotel was doing by giving these people a chance, and I told him that Alex was really trying and doing a good job. He had a look of astonishment about him. I don't think they're used to compliments and praise.

"Thank you very much, sir," he said.

Who benefited most? I don't know, but it sure felt good! Bad dinner? What a nice ending to a super day!

Sunday. At breakfast we met Alex again as our waiter. He's learning both English and Hebrew he told me. His name is Alex Mendelevitch (Mendelevitch meaning, in Russian, son of Mendel), and he's from Kiev. He's a real Jew with a long Jewish heritage, and he's thrilled to be in the land of his people. It seemed like he couldn't do enough for us this morning. Was it because we talk to him, unlike other tourists or did the manager tell him we said nice things about him? I don't care. I'm really proud of the country and the opportunity it offers people like him.

Monday. We head off early for Hadassah Hospital. We learn from Zvika that Hadassah Hospital was originally built in Jerusalem, but after the 1948 war was in occupied territory. It was abandoned, previously a state-of-the-art medical center for the Middle East.

With the help of American women, a new complex was built outside Jerusalem. It's the finest medical complex in the Middle East today. We saw a video about it. Boring? No. Riveting! What wonderful things they do. The doctors they train are required to serve two years in villages in Africa, community service to help underdeveloped countries in dire need of medical support. The doctors who go there are treated like gods, saviors, by the people, loved for what they are and what they do: treating babies, bringing vaccines, treating blinding illnesses. There's a lot I didn't know.

They've had major turn-around in care in those countries, and they bring doctors back to teach and train. They treat the Arab population. They work with the incoming immigrants. It really makes you proud to see the wonderful things a country can do!

We catch a flight to Eilat from a small airport in Tel Aviv. It's a one-hour flight in a small plane. From the sky, you can practically see the width of the country with the Mediterranean Sea on one side and Jordan on the other. Such a small country! We pass the Dead Sea and look to see if we can identify Masada from the air. There is so much desert, so many mountain plateaus that we can't be sure. What arid lands, but even here you can see settlements, Kibbutzim, tilling the land and serving as early warning against attacks.

We land in 100-degree heat! Eilat is at the Red Sea with Jordan on the Eastern border. The city of Aqaba, Jordan can be seen across the bend of the sea. The Jordan Israel geological rift forms mountains and valleys between the countries. Further down from Jordan and bordering the Red Sea lays Saudi Arabia. On the western border of the Negev lies the Sinai Peninsula and west of that the Suez Canal connecting the Mediterranean Sea to the Red Sea.

Tuesday. We visit a malachite factory. Malechite is called the Eilat stone. It's a beautiful dark green smooth stone that they mine there and craft into jewelry. They don't export any of the minerals, only finished jewelry.

We started with a brief tour. The factory showed us how they cut the stones and make settings. Then the main event: shopping! They had gorgeous jewelry and religious items, and some people made purchases. We looked at everything, lots of beautiful things for both men and women, stones set in silver, stones set in gold, candelabras, designs, stars.

David was looking very hard. I think he wanted something of his own because he saw us get those special engraved gold wedding bands in Jerusalem and presents for people back home. I think he wanted to bring a special keepsake for himself too.

I didn't know what he was looking for, but he was looking for something. I showed him a beautiful Eilat stone in a silver menorah setting. No sale. That wasn't what he was looking for. Eventually, he focused on a Star of David. So many kinds. One, in particular, caught his eye. A star with the points and center out of Malechite stone and held together by gold. I wouldn't have seen it, but he was right. As I looked at it, it was beautiful. But expensive! He looked and looked. David whispered with Rhoda. I guess he figured I'd say no! Negotiations on how he'd pay us back with the money from his bank account when we got back. "Please!!"

"Well, maybe. Do you have a gold chain?"

Looking for gold chains. He picked out a beautiful one. Gorgeous with the star!

"Please?" quietly.

Certainly there was no chance of spending so much money on himself. Down to just a few people in the store now.

"Please?"

Looking at him, wanting it so much, me, proud of all he's accomplished in being Jewish, all he's learned. How not to let him have it? Was it asking for a toy, something that would be forgotten? How not to give him something so important; so, like a Jewish identity?

"I want to buy it for him," I whispered to Rhoda.

Did she feel about it like I did?

"Look at him."

"Ok."

We said to him, "You can have it. We want to buy it for you. Every time you look at it, for your whole life, we want you to remember we bought it for you and to remember this trip and everything good about it. And to remember that we love you."

I think none of us could say more. He hugged us both, and I think for more than the present.

They brought him a box for it, but he wanted to wear it, and we put it on, and he wore it outside his shirt to show it off and so he could see it.

Zvika came over. "Let me see what you got. It's beautiful. Wear it in good health."

David bursting with pride. Zvika put his hand on it, looked David in the eyes and said quietly, "Always wear it on the outside, not inside the shirt. Show them you're proud of your heritage."

David looked back at him, and silently nodded. What a light and pride in his eyes! We bought a lot more than a necklace. Something for all of us to treasure forever.

We taxied back to the hotel. David's friends stopped him. "Show us what you got! Oh, how beautiful. I didn't see that there."

Throughout the trip, he wore it. Always on the outside of his shirt. And always, "David, how beautiful." And even when we were back in Illinois and David was back in his school, it was always worn on the outside of his shirt. Proud, beaming.

We returned by plane to Tel Aviv the next day, were met at the airport by our bus, and started driving north along the coastal road.

We all settled in. Zvika got up and started to talk to us again. This time about immigration – the Ethiopians and Russians coming in, the responsibility of all to ensure a safe haven for those in the Diaspora needing to return. He told us the plan was to first save the kids, to integrate them to give them the greatest chance for a positive future. They're immersed into regular classes and respond beautifully. They learn quickly and within six months they're already speaking the language. The parents are a different problem. Depending on their ages and education, they learn more slowly.

Many of the Russians came with big expectations and have a hard time. There are lots of educated people among them, lots of engineers, scientists, doctors, musicians, more than a little country can absorb right away. So, they have to take alternate jobs and try to adjust. Zvika told us of one little town that had a sudden influx of Russia immigrants with many excellent musicians. Overnight they formed an excellent Philharmonic Orchestra. Incredible!

We saw signs of some of this, too, when we were in Jerusalem and strolling around Ben Yehuda Street on Saturday night. We saw some very talented street musicians who looked like they were Russian immigrants.

Zvika told us the current absorption cost for immigrants was $11,600 per year. Multiply that times the 400,000 immigrants they got and it's $4.5 billion per year absorption costs alone! Incredible!

Zvika spoke about the special challenge of absorbing the Ethiopian immigrants. When they came, they knew nothing about modern houses or conveniences. They had to learn about doorknobs, toilets, bathing, washing clothes, working, everything. It's like trying to teach 3,000 years of civilization. What an enormous task for a country to take on willingly!

The first Ethiopian airlift, Operation Moses, happened seven or eight years go. But in that operation, word of the evacuation leaked out and not all the Ethiopian Jews could be taken out. Some families were separated, sending their children out while parents stayed behind, not knowing what would happen to them, but wanting to ensure their children's future.

The second airlift, Operation Solomon, happened just seven or eight months ago. 20,000 people were airlifted out in one weekend. Unimaginable! El Al airliners were converted to carrier status. All seats were removed so people could be packed in, and they flew around the clock.

We saw video footage of the arrival of those flights in Israel. What happiness. Arrival in a safe land; families united with children from seven to eight years ago they thought they'd never see again. A modern-day Exodus. To those people, especially to families re-united, it must have been no less a miracle than those during the exodus from Egypt thousands of years ago.

When you hear those things, see those images with your own eyes, you can better understand how miracles can happen and the connection between the readings of the bible and the events, and the meaning and significance of events, today.

As we drove further on, we saw several aqueducts that the Romans had built to carry water from the north. They were huge and went for miles. It's amazing to look at them and reflect on the technology and engineering skills they already had so long ago.

We drove on to Megiddo, an ancient historical site. It is one of the older tels in Israel showing levels of civilization. The hill stands out in the open and is surrounded by many other large hills. The view is inspiring; you can see a long way.

On top of the hill is a tunnel leading into the depths of the hill itself. Long steep stone steps in front of us and most of us dare to enter the tunnel. After a long trek down, the tunnel leveled and became momentarily horizontal, leading down eventually to an aquifer, where an old well stood.

The residents of Megiddo were protected on their hill, surrounded by sturdy walls. Their water supply, however, was on the outside and used to water their crops. To protect themselves in case of a siege, they built this system of tunnels. It led from the well outside the town down by tunnels and back inside the wall. By moving an immense boulder, they could divert the flow of the aquifer so that the well water was diverted inside the city walls.

What amazing skills these people had so long ago, to be able to dig underground in so true a path to know where they would wind up speaks to amazing mathematical and engineering knowledge. To dig out the tunnels alone and control the water flow must have been an immense task. It just goes to show that we're not so much smarter today than we think. We just have better tools.

Thursday morning. After a lengthy bus ride, we start our day with a jeep tour of the Golan Heights.

Looking westward from there you could see for miles across the narrow thread of the Jordan River to the north and across to settlements on the other side. Just a few miles to Syria on the east.

As we rode back with Zvika, we asked him if Israel would ever give any of the Golan back. His answer was surprising: "There are many who wouldn't give back an inch. They don't trust Syria and would give nothing. But it's a new time now and you have to gamble a little to get peace. Maybe we wouldn't give anything back. Maybe we would. The important thing is to start talking and see where it goes. If we can build confidence that we can trust, then anything is possible."

How that affected me: "Anything is possible if we can talk." For peace. It's time to try some new things.

We learned some things each day, felt we understood the people a little more the more time we spent there. We were dirty and hot and tired, but it was a good morning.

We drove next to Safed. The drive to Safed was pretty, winding through hills with pine trees. Safed is an old city that's famous for its' role in the development of Talmud and mysticism.

We only got to spend a short time in Safed. A huge song fair was scheduled for that night, roads were blocked off, and we had to get in and out before things got crazy with crowds and traffic.

We walked around and saw one of our group dickering and having fun with an artist at a small stall. He had cartoon-like graphic prints. I listened in to what they were haggling over – a print with beautiful colors, sort of primitive art (reminiscent of the Caribbean) and this print told the story of a life – family, birth of the first child, more children, growth, marriage, family, growing old, beautiful in style and concept. If he wasn't going to buy it, I wanted it! I wouldn't have bargained over it as much as he did; he apparently got as much out of the process of bargaining as he did out of the print. He bought it! I asked the artist if he had another. Yes. Bought it on the spot at the same price with no haggling. The artist laughed. Others came up who wanted copies too. The artist couldn't believe his luck.

Friday. We took a long drive from Haifa to Rosh Hanikra to the grottos.

We got to Rosh Hanikra and climbed up to the cable car. Taking the cable car down to the sea, we go through beautiful grottos, like beautiful windows on the Mediterranean. The sea-breakers force their way into the underground grottos, beautiful blue-green waves, and beautiful blue sky above it all. We climb back up from the grottos and take the cable car back up to the heights and drive south down the coast.

Next stop is Akko. Akko is halfway back to Haifa and also on the coast. Akko was an old Crusader town built underground to provide security. Even before that it was an ancient port. Both Akko and Jaffa are mentioned as ports as long as 2500 years ago. Today it's a mixed city of Arabs and Jews.

Underneath the town lay old Crusader outposts which have been excavated and which we toured. It really is incredible how much has been excavated. When I was here the first time, you could see just several of the rooms, and they had rubble in them. Now, layer after layer is cleaned out and restored to show what the Crusader city looked like. It is really incredible that it was done, and paid for, by a Jewish state.

On the way out of Akko, we visited an Ethiopian/Russian caravan village. It has just the basics, almost like a trailer village but with playgrounds for the kids. We stopped and talked to some Ethiopians. The kids are beautiful with beautiful smiles. They spoke pretty good English as well. They look happy and ham it up for the cameras.

How could these immigrants have survived anywhere else? Where else could they have found a permanent home for themselves and a potential good future for their children? For them, immigration to Israel had been an answer; for us, immigration to America had made everything possible.

Friday afternoon. We check in at the Tel Aviv Dan Hotel in Tel Aviv.

Uh Oh! There's a message waiting for me from my company: "Fred, we know you're on vacation in Israel with your family, but we need you to urgently divert from your trip and go to Paris for a critical business meeting. Instead of returning to the U.S. with your family, we need you to fly Sunday to Paris to make an important presentation."

I'd waited for so long for this trip, this opportunity. Diverted again from exploring my family history, my family relations? How was diverting to Paris going to happen? I had made no plans for business meetings on this trip. I had neither suit nor business clothes with me; nothing to prepare me for an important business meeting and had no plans for presentations in Paris. How did they want me to do that? Besides, it was late Friday afternoon and all stores were closing in preparation for the Sabbath.

The message included, "Buy suit and whatever clothes you'll need in Paris in Israel over the weekend. We've booked a flight for you from Tel Aviv to Paris and all arrangements are made. Don't worry about putting together a special presentation. We know you'll be fine meeting with our representatives there."

I quickly found an open men's store, picked out clothes, and explained I desperately needed them altered and ready for Sunday. They were incredulous but promised to have them ready.

We washed up, changed clothes, and Ephrayim picked us up for Shabbat dinner at his house. I had really been looking forward to this. I think some of the other families from our trip are jealous of us that we have family here that we can celebrate with. Clearly, it's more than just a tourist trip for us.

Ronnie and David meet Ephrayim's children. Ephrayim and Tamar can't do enough for us. Ephrayim's kids are Orit, the oldest born 1966, Alon, born 1969, and Shai born in 1973. Orit is there with her husband Meier Atiya and two children, her little boy Naor and baby girl Lital. Special people.

We have a fantastic dinner, salads galore, chicken, fish fillets, and no end of good things. The feeling of family is strong, really the whole reason for the trip. It feels wonderful.

Shoshana and Rachmil come after dinner. They finally meet Ronnie and David, a bridge now firmly linked between the past and the present. How wonderful for Shoshana to bridge the years from leaving Poland until meeting Mendel's grandson in Israel. Could we have not come?

Bridging Lifetimes / Bridging Worlds

We spend long hours talking. I talk to Rachmil and Shoshana in Yiddish and translate back and forth to Ronnie and David. We look at old pictures, hold hands, and laugh together. I think David really feels now that he has family in Israel. He's found a friend, and they're playing chess together with his brother looking on. From the time I already spent with my father, interviewing him, looking at old pictures together, the past and the present come together.

It's striking how the image of David and Alon, intense at the game, looks like the picture of Mendel's brother Fischel playing chess with his friends before the war. What a picture!

Saturday. August 15th, 1992

We finally get to sleep a little late, have breakfast, walk around a little and swim a little. It feels wonderful to relax.

In the afternoon, my cousin Bat Ami's husband, Meier Engel, picks us up and takes us to their house where everybody else is waiting. We eat, talk, and fill up on memories until we can see each other again. Eventually, we have to go back to the hotel. We say goodbye to Shoshana and Rachmil. Will we ever have an opportunity to see them again?

Tomorrow is the end of the trip. I have split feelings on whether I really want the clothes I'll need for Paris to be ready or whether they'll give me a good-enough excuse not to go. Not much choice. The clothes were altered and ready. At the end of the day, I accompanied my wife and son to the airport. They flew home to Frankfort, Illinois alone. I flew to Paris.

That's what work had become by August 1992. Many downsides, but still spectacular opportunities that I might never have had otherwise to connect with family.

When I returned home to Frankfort, Illinois, life continued as it had before. Rhoda commuted to Chicago where she had a job as a Research Associate/Research Assistant Professor at the University of Chicago. David went to high school in Frankfort, Illinois.

And for me? I had to keep working, but I couldn't stay away from my family history that I still didn't know enough about, work or no work!

Picture by picture, my precious collection of photographs and documents of the family before, during, and after WWII grew. It started while growing up listening to my father's stories of family members before the war that came to dominate everything. I saw an occasional photograph. I would make a copy of it and put it away. In time as my interest grew stronger and stronger, father would give me the original and tell me to put it away for future generations in a safe place. I did that and also set up a photography gallery for those pictures on the Internet where I could post each one as I got it and where they would be on display for others to find with a history of our town.

It didn't take long. Within a year, I had several comments posted to the site, one of them from an Israeli woman, Shoshi Shatit, whose father had lived in Sokolow, who had survived and was with her in Israel. I responded to her and we began to correspond. Several others also found me via that source, and I started to accumulate a list of those with a link to my city. I could now call it my city. Little did I know that, years later, I would meet Shoshi Shatit at a special gathering in Sokolow itself.

I had previously become a charter member of the United States Holocaust Memorial Museum, and in my first of many trips to the museum, I was overwhelmed by the horrors on display and the massive atrocities committed. While wandering from one horrible exhibit to the next, I glanced at the document that I'd been given when I entered, a simulated "passport" (story identification cards) of victims of the Holocaust. All visitors to the Museum, on entrance, are given what looks like a passport of someone who perished in the Holocaust. Somehow, during my first visit, and beyond all explanation, the "passport" that I received was of someone I knew.

Shock! Beyond all belief, in my hand was a picture, a document of Moische Velvul Felman, my father's younger brother, born 1926 and murdered in Treblinka on September 22nd, 1942. In another room, I saw an exhibit of pictures of a family from another small town in Poland, completely wiped away, with pictures of those lost covering an entire wall. It became clear to me that here was where the photographs I'd scavenged ultimately belonged.

I searched the museum's archives for other photographs that they had from my family's home town, but only found two, pictures of a survivor returning to the town at the end of the war and finding only a large mass grave where some of the victims had been buried during the war. After returning home, I contacted one of the archivists at the museum, Teresa Pollin and inquired, "I have many more photographs from that town than the museum has. Could I donate copies of the photographs to be preserved to the museum?"

Overwhelmingly the answer was yes. "We'd love to have your pictures in our collections. Let us know when you're ready to donate them. You're welcome to visit us and discuss donating them."

But the pictures weren't mine alone. I had to discuss donating them with my brothers and sister. Could we give up the only precious records of our family left to us? To my siblings I offered to scan each photograph, document the names of each person and make copies for each of us of the original and carefully restore versions of each and provide those to all of us. Only when all that was done, could I consider going back to the museum.

Work and travel again caught me and kept me busy and diverted me from connecting my history and answering the questions of our past that kept coming back to me. So frustrating not to be able to pursue this!

10

THE YEARS CATCH UP

Family Changes

So much had changed for us all and so much change continued in all our lives.

There had never seemed to be a place for my family that they could call "home" during their treks from Poland to Russia, from Russia to Azerbaijan, from Azerbaijan to refugee camps back in Poland and from there to displaced persons camps in Austria.

Even in America they moved from one temporary place to another until they finally were able to buy and live in what became their real home in 1953 and where Mendel and Frieda raised their family. With their family dispersed to the winds and no longer needing a large house, Mendel and Frieda moved in South Bend, Indiana from Sherman Avenue where they had been for over 20 years into a smaller bungalow south of the city.

Wherever we all were, home was where Mendel and Frieda were, but their house now was empty of the children, who were scattered throughout the country. As in many families, all our lives were busy, and visits home became sporadic. Only occasionally were we all at the family home together.

This was often at a major holiday, typically at Passover, when we all sat around the family table, when Frieda would create a massive traditional meal. Mendel would read the traditional service, missing no part of the old readings, and all would sing the old songs together, reminisce of the past and relate what was new with all of us. What precious memories to recall at these gatherings. Remembering celebrations in the first home that my parents bought in South Bend, with my mother and father in charge of their fates, with my young brothers and sister, with my grandmother who had gone through so much to be with us.

What a wonderful time for all of us to be together before the duties of job and home dispersed us all and left our parents home seeming empty again.

Mendel retired from the railroad in 1981 after his heart attack. Frieda's mother Ida, my beloved grandmother, passed away in the same year. Mendel and Frieda lived contented lives in Indiana, but missed having their children, who visited with every opportunity, near them. While Rhoda and David and I lived nearby in Illinois, we, too, could be only infrequent visitors and, in-between, their house continued to feel empty.

For both Mendel and Frieda, retirement was a new way of living. Father had never had free time to do what he wanted. What he'd known in Europe was a world of running and working. What he'd known before in the U.S. was unending and back-breaking work, work to feed his family, work to put his children through college, just enough time to keep things up and still get some sleep in between. "Free time" wasn't something he ever had to think about and being home was something with which he had to adjust.

He started by helping Frieda with her chores and with her cooking and baking. That drove her crazy. She had her own way of doing things; after all she was a professional homekeeper. She had always managed to make things work, no matter what the circumstances, no matter how primitive and stressed they had been in Europe, no matter how little money she had to pull things together as she had when they were first in America.

Over time, Frieda became fragile and ill and finally, after more than 40 years, they left South Bend and moved to Rockville, MD in June 1991 to be close to Charlotte and their grandchildren. Little by little as they aged, they managed to accommodate themselves to their new reality. And little by little, the infirmities of aging took their own toll.

Frieda gradually began to forget little things and had to be reminded and helped by Mendel, which disturbed her greatly and worried her absentee children tremendously. As time progressed, we children, and even Mendel, could see that Frieda was succumbing to some form of early-stage dementia, and none of us knew how to deal with it. Frieda and Mendel had overcome so much, had more than once been on the brink of disaster and death and survived. How unfair it was, now in safety and in comfort, to be faced with a disease that offered no place to run, no place to hide, no place to escape.

With time and increasing loss, Frieda was enrolled in an adult day care facility where she could spend her days with supervision. Mendel could be freed from the burden of being the caregiver 24 hours a day. Frieda, resisting the concept at the beginning, found enjoyment in being with others like her and with the social programs. She loved the little group that she became part of that spent time together singing old Yiddish melodies, songs that she'd learned and sung as a child.

But increasingly, the time when she returned home became more difficult as her memory became lost. When left at home for short times, she could wander away and forget how to get home; cooking became dangerous when she forgot to turn off the stove. Even personal care became difficult, and the time gradually approached when the only solution appeared to be a full-time nursing home for her.

Nursing Homes / Moving Again

By that time, Rhoda and I and David had also moved. My job became centered around Philadelphia and we'd moved near there, both because of the job and because it put us only a three-hour drive away from where Mendel and Frieda lived. All of us children caucused and agreed that for both Mendel and Frieda's sake, for Frieda to have adequate care, for Mendel to have some semblance of quiet life, that Frieda needed permanent day care. Frieda was highly resistant to this and rebelled from leaving her home. A nursing home seemed out of the question.

After much time and deliberation, an intermediate solution seemed to offer itself. Nearby, a home for a small number of occupants was found, with all the services of a nursing home, but with a home environment, and with a great deal of persuasion, we convinced Mendel that this was the only solution.

One weekend, Rhoda and I drove to Maryland and with Mendel we drove Frieda, very reluctant and tearful, to the home. We convinced her that she needed to stay, that Mendel would be not far away, would visit frequently as would we, and that it would be good not only for her but also for Mendel. Tearfully, she stayed behind. We left, also very sad that where time and the war hadn't been able to take them apart, that failing heath required their separation. Thankfully, though, a solution seemed to have been found.

Days later, we received at home a phone call from Mendel telling us that he'd taken Frieda out of the home. She had cried there constantly. After all the years, she couldn't be separated from Mendel. Mendel, too, missed her and felt guilty and had finally consented to terminate her stay. She was home again.

Things deteriorated even further. Frieda's memory became even more lost. Mendel's time was entirely swallowed with full time care. To leave the house, he had to lock the door or risk her wandering away and getting lost or hurt. It didn't take long to realize that the risk to both in their current situation was intolerable, and all of us convinced Mendel to enroll Frieda in a nearby full-service, full-time nursing home.

While it gave Mendel some semblance of freedom and assured Frieda that she would be safe, the nursing home was a terrible compromise. To her, it was like being in a prison. Frieda was constantly agitated. She became mean to her caregivers, the nurses, and frequently required restraints. The nursing home was only minutes from Mendel's house, and he was there constantly. He wore himself down and became at risk himself for having a physical and emotional breakdown.

The two who had suffered so much, who had kept each other alive through every dangerous scenario, now were at risk for not only losing each other, but losing themselves as well. How could they be left to this end! Was there nothing else that could give them peace and some happiness in the final stages of their lives?

Charlotte, who had born the brunt of her mother's mental decay because of her proximity to them, was out of solutions. Boris and I, separated by the distance of a continent, struggled to find a better answer. During a visit by Rhoda and me to Boris and Robin, we struggled to find a way.

Boris: "What if we moved them to Palo Alto? Maybe we could find a home nearby where Frieda would be comfortable, close enough so that Mendel could visit every day. What if we moved Mendel to our house where he could be near us and near to our kids, where he could still have a normal life, have no daily responsibilities and could visit with Frieda whenever he wanted, but not be burdened with her care?"

Me: "It sounds wonderful, but I can't imagine father would ever agree to it. Give up his house and potentially give up his independence to come live with you? Move across the country at his and mother's age? He's so stubborn. I just can't imagine he'd ever consider it. But to leave them like they are, they'll both rapidly go downhill. Even if it won't work, we have to, at least, give it a try."

Days later, when Rhoda and I returned home, we got a phone call from Boris. "I talked to father, and he'll consider it. If we can make it work, he'll come live with me and Robin and the kids. Robin's all for it too." I was so relieved. Finally, this had a potential for a good solution for my parents where both could benefit, where my mother could have good care and where my father could be happy with it and with her.

And the process started. A wonderful environment was found for Frieda in a house less than a mile from Boris in a quiet neighborhood with only a few occupants, but with full-time care. It didn't look like a nursing home at all but had all the resources that would have come with one. Boris and the kids emptied a room in their house that would be Mendel's own, and the children were highly enthusiastic of having their grandfather come to live with them. Robin, always kind, always loving, prepared for her father-in-law to be welcomed and to be part of their lives.

Mendel was told, "We need your help anyway. Both of us work; we need help taking care of the kids. You can help us with the cooking or cleaning. It will be doing us a favor for you to come live with us and all of us will love it."

Was it a done deal? How hard would it be in February 2000 to move the two of them across the country, Mendel and Frieda at 83 years old, and Frieda not well? Even for Boris, at age 45 and Robin 39, life would get more complicated. And their children, would they adjust? Especially for the youngest, Sam, moved out of his bedroom to make room for Mendel, how would he feel toward his grandfather?

Amazingly, Mendel agreed to move once more, to move again across a continent. How many times and how many distances he had traveled and moved, from temporary shelter to temporary shelter, from apartment to apartment and eventually to a home. Now again, after more than 50 years in South Bend, Indiana and then in Maryland, at the age of 83, he was prepared to relocate himself and Frieda one more time. Each time he had moved as a young man, it was to protect Frieda and then his family. In America, it was Frieda who had prompted him to move, even when they lived in South Bend, and now the final move was again to protect Frieda. To stay behind in Maryland, with Frieda miserable and isolated in a cold and inhospitable nursing home with no connections to anyone, and even hardly to him, was impossible for him. He was prepared to do whatever he had to do to change that and make her life pleasant and happy, even in the last stages. And in Palo Alto, while only a short distance would separate both, they would be near children and grandchildren and with vibrant life surrounding and including them.

And so, Boris, the youngest of their children, flew out to collect his mother and father to bring them back to a better place. Mendel to come to his and his family's home; Frieda to go just a short distance away in happy surroundings where they could all visit. The grandchildren were ecstatic, especially having their grandfather as one of the family, Natalie the oldest daughter at ten years old, Talya her sister at eight, Eli at six, and Sam, the baby, only one year old. For Mendel especially, Sam was a joy. For Sam especially, Mendel was a joy. He lived just across the hall from Sam's bedroom, and every morning when Sam got up, the first thing he would do would be to walk over to Mendel's door and go to

Mendel. They were inseparable, and for Mendel, it was life re-found, participating in every aspect of the family from feeding Sarah, the cat, to doing dishes every night and telling his stories at the Friday evening meal when the family invited a host of others to join them for Shabbat celebration.

He visited Frieda every day, just a short walk away. It was the highlight of her day, especially when he could take her in a wheelchair for a walk around the neighborhood. Two old people, appreciating each other and loving each other more than they had ever known, spending their time together. Periodically, I visited as well although the times were heart-rending as Frieda lost more and more of her memory and, eventually, she passed away on June 3rd, 2001.

Family Gathers / Frieda (2001)

It was a difficult time with all four children assembled for the funeral with both sad and happy memories pouring out.

In a small room at the funeral home, I could hardly hold back tears as I remembered her:

Frieda was above all else, a loving wife and mother. Coming from Europe in 1949 with her husband and two sons and mother and little else, she quickly made a home for them out of a small rented flat in the heart of a run-down black ghetto in South Bend, Indiana. She enrolled her oldest son, me, Fred (Ephrayim), in a public school and walked with him there for miles to get him started. She enrolled both me and Irving (Yisrul) in Hebrew schools. Charlotte was born in that flat in the ghetto, and she was the love of her life. She saved the little money that her husband Mendel earned as a laborer so that they could move. They moved first into a rented house around the corner and then into the first home that they bought for $8,000, a rambling old two-story house with an attic that Irving and I shared. Boris was born in that house, and because he was the child of her middle age, she loved him all the more. We all grew up in that house, and the memories are wonderful. Frieda was always a loving daughter and she and Mendel moved her mother Ida, whom she had taken with her and cared for throughout their entire journey, into a tiny house only two blocks away.

Passover was such a wonderful happening as an extended family in that old dining room with the furniture for which she had scrimped, bought, and was so proud of. Every year, Frieda would clean and make everything kosher by hand while grandmother would make cherry wine for Passover. Passover songs rang late into the night every year.

We lived about three to four miles from the synagogue, and walking back and forth on High Holidays, hand in hand, brings special memories. Friday nights were special. Frieda always kept track of the time so that she could light the Shabbat candles before dark. Chicken soup and a special Shabbat meal were ready when my father finally came home from his work on the railroad, bone-tired and dirty. But when we were all cleaned up and sitting around the Shabbat table, everything was right with the world.

In time, we all went our separate ways. Somehow Frieda and Mendel found ways to put us through school and college. Love of learning and respect for education was something they drummed into our heads. At every graduation, they were there, beaming with pride. And how proud we are of them of what they accomplished.

Our accomplishments are their graduate degrees.

None of us left without keeping our connection especially to her. She worried about us constantly, when we lived at home, and years and decades later when we were far away. We were always her babies. And she loved us all and was proud of us – Irving ("S'rulikyl") with the wonderful family he raised in Ottawa; Charlotte ("Chinkale") who brought her out to Maryland to live near Aviva and her other grandchildren. Charlotte who accomplished everything that Mother never thought a woman could. Boris ("Burach-aly"), the joy of her life, full of life as a child and accomplished as a man beyond anything she imagined. And me, Fred (Froymele) the oldest and first loved son, and my wife Rhoda, and Frieda's first grandson David Moses Fischel.

Frieda never thought of herself as anything but a simple plain housewife and never really thought she personally had accomplished much. But what stamina and fortitude and courage this woman showed. How many worlds she traveled. How many times she had to rip up home and try again, never knowing what the future would bring to her and her family. As a young girl, leaving Poland, surviving the Nazis, keeping her family together in Russia, always just ahead of the German army. Always waiting to see if her husband would survive another day and come home to her. Leaving Russia, making a new home in a displaced person's barracks in Austria. Leaving Austria and making a difficult journey by decommissioned troop-carrier to New York and then by car to Indiana, where she finally could settle down and start a real life. And late in life, leaving Indiana to move closer to Charlotte and her grandchildren in Maryland. Stamina. Courage. Faith in the future.

She never thought she was anything special. But she and her generation that endured and prevailed turned out to be among the giants of the earth. She'll be long missed and remembered by us all.

And the first-born child in America, the little girl that Frieda so loved, Charlotte (Chinkale), recalled the immensity of her mother's life.

In life, as in art, we sometimes stand too close to the people we love and miss seeing exactly who they are. My whole life I thought of my mother as someone who was just always there to cook – as no one else could – to clean, to take care of four kids, a husband, a few boarders, my grandmother. She didn't work outside the home. She didn't drive and didn't have a high school diploma. She was embarrassed about her English.

But in preparing to say good-bye to her today, I take a step back and see such an amazing woman! As a young woman in her early twenties, she had the courage and resolve to lead herself, her mother, her sister and future brother-in-law, and her then fiancée (my dad) out of Sokolow, out of the jaws of the Nazis. She did not freeze in the fear of "what if"; she did not allow herself to be comforted by false hopes of "maybe it'll be alright." We are leaving, she said to my dad, "choose". My brothers and I were trying to figure out last night how many people's lives that courage saved, in addition to the five who left, and we counted 27 already with, G-d willing, many more great grandchildren and great great grandchildren to come.

And her courage didn't stop with their leaving. There was surviving the Russians, planting herself in a Russian police station until they told her where they had sent my father, trying to create normality in a DP camp, coming to a new country – America as a life-marked woman in her 30s with two little ones and little else. And almost immediately giving birth to the daughter she had so wanted.

And I often marvel to my own children today that little more than a decade "off the boat" she and my dad had established a home, had a fourth child, found a way to make life seem normal and anything possible.

One humorous scene keeps popping into my head as I wonder at my mom's adaptability. Me at the age of twelve, them still little more than a decade off the boat; me a very Americanized adolescent going off to school in a tight orange cashmere sweater, with white lipstick and a teased bouffant hairdo out of Grease. And my mom letting me out of the house with not a word of criticism, although I must have looked like a space alien to her. I have used her lesson of forbearance very often as I allow my own daughters to grow and develop on their own.

So, in ways big and small, as I step back and see who my mom really was, I realize that she was truly an 'Eshet Chayal,' A Woman of Valor. She saved so many and gave so much in life. I only pray that life gave back to her some small measure of what she deserved.

Frieda was the glue that had held the family together for decades, across continents, across immeasurable distances and through the evolution from refugee to immigrant and from immigrant to citizen, and to a family assimilated in the rapidly flowing stream of American life. Without Frieda, with Mendel feeling alone, even at the center of Boris's family, where would the family now turn? As we left her funeral, would the memories and reality of all she and Mendel had gone through and survived gradually fade like a dream and be forgotten? How would we stay together as a family and what would we become next?

As we returned to our homes, Irving and Linda to Canada, Charlotte and David to Maryland, me and Rhoda to Pennsylvania, our lives continued on their separate courses, always busy, always immersed in our own family goals and struggles, and our lives occasionally intersecting with Mendel and Boris and Robin's family.

I was busier than ever traveling extensively around the world. From 2001 to 2003 and while working as a Senior Vice President at my job at Aventis Behring, I was asked to spin-off a new start-up business. As a Chief Executive Officer of a small biotech company, Genesis Therapeutics, LLC, I traveled throughout the United States and Europe and even Saudi Arabia, forming a business partnership with a highly skilled research genomics group based there. The company required $50 million to launch its research and development activities, an impossible task during the financial meltdown of 2001, and I was forced to close the company. Taking an early retirement from the company where I'd worked for over 25 years, I formed a consulting company while deciding what kind of future I could still fashion.

In the summer of 2003, and with Mendel increasingly showing his age, I decided, finally, I could wait no longer and abandoned everything else to finally extend my family history research and reconnect with my father. I left Rhoda in Philadelphia and flew to spend a week with Mendel at Boris's house. I brought all the documents and pictures I'd collected over the years, borrowed Boris's video camera and tripod and got ready to continue the formal interviews I'd started in 1986, 17 years earlier.

11

HISTORY REMEMBERED. PALO ALTO 2003

Interviewing My Father – How Much I Didn't Know!

July 2nd, 2003.

It's a beautiful day in Palo Alto. The clouds, some dark, some bright, mixing, folding in and out and finally thinning out as the sun breaks through. Below, Boris's house in modern-day Palo Alto is a large old Spanish-style house with a tiled courtyard in the back adjacent to a fenced-in yard. At the back of the yard stands a large pergola that could hold grape vines. Next to it are several lemon trees in full bloom bearing large fruits. In the middle of the yard stands an old round Spanish fountain. From above the house, the large palm trees in the corner of the L of the house can be seen with the fronds rustling gently in the breeze. Bushes in full flower are adjacent to them and send vines up the walls of the house, the vines full of brilliant red flowers. The palms and the red tiled roof make a pleasant and serene contrast with the bright blue sky that unfolded.

At the large tiled patio my father, now an old man, and I can be seen. We're seated in black wrought-iron framed chairs with straw cushions around a large wrought-iron table with a glass top. Even before beginning, my father looks worn and tired, and I wonder if the interview will really be too much for him. Asking him to go back and relive it in all it's detail, answering all the questions I've collected over the years may just be too much for him to do.

We look intently at each other, and adjacent to the table is a camera on top of a tripod with camera gear around it that will record our conversations. On the table lies a large collection of maps and papers that I've collected.

We finally begin what I've been preparing to do for ages.

I say to my father, "We're going to do some more taping. You remember, like before. When I taped you in South Bend? Seventeen years ago."

"How long will we do that?"

"As long as it takes. I'll be here all week. That's all I'm doing this week. I'll be here with you, talking and remembering, like we did before. I have lots of questions for us to talk about and I brought maps and pictures we can look at. Is that ok? We'll rest whenever you get tired."

Mendel seems to be getting used to the idea and looks at all the papers and pictures laid out in front of him. We've never had time or made time for anything like this before. This is different than we've ever done before.

I start with a recap of the prior interview in 1986 that I'd videotaped, leaving Poland and going to Russia, then to Crimea, then Azerbaijan, then back to Crimea. After the war, going back to Poland, then to displaced persons camps. That interview and the first tapes stopped mostly at displaced persons camps in Austria. For decades after that interview I had intended to continue from there, but work, my family, the rigors of daily life always kept getting in the way.

I believed, anyway, that I knew all about those times and didn't want to wear Mendel out repeating things.

Father will have none of that and starts to tell his story his own way, starting with their return from Azerbaijan to Poland to the refugee collection center in Southwestern Poland. There he'd met one of the men whom he'd known in his hometown before the war who was now in charge of a committee. He tells the story of Yitzhak Bylalef who helped him as they returned and were looking for other survivors who they might know from their town of Sokolow Podlaski. As he says, one day, another survivor from that town found Mendel and was searching to see if his father had survived. His father turned out to be Mendel's friend Yitzhak Bylalef. Mendel brought them together; neither knew they had survived, and they had changed so much, neither could recognize the other anymore.

I thought I had heard all the old stories, but had never heard this story before, and it was so filled with pathos that it almost made me cry. Mendel says, "All that happened in the town of Kamienna Góra."

I had heard of that town many times as I was growing up but had never been able to locate it on maps. For this interview and after years of preparation for this, I had brought detailed country maps of Europe, and we searched them together. I knew that town was the gathering place for refugees from the war, and I desperately wanted to know where it was, to actually see it as real on a map. "Where was Kamienna Góra?"

Mendel, "When we came from Russia, they put us in the town of Kamienna Góra."

"Was it near Warsaw?"

Mendel, "The Russians gave away to Poland some territory after the war, Niederschlesien. It wasn't near Warsaw. It was near Bratslav: Walbzich. It's Poland now, but was Germany before."

I wasn't sure what the towns were or how to spell them from Mendel's pronunciation and started searching on the map. "No, I can't find it."

Mendel, not content to give up, "No, let me look."

"Here's Breslau. Kamienna Góra's probably too small to be on here. But I can't find Bratslav; I can't find Walbzich. No such towns on the map."

Mendel, "Do you see it?"

"No, not yet."

Mendel, "Wait, keep looking; you will."

I'm ready to give up and go on, "I'll find it on another map. But that's the first time I heard where Kamienna Góra was. So, it's near Breslau in the south of Poland."

Mendel absolutely won't give up and looks even more closely at the map, "Wait, let me see it.... Walbzich. Walbzich." And he points his finger on the map.

I'm astonished, "Did you find it? Oh, there's Walbzich, but it is spelled as 'Walbrzych'. Is this where you went when you came back to Poland?"

He's still not willing to give up and continues, "Wait. Look for Kamienna Góra near Walbzich. Wait." He never gives up. Tired, worn, but even at this advanced age of 86, he has such a life force that it keeps him going and shines through the old body.

I let him keep looking although I'm convinced it's not there, and he'll never find it.

Suddenly I shout, "HERE IT IS. INCREDIBLE! Right here it is. Kamienna Góra. Right here on the map! Kamienna Góra. I NEVER SAW THAT BEFORE. RIGHT HERE. KAMIENNA GORA. RIGHT HERE! So that's where you went when you came back to Poland?"

And with that, the interview flows on with more questions and dialogue.

Mendel says, "That's where they put us. When we were making our way back, they didn't let us go back to Sokolow. We learned later that they didn't want the Jews when they came back from the war to go back to their towns because they killed Jews when they went back to those places."

We go back and forth between my questions and Mendel's memory. Mendel talks about how they miraculously met Eli and how they were finally reunited with Leah, Frieda's sister and their family. The miracle was not only that they had survived but that in the tumult of post-war chaos, of people, of families wandering from country to country, across the devastation that the war had left, that any were able to find someone who survived. As each finally made it to a refugee camp, each registered that they were still alive, that they had survived, who they were, where they were from, and who they were looking for that time and the war had torn apart – parents, brothers, sisters, aunts, uncles, neighbors, friends.

Many found that all had been lost, murdered, destroyed with their town. And many never could find, never locate, never learn what had happened to those they had known, had cherished in their former lives. Some were lucky to find one who had fled, one who had been hidden, one who had somehow survived the death camps.

And in the bright sunshine of the day, in the serenity of our surroundings and almost 50 years after the difficult times that Mendel survived, father and son now share what it means to have gone through that time. Even with having survived it all, the uncertainty that they faced not knowing what the future next had in store for them, and especially for Mendel in 1946, not knowing where they would go, what would happen to them all. They never knew if they would remain refugees and homeless for the rest of all their lives.

I've been saving questions and pictures and scraps for this opportunity all my life, little notes written by pencil on paper, copies made of precious old pictures as my parents talked about what their life had been and what they had experienced. And across the decades, there were holes to be filled in, people in pictures to be identified, stories to be linked together so that those who were lost could be remembered, their lives and stories preserved forever.

The father, now 86 years old, tired, worn, but re-invigorated by the telling, the son, now 69 awash with questions held for so long, pictures to be deciphered. Finally, both have the time and the will to sit and talk, to share, to embrace what they've been missing, and to preserve the memories and the relationships for all yet to come.

In the first telling by my mother and father over 17 years ago, the stories were of their early lives and the lives of their parents and their ancestors that had lived in those towns for generations. The story then wove the thread of Mendel and Frieda's misfortunes of war, of fleeing, of running, and never knowing whether there would be survival or any future for them. But even with that, the thread of hope stitched their lives together and they never gave up, even having children in the midst of complete uncertainty and devastation. And ultimately as the war died, they lived and managed to escape war-torn chaotic Europe to a new land.

And here my father's story swerved, and new threads made their way into what had been the torn fabric of their lives, the fabric that had shown the difficulties and prejudices they had faced and would now have to be overcome with the new challenges they would encounter in what they thought was the golden land.

Without resources, without speaking the language, without a real home, they slowly put a new life together. Starting with menial and temporary jobs, living in an infested rag shop, and finally in a bare apartment in the center of a black ghetto, they raised themselves up. They learned the language. Mendel got better jobs. They raised children and instilled in them their values, their drive, their belief in learning and education and hoped that their lives and future would be better.

As we pore over each of the pictures that I reveal, Mendel identifies where each came from, who's in the picture, and what story it contains, and I meticulously record each one. Finally, this is what I've wanted to do for so long. As we finish, Mendel looks intensively into my eyes and tells me, "I want you to have the originals from all these pictures. They've come a long way. You decide what to do with them. You're the only one I'd trust them to. You're the one who wanted to know what all we experienced and all we went through and the one that wanted to save it all."

Mendel has never been an emotional father who spent a lot of time talking with his children. He's loved them, but has never been openly tender, or affectionate or demonstrative of his feelings, and this expression catches us both by surprise so that I can hardly speak.

After days of reliving the past in Europe and Mendel's jobs and progress in America, Mendel starts to talk about how the children grew up and what it was like as each grew up and left home and each of us learns something new about the other. We've never found time to talk to each other like this.

"So, I was the first one to go away. I got accepted and went to school and you and mother drove me to school – to Chicago. Mother had a hard time."

"Yes. We cried that day when you went to college. It was the start of the family growing up and starting to separate. Then you found Ronnie. When you came home that summer, you said, 'Ronnie wants to marry me.' I told you to wait until you were graduating. And in 1965, even before you graduated, you got married."

We both chuckle at that memory.

"Do you know why we got married early?" I'd never really told him before.

Mendel guesses, "Because you were going to apply to graduate school together?"

I laugh, "No. That wasn't the reason. It was because you were all going crazy planning the wedding with 200 to 300 people. Mother and Ronnie's mom, June, were planning a big wedding and neither of the families could afford it. It was getting out of control. So, Ronnie and I talked it over and said, 'This is crazy. They shouldn't be spending money like this. Nobody can afford it, and we don't need a big wedding.' So, we changed the date and got married early. We didn't want you and Nate to spend a lot of money for a wedding and go into debt because of us."

Mendel looks at me astonished, "Oh, I never knew that before. Nate told me if he had to make another wedding like that, he wouldn't do it. He had to go to the bank to borrow money. Nate was a very poor man, a very good man."

"He didn't make much money. He worked for the electric company, first reading meters and later in the office because he was sick and couldn't work outside anymore. Yes, he was a good man, and he loved Ronnie very much. So that was me. The next person to go to college was Charlotte. Was it hard on you when she went to college too?"

Mendel struggles a little with that memory, "Yes, we had a hard time, especially Mother. She was the only girl, and it was very hard on her when she went away to school. She cried. When it was Charlotte's turn, I told her. Fred's in college. I have to pay to help him. I'm paying for Irving in business school. Why don't you go to the school in Bloomington, to the state college? Charlotte was a top student. She said, 'Daddy, top students don't go to the state.'"

Mendel laughs with the memory. "So, she went to the University of Wisconsin. She got a scholarship, but I gave her money. The third year, she went to Hebrew University. I gave her money to go there too."

"So how did you do this to put us through college? You never made much money. How did you do it?"

"We saved our money. We didn't buy a car every year. We never bought a new car. We didn't spend a lot. We bought wholesale, and bought at sales wherever we could. We didn't pay a high rent, maybe $50 a month. We'd go to the butcher to buy a quarter of a cow to cut it up. We'd make hamburger and put it in a freezer. We'd go to Chicago to buy hot dogs and salami."

I shake my head and remember it all, "Yeah. I'd go with you. We went to Chicago on the South Shore..."

"No! We went on the NY Central railroad. I had a pass. Then we took the cable car with electric cables. We went on the bus. We had a suitcase full of salamis and hot dogs. People said, 'What smells so good?'" Mendel laughs and laughs.

"So, Charlotte went away to school. She was the second one to leave home. I was already gone by then. I already graduated from College. I was at Purdue."

Mendel says, "I bought you a car when you got married."

"Two cars. First a Renault Dauphine."

"It was no good. It went for two days. The next one was a Volkswagen. That was good. I had an old car that I'd bought from a neighbor, an Opel Kadett. The Renault was no good. It used a quart of oil just to go downtown. So, what I did, I took the car home. I drained the oil. I filled it with STP. Then I took it to the dealer. I said, "I want to trade this in for the Volkswagen. He wanted $900. He gave me $500 for the Opel. I paid the rest and was glad to get rid of that car. I left the Opel and took the Volkswagen home. I called you and said, 'Now I have a good car for you.'"

Time stands still as we sit and remember and enjoy the memories that flowed past so quickly. Back then, there was no time to sit and talk. Time zipped past. Now, there's all the time in the world to savor what escaped us in the past, and we sit and sit and talk and relax and enjoy the memories together with nothing more important.

I chuckle, "The first car, that was a little black Renault. It was shaped like a cigar and it smoked like a cigar."

We both laugh.

Mendel remembers, "I called you when I got the Volkswagen and you came right away the next morning. You got a good car. You had that for a long time."

"You gave that to us as a wedding present, and we made a lot of trips from Purdue back and forth to visit you in South Bend and Ronnie's parents in Chicago. Lots of times the trips were during huge snowstorms, blizzards, and I remember times when we could hardly see anything in front of us. But each time, we didn't let it stop us. We'd come anyway. Then Boris went to college. How did Boris get to go to college to Yale? How did you ever afford to help him too?"

"Boris applied to Northwestern. Boris used to go in the summer during high school to Northwestern. He was a smart guy! Northwestern told him that if he went to college there, he could get his Bachelor's in three years, not four. But he applied to Yale and others. Yale didn't give him a scholarship. He told me they put him on a waiting list for a scholarship. So, he accepted Northwestern, and I sent them $300 for a deposit."

While we're talking, Boris's youngest, Sam, only four years old, wanders by, and I pick him up and put him on my lap. Sam is mesmerized with what's going on. He looks at the camera, at Mendel and at me and looks kind of puzzled at this dialogue going on, trying to understand why we're talking to each other like that. Mendel fondly strokes Sam's arm, and it's clear that the grandfather and the grandson have a very special relationship.

I hold my arms around Sam and say, "You can listen to some of this. Dad tell me more. Sam, grandpa Mendel is telling me about your daddy and when he was going to school."

Mendel continues, "Later, Boris had a girl friend. Her father was a doctor."

Mendel says, "Boris said, if he knew, he would have given her that name Annyalle." Mendel says, "She was short, too."

Talya chuckles. Sam yawns.

"Are you tired? Did you have a nap today?"

"I just woke up."

Mendel says, "We're all done."

"No, we're not all done. There are lots more. I have more to do tomorrow."

Eli comes by and I reel him in also. "Eli, Come here. We'll do a whole bunch together."

Eli comes in. They all wave at the camera.

"So, here's the whole bunch. Three generations." I point at Mendel. "Generation One." I point at myself. "Generation Two." I point at them. "Generation Three." And I tell Sam while he's on my lap, "And there's a number three right here on your back," while I pull the shirt off his back and point. Sam squirms and laughs. He loves the attention.

We're having fun together.

"So, do you guys know what we were doing today?"

Eli says, "What?"

"We were doing videotaping all day again. This is tape #4."

Talya says, "Oh, my gosh."

"And this is set B. Set A was done in 1986."

Talya says, "Wasn't bubbe Frieda in that? Daddy showed it to us. He showed us parts of it."

I'm astonished and gratified that the grandkids even now have started to ask the same kind of questions I did when I started to dive into our history, and say, "Sometime when you grow up, you'll watch the whole thing. I'm going to make copies of this and give it to you too. This is for you. And when you grow up, and 50 years from now," and I whisper emotionally, "this will mean a lot." I laugh and say to Sam, "And you'll say, was I ever that small, and who was that squirmy kid on his lap anyway?"

I turn to Mendel. "See, we only did two pages of my questions. I have more. When you retired, were you glad to stay home? What did you do? You didn't have any hobbies or anything."

Mendel equivocates, and then says, "Yeah, I was glad to stay home."

All the kids watch Mendel intently. This is something they'll always remember. I say, "What did you do then. You never had time before. What did you do with yourself?" Mendel says, "I read newspapers all the time. I read Yiddish books. I read now more than before. I read books in English."

It's been a long day. Mendel's tired and says, "Leave more for tomorrow."

Sam's been listening to Mendel and me talk. The four-year-old wants to get in the conversation too and says, "So how did Boris go to college and Yale, anyway?"

"We just did that, Sam. Did you miss the whole thing?"

And the taping session finishes with a picture of Talya, and Sam and Eli, with Talya telling Sam to sing a song.

Sam starts to sing, and I say, "No, Sam. It has to be a clean song."

And the tape finishes with Sam singing a silly song.

It's been a good day for father and son to bring back memories together and for the next generation to start to also be involved.

The interview, the history, the remembering continues again the next day. Father and son are on Boris's patio in the shade. Even starting early in the morning, Mendel looks tired and, even in the California heat, he needs a sports jacket around his shoulders to be warm enough and comfortable. The camera has already started and, as yesterday, documents and notes are spread out on the table in front of us, only today, there are a lot of pictures.

I start, "We went through a lot of history yesterday. It was wonderful to go through that together. I still have a lot of questions, but today we'll try and do a lot of pictures. You can tell me what you remember about them, and I'd like to get as many of the names of the people in the pictures as I can. We can't leave anybody behind."

The first picture we start with is one of my favorites that I've known for a long time, but one we've never talked about before. It shows Mendel and Frieda in 1938 with a large group of friends. Mendel and Frieda hadn't married yet but had found each other in a youth group in Sokolow in which Mendel's older brother, Fischel, was very active. They were part of a youth organization called *Hashomer Hatzair*, a secular Jewish youth movement founded even before WWI. The movement believed in the Zionist vision of the Jews' return to Palestine, tilling the land as pioneers, and freeing themselves from the antisemitism rife in Europe. Even by 1938, the actions in Austria, Germany and other countries raised their fears in remaining in Europe. Many meetings such as these were being held in Eastern Europe to prepare for large scale immigration to Palestine before things became worse for those who stayed behind.

Mendel's voice is very quiet. He starts to look through the picture and seems just to be thinking about it to himself. I look for a copy I made of the back of the picture that had the names on it. Mendel starts getting more involved.

I hesitantly ask him, "Did everyone in this picture survive?"

"No!" Mendel says emphatically. "Just me and Frieda, and mother's friend, Shayndel Pfeffkranz, and this man Pesach Rubenstein."

One by one, we go through the names of those who didn't make it. I record each one, to make sure their lives aren't forgotten, that they're not forever lost to memory.

And as Mendel identifies each one, it's as though he's back in his youth, seeing each one and their family and how they fit into their lives before the war. Especially Pesach he remembers, because he found him after the war, had reconnected with him, had met his brother and his son and even attended his son's wedding in Montreal. Pesach had lived in St.

Louis after he immigrated and had even visited Mendel once in South
Bend.

This picture linked traces from the past, traces after we were all safely in
America, traces I had never known about in my parents lives even after I
had left home to go to college. All now assembled themselves into a
complete story, as I continued to connect the fragments across my family's life.

And as we continued for hours, the photographs I compiled and which
we studied, assembled themselves into an even clearer picture of the
lives of my parents and those who lived happily in their town. And
with each remembering, Mendel laughs at the good memories and
what was happy when he was growing up until the war exploded
everything.

When we finish with the first set of pictures, Mendel asks, "You got
more?"

"Hours more!"

Mendel is totally into this now. He chuckles and points at the camera
and asks, "Is this all going in there?" You can see Mendel loves this.
Unexpectedly he turns directly to me and points his finger at me and
says, "Listen. This is the best interview I giving. I don't give another interview to nobody. I tell you things I don't tell nobody.

I'm in near-tears, "I love you Tah (dad)."

"My brain is good. I remember every detail. I tell you everything."

We stop for a break. Mendel says, "You're the only one I trust to do this.
Other people bother me for interviews. They send me letters asking. I
got a letter from Eli Wiesel saying he wanted to send people to interview
me. I said no."

We take a break and come back. We keep working on pictures. I take out
a picture of Frieda and two friends (**Photo 2**) that I titled, "Three
Friends," taken in Sokolow in 1937 or 38. It's late autumn and the three
friends are standing in front of a large building that was old even at that
time. They're clearly friends with arms locked together, nattily dressed
and wearing full-length winter coats. The picture is one of Frieda on the

right with Ytka Vloss on the left and another girl, Elka Rosenstein in the middle.

Mendel points at Frieda: "Frieda Altman."

I can hardly talk. "I know her," I say.

Yitka and Elka are both wearing caps, rakishly tilted to the side. Frieda has a beautiful woolen scarf tucked into her coat and Elka, in the middle, has a beautifully embroidered scarf. All three are smiling and happy to be alive and with friends out for a stroll, completely unaware of the dark clouds gathering that will alter their future and condemn two of them to a brutal death in a concentration camp.

Mendel continues, "You can take the pictures, all the originals. I'm not going to have any more interviews. I enjoy with you. You talk slow with me. You understand me. I relax. You look over my papers. You take them." Pointing to the faces of the three friends, he says, "I have the books from the Holocaust Museum that they hand out, booklets that look like passports. Their names and histories are there in those "passports." He takes the picture of the people he knew from that time and holds it closely to his face, remembering, remembering.

I can't imagine how all these photographs could have survived the war and the distances they traveled and ask, "Where did you get the picture from? From Shayndel?"

"Yeah. I think so."

"Did she send you more than one picture?"

Mendel gives an emphatic yes.

I'm afraid to ask, "Is Shayndel still alive?"

Mendel quietly, "I don't know."

With all the distances my parents traveled, with all the separations they encountered, with Shayndel eventually winding up in Israel, I want to know, "How did you find her anyway in Israel?

"I knew where she was. I wrote her in Israel. She had an uncle in Chicago. I told her to come, that she could stay with us, but she didn't."

"So, when you went to Israel, how did you find her?"

"I find her. I find her. We went to Lud on our trip to Israel in 1968. We stayed with her four, five days. She has a daughter, grandkids. Her daughter's husband is from Schedjetz (Siedlce), next to our town in Poland."

"Her daughter is in Israel, yes?"

"Yes."

"Does her daughter speak English?"

"I imagine."

"Do you have her address? Maybe I'll make another trip sometime to Israel and try to follow up with her or her family."

"I don't know. I have Shayndel's address. You can find her address if you want. If you want, your cousin Aharon Schwarzbard has her address. Whenever he'd make a *simcha* (a celebration), he'd invite her. Shayndel's daughter wanted to marry Ephrayim, but it didn't work out. Shayndel's last name now is Kneiper. Shayndel Pfefferkranz Kneiper."

And we return to pictures and again to the one of the three girl friends in Sokolow. Mendel doesn't know what the building was, but years later, I get a picture from my friend Kasia that shows the exact building in the picture in current Sokolow. The building survived even though all of them didn't. But their names and the memory of them are resurrected now forever.

Another picture comes forward, an even older one, one probably taken around 1920, very formal, clearly taken in a photo studio. In the front sits a serious-looking woman in her early thirties with a child standing on either side and, in the back, three grown people, a handsome young man with two pretty young ladies at his side (**Photo 12**).

I've seen this picture before as I was growing up, but never identified the people. Now their names come alive as Mendel points to each of them. The woman in the chair is Chaya (Rosenbaum) Altman, my grand-mother, and her two young children that stand there are Frieda, my mother, barely two or three years old and my aunt, Leah, around eight or nine years old.

In the back stands a young man dressed in a handsome dark suit, white shirt, and beautiful tie with dark curly hair. In prior years, I had thought this was my father's uncle, Joe Rosenbaum. He's now identified as my Uncle Bernard, Chaya's brother who fled Sokolow not long after this photograph and immigrated to Chicago. Bernard was my favorite uncle who visited us many times in South Bend, gave me my first Brownie camera and started me on a life-long love of photography. Most photographs of my family came from that camera as I was growing up.

Next to Bernard is a beautiful young woman, Bryna Rosenbaum, a sister to Chaya who later became Bernice Goldberg. She sports long dark hair, pearl earrings and a sportily fringed dress with a pretty pin in the bodice. She also escaped Sokolow and immigrated in 1921 to America, settling in South Bend. She played an important role in my family's early life, treating them with love on their own arrival after the war, in South Bend, even while she had tragically been separated from her husband.

And next to Bernice stands a lovely young woman, Sarah Rosenbaum, born in 1901 in Sokolow and who immigrated to the United States in 1914. She died in 1966 but has a daughter Myrna Berkowitz (now Myrna Millman) who still lives near Chicago and is one of my family genealogy resources.

As we continue to talk with each other and look at all the photos that somehow had survived, I'm fascinated by the world that the pictures reveal – a world different from the images of poorly dressed peasants, wrinkled and old, the men with long ragged beards, the women always looking old no matter how young. But the pictures I see now spread out before us are strikingly different, young people beautifully dressed, vibrantly alive, modern even if many years old. Beyond the differences the pictures showed, knowing the journeys that my parents had taken, the distances traveled, and the fog of war, I'm astonished both that the photographs survived, and that Mendel still had them.

"Your family always took lots of pictures in Europe. How did this picture survive and how did it come to you?"

Mendel says, "Uncle Joe must have given it to me."

I'm puzzled, "Joe must have had a lot of pictures. Maybe pictures from Poland before he left home for America, pictures of his family and friends, pictures of life in Poland in better times. I would love to see those. He's long gone now, but what would have happened to his pictures or any papers that he had from those times? Could they still be somewhere? Or who must have gotten them when he passed away? Maybe my cousin Bonnie might have the pictures. Those pictures tell a history!"

And as we talk more and more, I resolve to continue my search for that history, to learn more about the generations that disappeared, especially to trace what happened to the brothers and sisters of my grandmother, my mother's mother's generation and to link anything I could find of their lives to any photographs that might still exist.

Even at this stage in his life, Mendel is still actively involved with others in many ways. He takes a break from the interview to go teach chess to youngsters at the community center and when he returns, we continue with the interview and taping inside the house. Pictures that I printed out for us to discuss are spread out all around us on the dining room table, and we start again to talk about the people and the lives they represent. As we start again, my father isn't tired anymore. His memories are vivid, and his mind is sharp. With each picture, he's transported back into his youth. It's as though time never passed, and he recalls each event as though it were today.

We talk about one very old picture that was taken in Sokolow when times were happy before the war. He's the only young guy in the picture and there are young ladies on either side, Frieda and her sister Leah and Frieda's girl friend Shayndel out for a walk in the countryside. The photo has survived but is badly damaged and has been painstakingly restored by me over time. I still can't image how something like that could have survived the times. My father says he got it from Shayndel. He tracked her down in Israel some years ago and while corresponding with her, she sent him that tiny photograph along with some others that he kept.

His mind travels back to those times and – as Mendel relives his memories – I learn more about life before the war.

"Shayndel and Frieda were girlfriends. Shayndel's father was a baker. Her grandfather was a painter. She and Frieda were friends all the time."

"Frieda and Leah were living with grandmother, right?"

"Yes, they were living together in Sokolow Podlaski in one small room. Before that, they lived in a *Bes Medresh* (house of prayer), where they *daven* (pray). Because their grandfather, Yisroel Hersch was a *gabbai* (sextant) in the Bes Medresh, they let them live there. Later when I started dating Frieda, and Velvul started dating Leah, they were able to rent a small house. I helped them move over whatever they had in 1937 to the new place. They lived on the same street where I used to live, but further away. A nice house. They bought new furniture for it. They lived better in the new house. They had a little business. Joe, Chaya's brother, used to send them money from America. Every Passover, he used to send them $10 that he collected from Chaya's sisters, her sisters, Sarah and Bernice, and also a brother Baruch. Sarah and Baruch used to live in Chicago."

"Shayndel, was she from a poor family too?"

"Yes and no. She came from a typical family. Her father was a baker. She had a sister and a brother. The brother survived, and lives in Israel. The younger sister was killed when the Germans bombed the city."

"And were you from a rich family?"

"No. We had our place from my grandmother. We had an apartment in a building downtown. The bombs destroyed our building. I went back there in 1946 when we were returning to Poland from Azerbaijan. It was once a beautiful building. It was two stories high with the store on the main floor. My uncle used to live in part of the second floor. The building was on a big lot. We didn't have money, though, because my father was sick and there was only so much we could do by ourselves. One time, we rented out half our store. It was a big store with one side for selling grain. We rented part of the store to a guy who sold whiskey. He paid us 500 zlotys a year. He was a nice guy. Later we decided against it because it was better to have the whole store. We took in partners for the business. The partners wouldn't help us at all. We kept track of everything ourselves. The partners didn't help. Later, I borrowed money from Frieda for the store, and we got rid of the partners."

"Your father died when you were young?"

"Yes, in 1936."

"So, it left just your mother Chinka. How did your mother run a business like this by herself?"

Mendel, now reliving a painful part of his memories, "She was the greatest woman in the world. She had seven children, five sons and two daughters. She ran the business. She made food for the kids. She'd buy a quart of milk and combine it with three quarters of water and make soup in the morning with potatoes. She couldn't afford to buy whole milk."

"But how did she run the business?"

"Because she was from business parents. Her father, Baruch Eli was so smart; had a factory from mead (wine), and she helped him with that business every day while she had her children with her. When Chinka was working, Moshe was born." Mendel laughs, "It was said that Moshe was born in the store while she was working."

"So, your mother was a businesswoman?"

"One hundred percent. Smart. Smart. She bought. She sold. I helped her. She'd buy 50 pounds of grain, a hundred pounds. She'd try to carry it. I wouldn't let her. I carried it."

"What about your brother Fischel? Fischel was older."

"Fischel couldn't be a businessman. He said, 'If I have to be a business-man, I have to cheat people. Business is cheating.' He went to the Yeshiva, for two years or so. The rabbi slapped him, so he came home and quit the Yeshiva. My father then apprenticed him to be a *stoller* (a carpenter). He was a good man, so strong. He'd help us so much, but he couldn't be a businessman. He was totally honest and wanted nothing to do with running a store or a business."

And so, we continue, father and son, father enjoying reliving the past with his son, the son hungry for the details of happy life before the devastations that came later.

Three pictures come forward, Mendel and Frieda, one before the war in 1936, happy times of a beautiful young couple, engaged to be married and out for a stroll in the streets in Sokolow. Another one is of Mendel, a beautiful young man in a sharp suit, and one much later in 1948, after all the running and hiding and pain. It's of Mendel and Frieda, finally safe in the displaced persons' camps in Wels, Austria.

"What a big difference between the two pictures of you and mother!"

"What do you mean, such a big difference? We got through the war; we had children; we got through the Russians. We survived. Look at the picture (**Photo 13**) from San Gilgal, the camp we took you to for sick children after the war in 1946 – you and me. I look like a dead man."

"They're wonderful pictures of the history that you survived. They really show what you went through."

"When I left Russia, I was about 70-80 pounds. That was September 1946. I looked much better in another picture when we finally got to Austria. You go with me. I'll go to San Gilgal."

Sadly, that was never to be. My father and I never returned to Europe together, neither to Austria nor to Sokolow, although that trip to Sokolow, a "return to roots" that I was to take years later, was a trip of enormous emotional charge.

The next picture we look at was one of my father's mother Chinka before she was married – about 1905.

"She was born in 1892. She was engaged when she was 18. She didn't like the guy because he was a Yeshiva man. They broke up. Later she married my father in 1910. Fischel was born in 1911. He was the first child."

"This is an incredible picture of your mother. How did the picture come to the U.S.? Did you carry it with you? All those distances and across so many countries?" I just can't imagine how those pictures could have been saved after all you experienced."

Father explains, "Chinka had a sister, Chava Yitka, who'd been born in Poland, married and moved to New York where her name changed to Eva Greenberg. After the sister, Eva died, two of the children, sisters, sent me all the pictures that Eva had when we were already in America and had reconnected with them. Eva's sisters were Mary Meister and Sarah Meister. You met them on a trip that we took.

"Chinka's sister in New York was Chava Yitka Greenberg (nee Schwartzburt). Her story itself was amazing. Her husband was named Yisrael (Izhik) Greenberg. They were married in Bialystok, maybe in 1885, before they finally immigrated to America where she changed her name to Eva. They had ten children – Ida, Sarah (later became Sarah Meister), Mary (later became Mary Gerstman), and Rose. They were four daughters and six sons. Some of them were born in the United States, some born in Europe. Sarah Meister and Mary Gerstman lived in Mountaindale, N.Y. Nancy Gerstman, whom you know and lives in Maryland, is a granddaughter from Mary. Mary's husband was Bill. (Two brothers married two sisters). One brother married Ida Gerstman; one brother married Mary Gerstman. Mary and Bill had two children – Alfred and a daughter who lives in Monticello, NY. Nancy's father is Alfred Gerstman. (He was at Boris's wedding). (Mendel doesn't remember the mother's name.) Nancy has two more brothers. One lives in California or Arizona. The other lives in NJ."

So many family connections that Mendel knows, and I'm connected to them! I've met some of them along the way and never knew our relationship. I wonder how many from the current generation from Chava Yitka, Eva, know their amazing history and how their lives are connected all the way back to mine. I am committed to find them and share our joint histories.

I'm just amazed by it all. Here is my father, worn and tired from all he experienced, yet at age 83 still able to remember, in excruciating detail, all the names and relationships and dates from his entire life. How much I would have missed by not doing this!

Mendel even has their addresses. No computer, no smart phone, but he has everything. The last name I know: Gerstman. I know Nancy Gerstman; Nancy just got married. She has a new address in Silver Springs. She's a director of Public Television, probably with a new last name and new address, and I have to find her to reconnect us.

As the afternoon wears on, we keep on looking at the old photos, the treasures of Mendel's life. Sometimes Mendel is tired. Sometimes the photos, the memories, and the dialogue revive him, and he brightens up as his memories take flight. One such picture is a picture of his brother

Fischel (**Photo 14**), long gone now, brutally lost in Treblinka. Fischel is dressed as a Polish officer when he returned on leave from the Polish army, a year after he joined in 1932. Mendel was very proud of his older brother, his intellect, sincerity, and his strength. What a treasure to have this photograph!

I marvel and still try to understand how photographs like this survived, and how those treasures of the past made it into the present. "How did the picture of Fischel come to South Bend? Did you take it with you? Did you even have time to pack when you left Sokolow? How did this survive?"

My question is simple, but the answer isn't.

Mendel: "Fischel had a girl friend before he went to the Army. She had all the pictures. After the war, she survived with her husband. They went to Russia. After the war, they went to South America to Montevideo, Uruguay. She and Fischel broke up. I saw her and her husband in the camps after the war. She gave me the picture."

I'm astonished at how fate brought all these things together. Blown to different horizons by the winds of war, people and their most treasured possessions were reunited again. Mendel and Frieda, separated from Frieda's sister, somehow found each other again years later and in a place no one could have predicted, in one of hundreds of refugee collection centers.

Mendel and Frieda, also separated from Fischel's first girlfriend by the war, who flung in directions far from them, had kept a key photo from Fischel's life, even though they had separated. She had left, married, and survived. Fischel, stayed behind, perished. And while both Mendel and Fischel's girlfriend would ultimately be scattered to entirely different continents, they met briefly in one of the displaced persons camps, and the precious picture changed hands, found the brother to give the picture of his brother, and the picture kept for future generations to admire and treasure. How strange and wonderful is fate!

Fischel and Faiga

Another photo follows of Fischel and a young woman.

I ask father, "Who's the woman in the picture?"

Mendel says, "This is a friend from the organization they belonged to. She belonged to a poor family and Fischel got to know her. He fell in love with her. It's Fischel and his wife. I used to say to Fischel, why do you take such a big girl? She was big like him. He liked her. They used to sit and read together."

I'm temporarily puzzled and look more closely at the picture, "Where did you get this picture? Oh. It's a New Year's card from Israel. I actually brought you this picture from Israel."

Mendel laughs. He knows that he's the source of all family pictures. He can't believe that a picture of his brother actually came from me. "You brought me this? From my sister? From Israel?"

"I brought you this from your sister. When I visited her on my last trip, I asked her about pictures from Poland she might have, and she showed me this. She said I could have it and give it to you. But I have more questions. What does the card say?"

"It says the same thing in Polish as it says in Hebrew. Congratulations in the New Year."

"When could this be from? When you left Sokolow was Fischel already married?"

"Yes, Fischel was already married. They married about 1937." And he added something I'd never heard before. "He had a son."

"You never told me any of this!"

Mendel shakes his head. "You never asked! I was at the wedding. Frieda was at the wedding."

"What was his wife's name?"

"Faiga, a tall girl like Fischel. Their son's name was Ephrayim Yitzhak. He was born about 1938, and he was about one year old when we left Sokolow in 1939. I can't remember Faiga's last name."

I marvel at the preservation of Mendel's father's name. I already know of three generations who received that name as a blessing – Fischel's first and only son, Mendel's sister's first son, and Mendel's son, me, the one weaving the threads of time and memory together into a tapestry.

I say again quietly, "I hate to ask. None of them survived?"

Mendel shakes his head sadly, his hands clasped tightly together, his eyes inward looking, and says, "No. No one."

"Not the little boy either?"

"No. No one."

I'm so saddened by this that I can hardly speak, and we sit together for a while in silence.

Mendel loved his older brother dearly, and he tells me more about him in those last years before Mendel escaped to Russia. We're so close together now as the memories of those last times transfer to me.

"Fischel and Faiga lived in an apartment in Sokolow. He was a carpenter; she was from a very poor family. Fischel was a very attractive guy and would have been considered a catch by any of the families. There were many wealthy families that would have wanted him to marry their daughter, but he loved Faiga, and to him that was the only thing that mattered. He married her. After they were married, I loaned him money to buy lumber for the furniture that he could make. He made beautiful tables, beds, anything that his customers wanted for their homes, especially the wealthy. He also took the things he made on Thursdays to the market and sold them. He got more money that way. Before he was married, he worked for carpenters to learn his trade. They paid him ten zlotas a week. Ten zlotas a week was nothing. He would give our mother five zlotas a week, and he kept five zlotas that he gave to Faiga. But he learned everything there was to know about being a master carpenter, so he could work for himself. His work was in high demand. He was a hard worker and worked six days a week to make money for himself and his family.

Mendel sighs, "He was such a smart man. He was a teacher to children in the school. He was a top chess player. He was a wonderful brother, and I miss him to this day."

It saddens me how much love and potential were lost in the Holocaust!

"Did he live far away?"

"No."

"Your mother saw the baby? She went to visit sometime?"

"Yeh. Yeh." He shakes his head and says to himself, "Time went so fast. Time went so fast."

So much to remember. So much to cover. A lifetime of memories to share, to digest, to preserve. Never have the two of us been so together, spent so much time with each other, trying to relate, to understand.

It's been a long hard day. We started early and continue into the afternoon. After a short break we continue inside where we look at picture after picture and then at documents that survived the long trek, documents generated during our stay in the refugee camp, documents generated while waiting to get visas to come to America, some of the documents I lost in my own moving around.

Where Was I Born?

"You were born in Azerbaijan. You have a birth certificate from there."

"We moved around so much, Ronnie and me. Somewhere I lost that birth certificate. I don't have it anymore."

Mendel says, "I got my birth certificate by going to the Polish Embassy in Washington. You can get yours by going to the Azerbaijani Embassy."

"But I don't even really know where I was born. Azerbaijan is a large country. You tell me I was born in Baku, but was it really in Baku?"

"Give me a map of Russia. You were born in a little town outside Baku. I can show you where it is."

"No. There are better maps on the internet."

Mendel, looking very skeptical, "I don't know how you do that, but let's see."

"I'll set up on the Internet. You can show me exactly where I was born."

We set up in the family room in front of the computer, two chairs in front, Mendel in one, me in the other one. And while we get ready to explore, Boris's kids are in the house playing, and Natalie can be heard in the background talking. Mendel and I are now in a world of our own. We've never done this before. Mendel's never looked at a computer screen before, and we're going to do this together.

Mendel looks at the empty computer screen and asks, "You have maps of Russia?"

"Yes. I started to look for this at home, but you can help me."

Mendel starts to get into this. "You have maps of Baku? I'll help you find it."

I'm muttering. "So where are my maps. Where did I put them? Right here." We're both looking to see what shows up on the screen. Mendel's transfixed to see if something's going to show up. He's never done anything like this before. Maps flash by. I point at the screen, "Here are the Caucasus mountains. Here's Baku. Here's Georgia. So, we're going to look over here," pointing at the Baku area.

Mendel's really into it. He gets out of his chair to get closer to the monitor, "Let me stand so I can see better."

I scroll the map and say, "I'm going to come to..." and Mendel says, "Baku." Now he's right at the monitor looking over the map, pointing out features with his finger. Remembering. Whispering names.

I can't stay back. I join him and point. "Here's the Kura River. You see this. This is the Kura River." I heard of that from his stories before.

Mendel looks and nods. "Yes. You were born by the Kura River." Points more at the map. "Where's the Kura River?"

"Here's the Kura River, the blue line. It goes like this and comes down..."

Mendel points and says, "You were born by the Sofros (agricultural farm)."

Looking for a Sofros, I say, "This map doesn't have Sofros on it."

"You were born near the Kura River, maybe a half mile from it." Finger points to the Kura River near a town called Salyan.

"But the Kura River is long, almost 900 miles. It starts at the Caspian Sea and runs all the way through to this lake."

"Yeh. Yeh. But you were born near the Kura River." He won't be distracted with where I'm pointing. "You were born near here," again pointing nearer to Salyan.

I again try to orient him and point further south. "Over here is Iran. Over here is Azerbaijan. And over here is Baku."

"No, you were born near the Kura River, near here." Again, pointing near Salyan, "I used to go there and fish; catch fish by the river." Finger still pointing at Salyan. And now he says, "Salyan. You were born near here."

I want to make sure that his memory is accurate and point further away again and say, "Here's another river. Aras River."

"No. No. You were born by the Kura River."

"But the Kura is all of this!"

Mendel keeps shaking his head and says loudly, "But you were born over here," pointing again near Salyan, "not over there, further away."

I point to another town south of Salyan. "This town is called Banka." Pointing some more, "This town is called Salyan."

"Maybe."

I go again, wanting to make sure, pointing at another town. "This town is called Karasal."

"No."

Again, "This town is called Ali Balramni."

"But you weren't born in a town. You were born on a farm."

"I'm asking you what town it was near."

Mendel's still looking closely at the map and moves his finger over. "You were born close to Salyan," he says, nodding his head yes.

"You think it was Salyan?"

"Yes. You were born close to Salyan. Close to the Kura River."

"You think so?"

"Yes," he says. "Salyan," he keeps repeating, nodding his head. "You got to go to the Russians and ask them to look in a book."

"Where will I tell them to look where I was born?"

"Salyan. You were born five *zoldhenyenes. Vaist vu a zoldhenyene iz?*" he lapses into Yiddish. "Do you know what a *zoldhenyene* is?"

"No."

Vaist vus a kolhoz is? he repeats.

"Yes. It's a farm."

"Farm," Mendel repeats, satisfied that I know. He shakes his head yes. He looks at me, looks at the map, remembering. Sits down. "There were five chapters (sections), five chapters on the farm. The first chapter was 'Centrale.' Where the officers were. Where they keep the files. You were born in Chapter 2. You gotta go to Russia and they'll give you the papers."

I change the screen. "Let me see if I can find another map."

Mendel, "I have Russian maps."

Mendel gets up to look at the screen again. We're back to the map where we can see Baku and the Kura River again. Mendel points at Baku. "From Baku, we used to take the train and go down (south), go down (and pointing further south out of Baku). Mendel points again near Salyan. "You were born near this town; half a mile from the Kura River."

I'm sure he's right, but I have to make sure his memories are not failing on this. I have to make sure. I call out other towns from the map again. "This town is called Karachala." Mendel looks.

I point again. "This town is called Salyani. This is Neftechala. And this is Banka..."

Mendel straightens up and points, "You were born here, but I don't know the name. You were not born in town."

"Near Salyani? This is about 50 kilometers from Baku. Let me look for more maps."

We flip around different maps, big and small. A map of urban Baku. Back to a larger map showing Baku, but also the country south of it.

Mendel points again. "Salyan. You were born near here. Salyan. Not far from Salyan on the Kura River."

"What do you think the birth certificate says?"

Mendel, shaking his head, "I don't know."

"Was I born in a hospital?"

"No. You were born in a house. A neighbor took you home. It was in the middle of the night. It was raining. I wasn't home. They sent me away to work. A good neighbor came in. She went to the supervisor to get a special *odzholena* (permission) to take you to the hospital. The supervisor said, 'Listen, it's night; it's raining outside. If I give you horses and the horses die, I go to jail.' He didn't want to give us the horses. So, the neighbor delivered you. She was a midwife. She was so good to us. She gave us food. Everything. She had sons. She was so good. I forgot her name. She delivered in the house. I came the next day, and you were already there."

He tries again. "If you go to a Russian place. The Russian Ambassador. Or any place. They can order a birth certificate for you. They'll find it."

"But I have to know where I'm from or they'll never find it. If my birth certificate says Baku, if I say Baku, they'll never find it."

Mendel says, "I couldn't spell the names."

"So, if I go to the embassy, I have to say Baku, right?"

"You have to take me with. Maybe we go tomorrow to San Francisco, to the Russian Embassy."

"Tomorrow's the fourth of July. They're closed."

"Next time." Mendel continues, "How did I find my certificate? I went to the Polish embassy in Washington, to the Ambassador. I told them my name, where I was born, when. I told them Schmuel Mendel Feldman. I paid them $30-40."

I've been flipping maps on the screen while Mendel talks. I find another map. "So, here's a different map. This is a map of Baku. It shows the railroad lines going out of Baku."

Mendel follows the lines with his finger. "Yeh, I used to take the train from Baku. It goes to this city, Alat. The train goes on to Salyan. And here's the Kura River. Yes, you were born right here by Salyan. I used to take the train from Baku and walk from the train."

I'm satisfied now that there's no question. "So, it must have been this city Salyan."

"Yes. Salyan."

By myself, I would never have known where I was from, and from the discussion, I could finally grasp how Mendel had been able to survive it all. His force of will, his stubbornness to keep going until he reached his goal was what kept them alive and brought them, time after time, to a better place. Many times, during these few days, during this exercise of trying to know, I would have been satisfied to stop, to know enough, even without getting to the final answer. But for Mendel, even at 83, he refused to accept anything but to get to where he needed to go. This was one of the final lessons he taught me, his son. Never stop until you reach all you need to know.

We still weren't done. I wanted to know more about all the places they went after that, Frieda and Mendel and me and then also with Irving. And Mendel related how after the war, they left Azerbaijan, traveled through Grozny in Chechnya, to Tbilisi and Chiatura in Georgia, vast distances, before finally making their way back to Crimea where later their son and my brother Irving ("Srul") was born and, finally after that, to the refugee camps in Poland.

Over the years, snatches of history were caught on the fly, in between going to school, going to work, never enough time to know, to appreciate the marvel of their lives. Only toward the end, with grains of sand dropping inexorably through the hourglass, was the decision made to wait no more, to talk to each other, to know each other and to make sure that each understood how much they were loved.

With all the discovery and history exhausted, father and son stand and just look at each other.

I look at him and say, "I'm done with the taping. This tape will be here for 200 years, for 300 years, so your grandchildren's grandchildren will look at this. What do you want to tell them? What do you want to say to them? Your grandchildren's grandchildren?" I have a tremor in my voice. I have a tear in my eye.

Mendel looks back, slow to respond, and begins to relate all he experienced, all he went through.

"So... So how did you survive all this? How did you survive all this?"

Mendel continues with all the memories we went through.

I interrupt him, and we look at each other, "I know this. I now have this on tape. But tell me, if you were going to do anything different in your life from all of this, what would you have done?"

"I should have taken my mother with and the brothers and sister."

Mendel finishes quietly and now I say, "A lot of what you told me, I remember. Some things I didn't know. A lot of the pictures I'd seen before; some names I'd forgotten, but it was wonderful to do this with you."

"Yes. Wonderful. I'm glad you did this."

"But you know, tah," and I look at my father, "what you and mother went through, is unbelievable. And it's unbelievable that you came from all of that and came to this country and made all this. Such a life!" I turn and look at Mendel and Mendel looks back. "We're all proud of you. We're all proud of you. We love you.'"

The time the two of us spent side-by-side sharing, talking, and listening to each other was something we had never engaged in during our entire lives and was something I would never forget.

Separating again, I returned home. More distractions again followed. More work, more involvement with family, more change. Our son, David, graduated from Brandeis and become a greatly valued IT professional, working his own way higher and higher in industry. I, myself, continued to advance up the corporate ladder, first as a Senior Vice President of Research and Development and later as a Chief Science Officer in the pharmaceutical and biotech industries, again getting more and more involved in my work.

The Family Gathers / Mendel (2004)

On March 2nd, 2004, Mendel passed quietly away, less than a year after the precious time we spent together.

The family gathered for the funeral in Palo Alto and wept silently throughout the eulogies.

The Rabbi, Yitzchok Feldman, not related to Mendel, had come to know him well during the four years Mendel had lived with his youngest son and his family. Of Mendel, he said,

"This was a scrappy man; a feisty, blunt, and determined man. Only someone with such qualities could have endured the tortures of the valley of death. This was a last link to another time, the living reminder of how the torture of being a Jew in the last century could give way to deeply satisfying Jewish pleasures like seeing your children excel and your grandchildren thrive.

"Those years – the harrowing years of Blitzkrieg, of brutality, of flight, of fear for one's life, and of anguish about what happened to those who were left behind – those years surely shaped much of Mendel's outlook. The events of those years became the greatest test of their lives. There was always a question hovering over them: Were they going to be consumed by those years even if they survived or were Mendel and Frieda going to overcome them?

"Mendel saw both a public world and his private world destroyed. But like some others, he rebuilt. He brought children into the world, even in the midst of destruction, and he worked with fierce determination to make sure that they would be educated and truly ready to thrive in America.

"And Mendel was able to negotiate the middle stage with his identity and faith intact. The flight from the Nazis and the search for survival in the east and west were the ultimate chess game of Mendel's life. Thankfully, his ingenuity, his tenacity, and some help from above, allowed him to prevail.

"Finally, Mendel was able to rebuild. The life of the immigrant generation is focused on basics, focused on day-to-day survival. Mendel spent his entire life working at jobs that circumstances forced him to take. They dirtied him up, but they didn't come close to defeating him."

My own eulogy ended simply, recognizing how much my parents had gone through and how much, despite all their sorrows and travails, they loved each other.

"We learned much from their lives about overcoming difficult hurdles, and we learned, as they became old, how much they came to mean to each other, even as they appreciated it more. We came to learn never to put off until the last days to tell each other how much we mean to each other and to treat each day as the precious gift that it is. In my mind's eye, I still see them as beautiful young people, strolling – locked arm in arm and enjoying eternity together."

The youngest of the children of Frieda and Mendel, Boris, described what was really the core of his father's being.

"Mendel was the most relentless person I have ever known. That is why he survived. That strength of will, that can-do attitude, triumphed over the Poles, the Nazis, the New York Central Railroad, and even the California DMV. As his body gave out over the last month, his spirit did not. He was determined to make it to his beloved Talya's bat mitzvah last week, and he did. Mission accomplished."

And the last to stand up and speak was Talya, Boris and Robin's younger daughter who loved her grandfather so much, and who remembered through her tears, "He was a huge part of all of our lives. Mendel had missed out on a lot of his children's childhoods, because he was constantly working, so this was his chance to experience it with us. To some people, my grandpa was a leader, to some he was a star chess player, or a wonderful member of the community, and to some he was a good friend. But to me he was my grandpa, an amazing, righteous, kind, and courageous person. And I will never forget all the wonderful times we had together."

The last year of Mendel's life had not been easy for him with difficulties in climbing stairs, in breathing, in everyday life, but he knew that Talya's bat mitzvah was coming, and he was determined that – hell or high water – he would make it to that.

The defining characteristics of Mendel's life were his perseverance and his love of family. It drove him to protect those whom he took out of the fires of the Holocaust and protected them until he could finally find a safe place in America. And with few resources, he drove himself to ensure that each of those he loved would have the greatest chance, not to just survive, but to excel. He was a quiet man who rarely showed his closest affection to those around him but who was ready to sacrifice everything for them and whose family came to understand how much they loved him in return.

Eleven months later, the family reunited again at the cemetery at an engraved tombstone, part of my mother's, and I recalled again our archetypical Mendel – crystal clear memory, strong opinions, driving his point home, loving to be the center of attention.

With the family gathered around, I said, "We're the beneficiaries of a lot from these two people, Mendel and Frieda. Everything we have came from them. And besides the miracle of their survival from the maelstrom of the Holocaust, what we've been able to do with our own lives because of them is also a miracle. They taught us... how to survive, how to never give up (part of the dominant "stubbornness" gene), how to always strive to be better, how to value family, how to value our heritage. And we learned in the last days of their lives, that they also learned how important they were to each other. What they taught us, even then, is the importance of us knowing how to appreciate each other, in our own lives, every day that we live."

"They made us a strong family and always wanted us to be closely knit with each other. With them gone, we need to maintain our links to each other to keep the world from shrinking with their passage and to keep their memories alive."

And as we dispersed again to our respective homes and lives, Sam, only five years old and who had been Mendel's closest companion from the time that Sam was just a baby, refused to leave the grave, so close had the love been between them.

Over the next years and even while I continued to work and travel, one objective, one goal finally dominated my thinking. The drive began to finally coalesce everything I'd learned about my family, about their origins and backgrounds, about the war that separated them from their beginnings and almost destroyed them and ultimately to write a book about their lives.

As I continued to travel, I now also diverted time to transcribe all my notes, assemble all the photographs I'd collected of their histories and document all those that were contained in them. I transcribed the intensive first video interview that had opened the book of their lives and spent more months transcribing and saving the last final interviews. I ensured that the final weeklong interview of my father in the year before his life ended was forever preserved. Copies of the tapes were burned into computer hard drives and finally into DVDs and distributed so one would always be found. And the original tapes were placed into a bank safe-deposit box as an ultimate resource in case of any failure. And all of that was really just a beginning, a new direction for me that had been suppressed for years and one that now rose to the surface.

The precious photographs that I had slowly squirreled away over time and eventually inherited from my father became a separate intensive project. I had long before become a charter member of the United States Holocaust Memorial Museum and visited many times. I resolved that ultimately those photographs should be preserved forever in those vaults. In preparation for that, I carefully scanned each of the precious pictures and, searching through the interviews I'd conducted of my parents over the years, recorded the names of all that could be identified. No piece of potential information was overlooked so that even the back of every photograph was copied in case it could reveal another speck of information.

In late 2004 and early 2005, I had few choices. I was between jobs and with Rhoda in our house near Philadelphia. I had no choice but to find another job, if for no other reason than we had to have major medical insurance with Rhoda as a breast cancer survivor. But even while working unendingly on job searches, uncovering and expanding my family history still drove me.

While returning to the Midwest on the retirement of one of my colleagues, I decided it was important to spend time with Rhoda in Chicago exploring her family history as well.

We visited her mother and stepfather's graves in Westlawn Cemetery, and then I said, "Let's go to Waldheim Cemetery where your birth father Charlie is buried and see what we can find."

The directions on the Waldheim map were vague, and we were completely uncertain if we'd ever find his plot. Suddenly we spotted a large smooth granite slab with "Taslitz," her father's family name, engraved on it and surrounded by smaller plain stones around its base.

"There! There it is," Rhoda shouted. "But it's so overgrown, we can't even make out the names of who's buried."

Nearby was someone with a weed whacker clearing out brush at another site and we borrowed it to clear away the weeds. As we did so, we could see the name Charles Taslitz appear with the inscription, "Beloved Father and Brother, Laid to Rest Jan 14, 1954."

Attached to the stone was what looked like a small closed picture frame made from metal, and when we opened it, Rhoda exclaimed, "It's my father!" Underneath the now open metal lid, under glass, a picture of Charlie could be seen.

Nearby we found his mother, Dasha Taslitz, with her picture also beneath a metal window and next to her Ben (Boruch) Taslitz, "Beloved Husband and Father." Rhoda had found not only her father Charlie, but her grandparents, Dasha and Ben. Also nearby was Leo Taslitz (husband, father, grandfather), Charlie's brother, and Lilly Taslitz (wife, mother, grandmother) Leo's wife. And, a surprise, she found Earl Taslitz (son and brother) Leo and Lilly's son who had died young at only age 20.

Waldheim Cemetery was a major find for Rhoda's discovery of her birth father's family; for me, it was an awe-inspiring site to see so many old and ornate dedications to family long gone. For me, it would not be the last time I'd visit and be inspired by my findings in that cemetery.

Far from having no family and little to no family history information, she'd found her birth father and his whole family. On top of that, she was able to find links from the cemetery office, and she followed those to start a major dive into her own family tree and genealogy that expanded and lasted for years and rivaled my own exploration.

Exhilarated by our findings, we returned home, and again the normalities of daily life took over, especially for me. Intensively looking for a new position and again uncertain whether I'd ever find one, I received a job offer while consulting on a project in New Hampshire. Just as my father had moved time and again during his lifetime, we moved again. Rhoda and I put our home on the market and moved overnight to New Hampshire where I took a position as Vice President of Research and Development and Chief Science Officer. Who would ever have imagined again that a young boy, who might have wound up as a goat herder in Azerbaijan, could have achieved such a position? I never stopped marveling at my fate.

We loved living in New Hampshire, this time only an hour from our son around Boston, a major advantage to us. The position and new research for me on a different treatment for diabetes was exciting with a major potential for a breakthrough in care. Again, I devoted myself, with unending hours, to my work, and again travel increased.

The Family Gathers / Irving (2006)

One morning, sitting at a conference on drug delivery in Dallas, Texas, I received an unusual call on my cell phone and exited the lecture to answer it. It was a phone call from my sister-in-law Linda, Irving's wife in Ottawa, Canada. She never called me, and I became immediately concerned.

Sobbing on the phone, Linda cried, "Irving just died. He was in the hospital a couple days ago not feeling well. They couldn't find anything and sent him home. He got worse and worse, and I took him back to the hospital, but they didn't do anything. He just died."

It was a tremendous shock to me. How could this be? It couldn't be real. There hadn't been any indication of serious illness when I'd seen him just a month ago at a family reunion.

Pulling myself briefly together, I said to Linda, "I'm at a conference in Texas. I'm going to leave now and go home. I'll call Ronnie and Dave, and we'll make immediate arrangements to join you in Ottawa."

At the airport, I called my brother Boris, my sister Charlotte, my cousin Aharon Schwarzbard. Everyone started planning to fly to Ottawa.

I was in a daze at the funeral. After everyone left and flew home, Ronnie and I stayed with Linda for the rest of the week to do what we could with arrangements.

I still couldn't come to grips with it. This was the brother who had survived with me after the war, who had been with me in the displaced persons camps, who had come with me on the ship to America, who had been my roommate until I, myself, had gone away to college. We had been at each other's weddings. I'd been there as Irving's kids had grown up. Irving, "Srul," Gone!

Sorrow gripped me. After Irving had gotten married and moved to Canada, we just hadn't seen each other enough. Had I done enough to help support him? Irving had become a bookkeeper, but never made enough money. Despite that, he'd raised a wonderful family. Kimberly, the oldest, became ill with Crohn's disease in her late teens and it had set her back badly, but she recovered. Mandy, the second child, was a brilliant young girl who could do anything and had a wonderful future in front of her. Danny, the youngest was still looking for a long-term career, but was doing fine. What would happen to them now?

During the week that we stayed with Linda, I learned so many things about my brother that I'd never known. What a kind and wonderful man he'd become. While never making enough salary to do much for himself, he had a clientele that depended on him and that he serviced whether or not they had much to pay him. He helped older people, who were his and Linda's friends, with everything, even if he didn't have the means to do so. I grieved forever that I hadn't been close enough to my brother in his late years and dedicated myself to doing anything I could to help my sister-in-law and her children as they grew older.

Coming back to work was hard, but unavoidable. I continued to try to make the treatment we were developing succeed, but the company was small and had few resources to pursue such a massive objective. Again, however, we needed the job for the medical coverage to protect Rhoda as a breast cancer survivor.

When Rhoda turned 65, and with Medicare coverage for our health plans, I could now finally retire, and I quit my job on April 1st, 2010. The pressures of work were now gone.

I set to work on what would be my main task in retirement, returning to documenting and recording my family history and genealogy.

PART III

THE BEGINNING OF A NEW MISSION

12

CONNECTING MEMORIES AND HISTORY

Finally! USHMM

After finally finishing my preparatory work, I was ready to discuss my plan with the United States Holocaust Memorial Museum (USHMM) staff. I made an appointment, and Rhoda and I traveled to Washington and showed up early at the Museum. I was astonished to see a long line waiting to get in, not just American tourists to Washington but people from other countries, speaking many languages, anxious to understand how the world had gone crazy. I showed my charter membership card to the guard, announced I had an appointment, and Rhoda and I were led to the top of the building, to the research wing. My appointment was with Teresa Pollin, the curator specialist with whom I'd previously communicated. Teresa was a congenial middle-aged woman, sympathetic to our interests, and curious about my history. Her responsibility focused on Poland and photographs and documents of its history during WWII about which she was highly knowledgeable.

"What brings you here, and what can I do for you," she asked.

A long explanation followed of my background, of my and my parent's history as survivors, of the journey we'd followed. Teresa patiently listened. I showed her the interviews I'd conducted and transcribed, the research I'd done, the original pictures I'd painstakingly documented and copied.

Teresa hardly interrupted, and when I finished looked at me and said, "It's incredible what you've done and the wealth of materials that you've collected. We continue to get more pictures, but the flow decreases, and we don't often get as much as you've collected and hardly ever with as much documentation as you've assembled. What is your intention to do with this?"

"I've discussed with my brothers and sister along the way. We have agreement that we'd like to donate this to the Holocaust Museum. I have carefully scanned all the photographs, and I'd like to donate those. You can have the copies, or if you prefer, you can scan them yourself."

"As much as we'd like to have this, the policy of the museum is to only accept originals. We can't accept copies. We can't accept the risk that, at some point, there would be an accusation that what we have isn't real. We can only accept originals. I'm sorry."

What a disappointment! It was a difficult condition I hadn't anticipated. Give up my precious pictures forever? Have them placed on a shelf or in a vault that might never be accessed again? Lost to my family? Lost forever? It was hard to consider.

"I'll have to review this again with my family. I very much believe that this is the place where they must be, never to be lost. So, I would consider it, but only on two conditions."

"What would those be? Maybe we can accommodate them."

"The conditions are that you would scan them once more in the highest resolution and provide a complete copy back to me. And second, that within one year after giving them to you, that you would ensure that they would be scanned, and the photographs made available for any researcher or family to find them on the Holocaust Memorial website. What I can never accept is that, though, they'll be safe here, that the memories will be lost forever in storage."

Teresa looked at my sorrowful face, struggling with what separation from the pictures, the heritage from my father, meant to me. "I'll do everything I can to ensure you of what you want. I'm sure I can accomplish that."

We continued to speak for a long time, exchanging stories of what we knew of those difficult times. We had established a strong relationship, a friendship that would endure for a long time.

"I'm going to go home, confirm with my brother and sister that they agree, check all my documentation that I'll provide along with the photographs, and come back to give you that and the original pictures."

With that we returned home and got agreement from my siblings. I spent more time numbering and scanning again all the photographs and compiling an extensive spreadsheet linked to the pictures of names and dates and places and events and returned on August 2nd, 2010 to turn over the precious materials.

Along with turning over the precious photographs, I told Teresa, "This is the culmination of a goal that I'd set over ten years ago to put my father's photographs in order and to memorialize them for posterity in the museum's archives for access to the world. Even so, it's also the start of the next ambition, which is to expand knowledge of that history to a broader base of family members and friends. Ultimately, I'd like to write a book covering this history and the people that were swept up in it. Teresa, I look forward to a long and fruitful relationship with you and the museum in my efforts and with continuing updates, as I'm able to uncover additional photographs, documents, and stories."

Less than a week later, I got an amazing email back from Teresa.

Dear Feldman Family,

It's an interesting world, and the coincidences are amazing. I was talking today to a researcher (Belinda Blomberg) for the upcoming exhibition on collaboration, and she mentioned that they (the curators) intend to use one small town as an example of collaboration and complicity of the local population. The town she was talking about is Sokolow Podlaski – what else. She already listened to your dad's testimony, so when I happily told her that you, Fred and Rhoda, were just here and brought these amazing photographs, I thought she would fall off her chair!

Just wanted you to know.

Teresa A. Pollin

Curator Art and Artifacts, US Holocaust Memorial Museum

A short three months later, all the papers had been scanned in ultra-high resolution, disks made and distributed to me, an album of them also sent to me, and the pictures loaded to the Museum's website for discovery by users in perpetuity.

A Global Sokolow Podlaski Havura

Early in my discussions with the USHMM, I received an email from Teresa Pollin telling me she'd read an article about a young woman photojournalist, Katarzyna Markusz, from my family's hometown of Sokolow Podlaski who had an interest in the Jewish history of her town.

It was with some excitement that I tried to contact Katarzyna. In years of traveling back and forth to Europe for my job and never more than a few hours air travel from Poland, I had many times considered taking some extra time and visiting Sokolow. But I didn't speak Polish, didn't know anyone in that town, and was very leery that I would know what to do once I got there or gain anything by going. So, I never went.

Now I finally had an opportunity to contact someone who lived in that town, someone to answer questions, someone who might be able to be a link to the past of my family.

Emails back and forth. Wow, she speaks English, communicates by email and has the same interests as me!

I found Katarzyna, her nickname is Kasia, to be a young lady with a keen interest in the history of Jewish aspects of her town, even though she wasn't Jewish, even though there were no longer any Jews left in her town. She worked for the town newspaper and was also an avid photographer. Through many communications, I learned that she had access to an old Memorial Book of Sokolow that was in Yiddish (in Yiddish a *Yiskor Buch*). I had the same book. In fact, I had three different Memorial Books of the town that I'd gotten from my father, two while I was growing up and one, the same one she had, the year before he died when I spent a week interviewing him.

The book was filled with the history of the town, with stories, a map of what the town center looked like before the war when 7,000 Jews lived there, and many pictures of the town, its schools and societies and people.

Kasia had copied key landmarks of the town as it existed before the war from that book and had searched out the same areas and buildings as they existed today. Beyond that, she had made an exhibit and published it online, of the before and after pictures of the Jewish presence. In addition, she was a proponent of teaching the town about its Jewish history and reconciling it with its antisemitic past.

It was during my communications with Kasia that I initiated a worldwide Internet community of people with ancestral links to Sokolow. Some had parents or grandparents who had lived in that town, and some had ancestors who had left generations before. Many were scattered around the United States, some from Israel, Argentina, South Africa, and Australia. And the list continued to grow over time, and we communicated for years by email.

All Steam Ahead: Genealogy and Family History

One-night Rhoda and I attended a special program at one of the Temples we belonged to with a lecture title, "What's Your Story?" An invited lecturer, Judy Faust, spoke of making a movie about her mother, who was a Holocaust survivor, from interviews Judy had done.

When she finished, I went up to her and said, "I have a lot of information about my own family who were Holocaust survivors. I have original old pictures, interviews, and lots of stories that I've collected since I was a young child. Could I do what you've done and make a movie out of that? I already have everything I need. I just don't know how to do videoediting and don't want to divert from what I'm doing now to learn that."

Judy, said, "Sure, why not? I could help you. Let me know when you're ready."

This was her business model and she followed up incessantly.

"Ready yet?"

"No. Not yet. I'm still putting things together. I'm organizing my materials. I'm transcribing everything."

"OK. Call me when you're ready."

Eventually, I called her. "I'm ready now and want to go ahead. I've put together a storyboard. I've put together pictures. I've put together a script. I don't want you to do any of that. I know what I want to do, I have the camcorder, and what I want is for you to do the interview and edit the movie." My plan was to have myself interviewed just as I'd interviewed my father in the year before Mendel had passed away.

I hired her. We signed a contract, and some weeks after, she came for the interview.

It was much harder than I anticipated. I went through all my material, showed all my father's pictures, talked about my own research, even showed video clips of interviews I'd done. To my great surprise, at many points, my emotions got away from me as I recalled the dangers and difficulties of my parents' lives.

Far from the hour or two that I expected the process to take, it took all day. Judy took the materials, promised to do an initial edit, send it to me, and contact me for plans of what to do with it.

Weeks later she called me. "You have a huge amount of material and it's all fantastic! It's impossible to cut out much of it. I've edited and spliced it together and it covers four DVDs. I know that's all you intended, but I think you should do much more. I think you should make this into a video-documentary, into a movie. I'd help you with that. You direct it. I'll control the software and processing it, and I'll be the producer."

I was wary. This was far from what I intended to take on and again opened the risk of delaying my starting to write the book that was my main goal. But the discussion started my thinking of what I could do with it. I could incorporate the major interviews of my parents that I'd recorded over the years. I could incorporate all the photographs that were now safe at the Holocaust Museum. I could incorporate wonderful pieces of music. It would be a testimonial itself, and I agreed to go ahead with Judy on hire as a formal consultant. Many drafts followed and much debate.

While working on the documentary, I started an email correspondence with one of my cousins with whom I hadn't communicated for decades, Howard Halasz.

After many email exchanges with my re-found Cousin Howard, who seemed mostly interested in old music records, I one day got an email that said, in passing, that he had Joe Rosenbaum's old 16mm-film projector and films. He'd gone through them and created a DVD of all of them.

He said, "Some of the DVD footage includes the Feldmans (Mendel, Frieda, Fred and Irving) and the Lopatas and Ida Altman. I can mail a copy of that DVD to you if you want it."

If you want it?! The immediate response to him was,

"Howard, we've been corresponding for about a year or more on all kinds of stuff (motorcycles, old jokes, old records, old movies, Roy Rogers, South Bend memories, nostalgia) but I never imagined asking if you had something like this. What else do you have? I'd love to have any family history or old pictures you have. Your grandfather Joseph came from Poland in the early 1900's along with other brothers and sisters of my grandmother Ida. Did he bring any old pictures of family with him from Poland? What was his life like when he came? He must have had some pictures of early life in South Bend, of his family growing up, etc. I'd love to be able to fill in all that information.

When Joe passed away, those materials must have gone to someone. I was hoping that your cousin Bonnie might know and have some of them, but now I heard that you have this. Most people wouldn't know what to do with old films, but you've taken what's really precious historical material and digitized it.

Yes. Yes! Please send me a DVD. What else do you have and what do you know about any other material he left behind?"

The DVD arrived, and I was astonished to see an ancient yellowed film clip of myself and my family and my Aunt Leah and Velvul Lopata at what was apparently a party for them shortly after they arrived in America. My expectations until now had been to, at most, find a few old photographs. I never expected to find actual film footage of our arrival in the United States, and it took my breath away. There was my father as a young man wearing the suit he'd brought with him from Europe. There was my mother as a beautiful young woman, skinny from all the hardships she'd endured, but smiling to finally be free, and there we all were, my brother, my grandmother, my cousins and me. We were surrounded by our American relatives who were dancing, drinking, smoking, and laughing, while I'm sure none of us could understand what was happening. What a prize to be found of our life at this most critical moment when we arrived in our new world. Never would I have expected to find a treasure such as this. I was overwhelmed!

In editing my documentary, this film clip became a major addition to which we added a klezmer soundtrack with its highly expressive melodies, reminiscent of the human voice, complete with laughing and weeping. What could have been more appropriate for them at this stage of their lives and especially in this setting?

I added special selections of music that I had collected while I had been at the Diaspora Museum in Tel Aviv. I picked specific video musical introductions and designed jacket covers and photographs for the DVD pictures and boxes.

It took a year of continual work, and I was finally done. The interview had taken one day; the project had taken one year. What I had was a finished wonderful documentary of my parents' lives – four DVDs taking three and a half hours to watch and a fifth DVD that contained all the photographs with which my father had entrusted me, in high resolution for posterity.

I'd learned a tremendous amount in the process and had indeed been the Director for the movie. I immediately made four copies of the full program, designed a book cover for it and gave copies to my son David, to my brother Boris, and to my sister Charlotte, while keeping a copy for myself. Masters of the entire project were burned to several computer drives for additional future copies as I already had planned.

Judy was thrilled but wanted to continue. "It's great, but three and a half hours is too long to present in a lecture. You should cut it down to no more than 45 minutes. I can help you with that."

But I resisted. "I don't want to go on the lecture circuit with this. I never intended to be a Holocaust lecturer. I made these for two reasons. I made these for future generations to know, to remember, to appreciate what their forebears had suffered and achieved. I also made it as a basis for continuing directly to write my book. What I'd still love to do is to find even more about our family history, to confirm what I've learned about it from my father, to sometime visit our family origins in Poland, and to learn more about my father's sister who immigrated to Israel before the Holocaust."

With that, the video-documentary project was finished. The set was titled, "From Generation to Generation." As major new life milestones occurred in the family, though, a full set of DVDs in a case would become the gift I presented. The first to get the gift was Natalie, my brother Boris's older daughter, on her graduation from Harvard. Others would follow as well.

Connecting Back to my Roots

But was my project of understanding my past now completed? No more I could do? I still had questions to pursue. I had been so close with my grandmother, but what did I know of her generation, her brothers and sisters? I had known those who had immigrated in earlier times to the U.S. Uncle Joe and Aunt Bernice had lived in South Bend, Uncle Bernard and Aunt Sarah had lived in Chicago. But all of them were gone now, and I'd never had the opportunity to interview them or learn of their past from them. Other brothers and sisters? I knew almost nothing of them. I knew from my dad that my grandmother's father, Yisroel Hersch Rosenbaum had been married twice and that he'd had 12 children with the first wife and 12 with the second. My grandmother and my uncles and aunts that I'd known had been born from the second wife whose name was Bayla Rechl. But I didn't know the first wife or anything of her children, my grandmother's half-brothers and half-sisters. I didn't even know who the other brothers or sisters of my grandmother were. And I had so many questions of the generation that had emigrated earlier out of Poland. After they left, had they stayed in contact with those left back? Did they communicate or ask what happened to those who stayed behind during the Holocaust? Were there any survivors or children of them? So many questions still to answer!

That entire generation of my grandmother was what I wanted to know the most about. And among all of them, my curiosity was greatest about my Uncle Joseph who had visited us in the displaced persons camp in Austria and who had signed visas that allowed us finally to come to America.

How much there was yet to know. Where to start on all of that, and was it already too late or should I now stop?

In interviewing my father, we assumed that whatever pictures or documents that Uncle Joe had might now be with his granddaughter, Bonnie Hoover, the daughter of Irving Rosenbaum, one of Joe's sons. Another possibility was that Don or Howard Halasz (who had provided the precious film clip that I now had), the sons of Evelyn Halasz, Joe's daughter, might be further resources to his past.

There was another resource to which I turned. Bernice Rosenbaum Goldberg, my grandmother's oldest sister had immigrated to America in 1921 and I had established friendship with her daughter-in-law, Dory, and with Dory's oldest daughter Judy, now Judy Jankowski. Judy had for some time been my genealogy buddy. She'd also been interested and worked on her family history, and we had already exchanged some family tree information. Judy even had a name for the first wife, Yuspa (which turned out to be in error). But she did have names of some of the children from that generation.

With those possibilities, I began a new project to reconnect with those children, now of my own generation.

Many emails exchanged and, despite the years that had passed without any contact, we all became comfortable again with each other. While few of the family of my generation had extensively pursued knowing more about their family history or genealogy, it seemed that my passion stirred great interest among them., and they wanted to know everything that I might find.

Research Our History Anew with Old Connections

When my older cousin, Barbara Lopata Hartman, my mother's niece who was the first born during our parents' wanderings in the Soviet Union, invited me to her granddaughter's Bat Mitzvah in Chicago in spring of 2011, I had to go. It was a rare opportunity to reconnect with relatives lost but found again in the mists of time. It was also the opportunity I was looking for to not only share the extensive history that I'd already unraveled but to also look for yet uncovered history. I was totally unfettered by obligations of work and now fully free to develop the history for which I'd been longing for such a long time.

We contacted relatives in Chicago and Indiana and said that we were coming and why.

Rhoda and I packed our car with gear, cameras to document where we were and a large scanner in case we'd find new old photographs and documents that would either corroborate what I thought I already knew from my father or modify or extend it. It was so exciting.

The first step was the Bat Mitzvah in Chicago. I'd never met the little girl before – Tara Bryce Hartman, an authentic American in name and person, born in Chicago whose father, Craig, I'd last seen when he was a little boy growing up in South Bend, Indiana. The same was true for Barbara and Phil's other children, Steven and Jennifer who were only small when I'd seen them last.

We stayed an additional day after the service to get an extra chance to talk with them all. While Barbara didn't appear to have a great interest in family history, her children were highly interested, especially in the family tree and their link to it. We separated afterwards and committed to be in touch again.

But we now had an opportunity to go far beyond this contact and we proceeded to visit several relatives in South Bend, Indiana, only 90 miles away from Chicago.

In planning the visit, I contacted Bonnie Hoover, who I suspected had photographs or albums from her grandfather, Joseph Rosenbaum. I had so many questions about him that had lain dormant for so long. This was my chance to potentially get answers to my anxious questions about his contacts and his communication with his sister, my grandmother Ida, when she was stuck in wartime Europe. Bonnie surprised me even before I started my trip. She told me she had a friend, Byra ("Honey") Warner, potentially also a relative, who had a great interest in our family tree and asked if she could be part of our meeting as well.

I knew that we had a Warner family in our tree, so sure, why not. Maybe another chance to learn of more family links.

We reserved a library conference room near them, and Rhoda and I were astonished when we arrived.

A family tree was taped and covered an entire wall. Honey was also a genealogy buff, who had separately been tracking her own family tree for years, and like me, was looking for connections between the families. We knew we were related but really didn't know the details of exactly how. I knew some of the family branches that she had – from my other genealogy buddy Judy Jankowski – and Honey had a wealth of information about those individuals, but she didn't know where the crossover to my tree was. I had a lot of information about the branches in my tree that she didn't have, and the real excitement was that I knew how our trees were connected! The connection was my grandmother Ida's father, Yisroel Hersch Rosenbaum and from him, Bonnie, Honey, and I were connected. It was amazing. What we could then see was that Yisroel Hersch had been married twice. Honey's tree stemmed from the first marriage. My tree, and Bonnie's branches, stemmed from his second marriage. That meeting instantly doubled our knowledge, although none of us knew who his wife was from the first marriage. That, it turned out, would take a lot more travel and a lot more work, although Honey and I were able to exchange a lot of information across the branches of our trees. It set up a long-term collaboration. Honey became another of my genealogy buddies that continues to this day.

On Monday, May 2nd, 2011, Bonnie brought to the meeting what I'd been hoping to find for years. Photographs that her grandfather, Joseph

Rosenbaum, had collected over years were neatly stored in several large photo scrapbooks. The photographs were in beautiful shape, but Joseph had notated none of them. There were no identifying marks on their back, no notes of the names of the people in the pictures nor when or where the pictures were taken. Without any information, could the pictures be of any help in adding to family history information or genealogy? As beautiful as many of the pictures were, the group struggled with what to do with them. To scan them all wasn't possible in the time available. I knew that I wanted to scan them anyway, to preserve them for some future opportunity, and I committed to return at some future time to do that.

We gained a lot at that meeting. We established a family bond, a bond and commitment of interest to continue to look, to probe for family history, and to stay in touch with each other as we made progress in understanding more about our historical connections.

Parisdory

The next day was, finally, a connection to one of my relatives whom I'd only known peripherally over the years, Dora Goldberg (Dory). I knew Dory as a Holocaust survivor, as the daughter-in-law of one of my grandmother Ida Altman Rosenbaum's sisters, Bernice ("Bryna") Goldberg, née Rosenbaum who had left Sokolow Podlaski as a young girl and immigrated to America. She had settled in South Bend, Indiana where she'd lived the rest of her life. I knew Bernice well and had always felt a strong and grateful connection to her since she had taken us in shortly after we arrived. I well knew Bernice's story. I didn't know Dory's much.

Rhoda and I sat around Dory's kitchen table to listen and learn. At the side was a camcorder, manned by Rhoda, to record our conversations for posterity. On Dory's table already were albums of pictures and notes. What an incredible wealth of history and information we learned. Dory was a consummate historian. All her photographs were carefully stored, and details attached. In addition to constructing her family tree, we went through all her pictures, one by one, with Dory relating who her parents and relatives were, where they'd come from, what had happened to them. And with each photograph, I was able to scan it as a precious document to her, and as it turned out, to my own history.

The first thing I learned, to my amazement, was that Dory's family, the Cybulski's originated from the same town in Poland that my family came from, from Sokolow Podlaski. From that very beginning, her story took my breath away. I had never known that our families came from the same small town in Poland. All I'd known was that Dory was born in Paris, and I had assumed her entire history was of France.

Her grandparents, Esther Beckerman and Moshe Cybulski had three sons and a daughter; Pesach (Paul) was born in 1902 and was later, for good reasons, called Eli. The second son, Ela (Eli) Cybulski was born in 1904 and the third son was Chiam Yisruel who died during WWII. Lastly, the daughter was named Devorah.

Ela, as he grew up, married Jenta Kierchenblatt and they had two children, Denise (Dora) and Henri (Harry).

The first brother, Pesach, was drafted into the Polish army where life for Jews was unbearable. He ran away, and using his brother Ela's passport, with the name Eli, made his way to the U.S.A to Illinois.

The second brother Ela (now called Eli), after he married Jenta immigrated to Paris, France in 1931. Jenta had a sister, Bela, who also moved to Paris. Dora was born in 1932 and her brother Harry in 1937 while they lived in Paris.

Dora's father Ela (Eli) might have emigrated also to the U.S but couldn't because he had lost his passport to his brother who had taken his name (Eli) to escape Poland.

I had known none of this. Incredible to be able to unearth family history in such detail almost 80 years later and to preserve it for future generations.

In 1941 with the German army already occupying Paris, Ela (Eli) was detained in a round-up of Jews in what history would later record as The Vélodrome d'Hiver (Vél d'Hiv) Roundup, the largest French deportation of Jews during the Holocaust. To preserve the fiction of a French police force independent of the German occupiers, French policemen carried out the mass arrest of some 13,000 Jewish men, women, and children.

Approximately 6,000 of those rounded up, including Dory's father, were immediately transported to Drancy, in the northern suburbs of Paris. Drancy was at that point a transit camp for Jews being deported from France. The rest of the arrestees were detained at the Vélodrome d'Hiver (Winter Cycling Track), an indoor sporting arena in Paris's 15th arrondissement.

In both locations, conditions were deplorable. History has indeed documented this travesty and novels have written of the events, but the real-life story that Dory relates as a survivor goes beyond fictional accounts.

Dory's mother, Jenta, was able to visit her husband in the camp several times, and the Germans wanted her to come back with the children. Her sister, Bela, warned her against that. Jenta sensed danger and moved Dory and Harry outside Paris to a nearby town called Goussainville as a precaution. On her way back, Jenta was arrested and also sent to the camp. She was told at that point that they no longer knew where her husband was, although later papers, discovered years after the war, showed that under orders from Eichmann, he had been sent to Auschwitz where he was among many who were murdered. Both Dory's parents died in Auschwitz on August 2nd, 1942.

The children were left with Bela in charge, who later moved them to a farm and non-Jewish family in another town in Fontenay-Parisis. Dory never left her brother Harry behind. She protected him always and they stayed in that town throughout the Nazi occupation where there were many run-ins with German soldiers in the town.

Dory said somberly, "The area farms-people must have known the children in town were Jewish children, but they never revealed them. They were good people."

After the war, Dory and Harry moved back to Paris. By then, Dory was fourteen and Harry nine. Dory realized there was no future for them in France and wrote her Uncle Eli ("Pesach") in 1945 to try to get her and Harry to America. Finally, January 8th, 1948, Dory and Harry arrived in New York City, were met by HIAS (the Hebrew Immigrant Aid Society), just as they had helped my parents in Europe during that time. They were put on a train to Chicago to meet their Uncle Eli and Aunt Ida. When Dory grew up, she married Irvin Goldberg, my grandmother Ida's sister's oldest son.

Dory's pictures were breathtaking and chilling. There are several pictures of her father as he was in the work camp in camp Beaune de la Rolande lined up with other men from Barague 19, Gr 1 on April 12th, 1942. Many groups, none of them, from their appearance and demeanor, had any idea that they would shortly be sent to die in Auschwitz. Chilling. But amongst her pictures, she has pictures that are heart-stirring that have somehow miraculously survived of her family before the war and of her and her parents shortly before the world went crazy.

Amongst the wonderful photos is a picture of her mother as a beautiful young woman amongst relatives and friends in a formal pose around a beautiful table set with wine and fruit, with everyone elegantly dressed and happy, looking at each other and the camera and smiling and happy. The photograph was probably taken in Sokolow more than 70 years ago and though miraculously preserved is one that suffered considerable damage. That was one that I worked on later, for years, doing a complete restoration of it. It's a treasure.

Other pictures included a photo of Dory as a beautiful little girl, maybe four years old, sitting in an old leather chair, posing with a smile at the camera while dressed in a beautiful little white dress with a fancy tied bow, frilly sleeves, a watch on one wrist, a bracelet on the other and pretty little shoes and socks. Magnificent. And another treasure, a photograph of Dory with her mother and father in Paris. Dory is dressed in a beautiful frilly white dress, a large gorgeous satin bow on her head, smiling un-intimidated straight at the camera. Standing on a tall round little table, she's in the crook of her mother's arm, her mother beautifully dressed wearing a pretty beaded necklace around her neck and with a lovely smile. Leaning against her, his head next to hers, is Dory's father, dressed in a smart suit, white shirt and tie, clearly happy to be there with his happy family, unaware as anyone could be of the disasters that fate had in store for them. Wonderful to see the picture, hard to take knowing what came next.

So much memory preserved, to be treasured or cried over. Two more pictures in my own memory now to share, one of Dory standing outside a shabby little house, with her mother and father squatting around her, holding her tight. Smiles on both her parents, bright with love, but Dory not smiling here, looking quizzically as though with a premonition that not all will continue to be as it is then (**Photo 15**). And the last picture to be described here in my notes, Dory standing alone, outside a house that looks little more than a shack, maybe six years old, staring at the camera without a smile and closely holding on, in front of her, to her purse.

Over two days, we scanned all her pictures and listened to so many sad and wonderful stories and asked her about her life when she reached the United States and after she married.

We learned that she studied hard to become an American, took courses to learn English, and took courses to learn to write. One of those required her to write regular essays. For her subjects she chose her own history as she remembered it, essay after essay about growing up that was a document of her early life. That was another treasure that we found that she'd kept and let us make a copy for posterity.

Finally, we asked, "Dory, are we done? We've copied all your pictures, listened to so much history, marveled at your amazing stories. Have we skipped anything? Is there anything else to see or ask about?"

We thought, as we found in many instances of our search for history, for family, that now, again, we were done, and again the answer surprised us.

"No," she said. "You've seen everything, although there are a couple big old pictures in frames in the basement. They're completely wrapped up in paper, and they've been there for years. There's been water in the basement. They're probably damaged, so I never looked at them. I don't know if there's anything to look at from them or if you'd want to see them."

"Why not? Let's not take a chance on missing anything."

When she came back up, we did indeed see two big packages wrapped in a lot of paper and, sure, there were water stains on the papers. Just as we recorded all the interviews with Dory over the two days, we recorded this on a camcorder as well. We said, "Shall we try to unwrap these and see what we can find? We'll be careful, so we don't add any damage to what's in there."

"Sure. Let's try," she agreed.

Layer by layer, we removed wrappings until the frame of a picture could start to be seen. From the back, the picture was sealed with paper and a wire attached to the old wooden frame. From the front, with paper removed, we could see there was glass, so covered with dust that we couldn't really make out what was below, but we could vaguely make out the form of some faces.

"Can I take the frame apart to see if I can get at the photograph that's inside," I asked. I think I can at least do that without damaging the mat that's holding the picture against the glass."

"Go ahead."

We peeled off the outer paper, pried pieces of the frame apart until the only thing left in front of us was the back of the picture mat and the back of the picture against the front of the glass.

Now what? Try to move the picture away from the protective glass that held it for so many years, maybe 60 years or more? If the picture was stuck to the glass, there was a real possibility, especially if humidity or water had penetrated to it, the image of the picture could be ripped away. Did we dare to take that chance? We all looked at each other uncertain what to do.

"Do it," Dora said. "I have to see what's there."

Gently, gently, I inserted a blade to elevate the picture slowly away from the glass. We all held our breath. Hallelujah! It pulled away intact. Clean. No damage, and in front of our eyes, we could see Eli and Jenta as young people before the outrage of the Holocaust! I could have cried.

The second picture still lay there in front of us, wrapped and in the same condition as the one that we'd just liberated. Did we dare?

An identical result, and this time, we could see again two people, but these were Dory's grandparents!

Astonishing. At this point in her life Dory was a cancer survivor, a wonderful feisty old lady who lived by herself while her daughters lived their own lives. Only she could have identified those pictures. And if by fate she had passed away before and her house had come to be cleaned out, those pictures in the basement, stained with water marks, might well have come to be considered trash and discarded. Even if not, even salvaged but kept, could anyone have identified them as the gems that they were?

In every instance where we looked for hints, links to our past, the result always seemed the same. When we thought we were done, when we were ready to close up and go home, the little added treasure would surface, the treasure of our hunt, the treasure of our lives.

We visited Dory a year later again. Those two pictures had been restored, reframed, and now adorned the main wall of her living room, never to be lost again.

We had visited Dory's daughter, Judy, my genealogy buddy, several times and even attended the Bat Mitzvah of her daughter Katie and later her marriage. Katie, now a PhD graduate in clinical psychology, has a family tree that, with her, currently encompasses five generations and includes pictures of her mother, grandparents, great grandparents, and great great grandparents. With it, and because of Dory's pictures, she can see exactly how she's connected to the generations of the past, those who contributed to what she is today. How wonderful is that!

Mystery Girl with the Ball

We didn't expect to find much material that we already didn't have or didn't know about when we went on to visit my cousin Barbara Hartman in South Bend. Barbara and I were part of the original group of nine souls that arrived in New York harbor in late October 1949, new immigrants in America. She was eight years old then. I was six and we'd been together with our parents in displaced persons camps in Austria since our families had been reunited in Poland in 1946. She had been born in Berezniki, Russia. I had been born in Azerbaijan and we became friends in Austria while our parents tried to find a place where we could go to call home. As children, we'd wandered around the camp and around the fields outside town. Wels in Austria. A wonderful picture survives of Barbara and me standing outside the town with Barbara holding a solitary flower, both of us looking forlorn (**Photo 16**).

Barbara had grown up in South Bend, as had I, but she stayed and became a successful businesswoman. We visited many times over the years to probe her memory of those early days in Russia and Europe, but this time we came to enjoy her company and Phil Hartman, her husband. Even so, after dinner, I asked again, "We're on a family history trip looking for old findings and I brought all my gear along to scan anything you think might be useful. Do you have any pictures or documents I haven't seen that I could copy?"

Barbara was very amused. "You know that most of my pictures I got from you. My parents never really saved much in the way of pictures, and I'm appreciative of the ones that you gave me. I don't think there's anything new you haven't seen."

It really wasn't a surprise at all. As we sat talking and relaxing and the evening wore on, I said to Barbara, "I should probably pack up my gear and put it away since I won't be needing it. You're sure I won't need it?"

"No. There's nothing I can think of. But I do have some old papers you might not have seen. I don't know if that's worthwhile to you."

"What's that about?"

"One of the problems my mother had was that when she applied for social security, she needed something to prove her age and someone to testify to the accuracy of that. It was a real problem. It was finally resolved because when Uncle Joe, who brought us over, signed a document, he wrote about how old she was. It's not a very interesting piece of paper, but do you want to see that?"

We had no reason to expect that what she'd bring down would really add anything to the history that we knew. But the old piece of paper, which was brought down, was, in fact, a testimonial to Barbara's mother age. Oddly enough, Joe didn't say how old she was. He could have done only that. Instead, he wrote a short essay about when she had been born, but also continued to talk about the time he visited her and left. He wrote, *"... and when I walked out the door, I saw her standing there, a little girl holding a big blue ball in her hand."*

To anyone else, including Barbara, this would have had no special meeting. I was dumbstruck though! I knew all the pictures that my father had and that we'd gone over time after time. We'd spent so much time poring over them, identifying everyone in every picture. Except for one. There was one where he didn't know who the little girl in the picture holding the big blue ball was. Barbara had that picture. So, did I. The little girl in that picture was her mother. But for that innocuous exchange of information, that picture and that little girl would have gone unidentified and potentially lost to memory. What a moment!

Again, a search through the threads of time and memory had brought forth another treasure.

How much we were getting out of this trip!

We weren't ready to leave South Bend yet, though, and visited the Jewish cemetery in adjacent Mishawaka, Indiana. There, my grandmother Ida was buried as well as her brother Joseph, and his family, as well as her sister Bernice. I photographed all the tombstones to secure their actual dates and names of their fathers that were also on the stones to supplement the detailed charts that I was now compiling.

We had notified the local newspaper of the treasure hunt we were on and a photographer and reporter were sent to the cemetery to explore our unusual mission. They were fascinated with my background. Being born in Azerbaijan and immigrated to America, growing up and educated in South Bend raised their interests. To have left that town and gone through an advanced education with publications and substantial professional accomplishments made me an unusual figure in their perspective. Beyond that, to come back to that small town to connect those who were still there, those who were no longer living, with those of the past merited, they said, a special story in their press.

I found months later that they had published an extensive story with photographs of me and my efforts in their Sunday newspaper. I started getting letters back with copies from my South Bend relatives who were somewhat surprised to see their names also in print. Far beyond that, and another prize found, was that a relative in Minnesota, Faith Weiss, whom I'd never known, with a link to Joe Rosenbaum from my tree, happened to see that newspaper and contacted me. The two of us spent months exchanging information and, while she had no family tree when we found each other, she had a full and comprehensive connection to my tree a year afterward. Another relative who'd been lost to us was found again.

Sarah's Daughter

We were still not done and headed to Chicago. There we met with Morris and Myrna Millman. Myrna was the daughter of Sarah Berkowitz whose name had been Sarah Rosenbaum when she'd been born in Sokolow Podlaski. Sarah was another sister of my grandmother Ida, and Sarah had immigrated to America early in the 20th century, had become a citizen, married, and raised a family. When we met, Sarah was no longer alive, but we spent a day with Myrna going over, and scanning and recording, old pictures of Sarah's family in early times in America. We met her son, Michael, and I could tell that he was the next generation candidate to take up the challenge of keeping the chain of memory alive.

At the end of that day, Myrna gave us a tour of her home. Again, at the end of a very productive day and potentially finished with our efforts, we made another major find. On her walls, Myrna had framed some pictures of very high importance to her family, including a photograph of her mother as a young woman while she was still in Sokolow. Another photograph was one in America of Sarah and her sister Bernice, the two sisters of my grandmother who had left home for America.

One photograph in particular was the treasure found of this trip. On one wall was a picture of an old couple, probably in their 80's, sitting together, separated by just a small table. The old man had a white beard and wore a heavy black coat buttoned almost to his neck. He had on a dark cap and was holding a cane that he clearly needed to support him. He had such a somber look on his face.

The woman, who was sitting in a chair next to him, was wearing a long dark striped skirt that came up to below her bosom. She wore a pretty long-sleeved ivory blouse with a long collar and wore a long-beaded necklace and dangling earrings. She had dark hair and sported a small fashionable hat. She held a sheaf of some papers, and also had a very somber look on her face.

I caught my breath looking at this photograph. At that point, I'd seen a lot of old family photographs and had a good recognition of most of them, but I knew I'd never seen this one before anywhere, not in pictures that others had, not in memorial books, nowhere. But I recognized the old man. I'd seen that face before, and I'd seen it in a Sokolow Podlaski memorial book as a very tiny picture. This was Yisroel Hersch Rosenbaum, my maternal great grandfather, my grandmother Ida's father. This was someone that I'd wanted to know about for such a long time. This was a page that had still been missing. Myrna confirmed my finding and identified the woman as his second wife Bayla Rechl. No other picture of her had ever shown up. This was the only one, and to have a photograph of the two of them in their later years was an unimaginable reward. I would never have expected this finding. The picture was securely sealed behind a frame, and I dared not take it apart to scan it, but I made many photographs, preserved the originals and restored this one to perfection. All the photographs and scans I took of people on this incredible trip made their way to a special gallery on my now burgeoning photographic web site dedicated to genealogy and family history that I shared with everyone as I went along.

The next day we went to the very old cemetery on Chicago's south side, Waldheim, the cemetery I'd visited with Rhoda when we discovered her birth father and his family. I went there now armed with all my data on those who might be found there. I found many of the Rosenbaum family whose progress out of Europe I was following, many born in Sokolow Podlaski, and many of their progeny who had grown up and had families in Chicago and who were also buried there. I found that many of the tombstones had pictures behind windows on them, and I photographed them as well as all the inscriptions on the stones. The inscriptions were of particular high value because they always showed the names of the fathers of the deceased, besides the dates of birth and death, and all of that information gave me linkages that I could use to further expand my knowledge and the family tree that was rapidly being filled in. So many pictures, so much information, so many ties now clearly linked.

This was the last stop in this trip, but not the last time I visited this cemetery.

Lost No More: Hyman

We had been trying for some time to make one more important connection. Hyman Kawer lived near Chicago not far from where we already were. Both he and Rose, his wife, had been important to our family for decades and we had mostly lost our connections with them. I hadn't seen them since the early 1960s, over 50 years before. The last time I even remembered them and my family being together was one of those vacations our families used to take together. It was the summer of 1962, and I'd just graduated from high school. We were in South Haven, Michigan at a rental near the lake. Hyman and his wife drove up and joined us for a couple days, and we enjoyed spending time at the beach while our parents reminisced about old times together. I would look at their faces, beaming at each other as they remembered being together in their youth, at the sadness that came over them remembering the long and suffering separation during the war, and at the brightness of finding each other again. They were the best of friends and would always remain that way.

It now could be my last chance to find them and to swim in the tide of memories once more. I had always kept contact with Hyman's son Aaron, and even a couple years ago had sent him a DVD that I'd made of an interview I'd conducted of his father in their house in Chicago. Hyman had agreed to be interviewed about his history and how they'd survived the war, but Rose absolutely refused. She wanted nothing to do with it and just didn't want to dredge up old unhappy memories again. But we went ahead with it anyway. Rose, still in their house, watched us set up around the kitchen table, but adamant that she wasn't going to participate and was going to leave as soon as we started.

As that interview began, though, Rose stayed behind the camera and periodically a voice would come out from behind, "No, Chayim, you have it all wrong. That's not when it happened. That's not where it was.

Here's what it really was." The pleading to come out and join us was to no avail, however. She finally left, and we spent most of the day interviewing Chayim.

Now 60 years later, we went to see the two of them. They had done well, running a successful grocery store in Chicago's poorer neighborhoods, had invested wisely, and had raised two wonderful children, Aaron and Pam. Pam had married and moved away. Aaron stayed in Chicago, was also retired and helped to look after his parents. Chayim and Rose lived in a comfortable apartment not far from him. He'd finally arranged that we would meet. We came with some trepidation.

As old as he was, I could recognize Chayim right away and also recognized Rose. It was like jumping out of a time machine to see how they were vs the pictures in my memory. Stooped, wrinkled, age spots, bags under their eyes, thin white hair – how unfairly time had treated them. But they were the same people yet. Chayim with a thin but pleasant smile on his face, just like always. Rose, more affectionate with Chayim than I'd ever seen her before, but still ready to debate him if she thought he was wrong. But overall, it was wonderful to get to this moment in time and once again share memories. How fortunate we were!

And even here, I again surfaced my old questions. "Chayim, do you have any old pictures from before the war when you were in Sokolow as a young man?"

My parents were gone, few remained from those times, but here was a direct link to that ancestral home and that time.

As with other times, I constructed a family tree with him, and we sat down and started looking at pictures. For this visit, no fancy tech gear, no scanners, only my camera and a small micro-cam recorder to record this milestone.

While his hearing had deteriorated, and I often had to repeat my questions, Chayim's memory was intact and still sharp. And what wonderful old pictures he showed us. One was of him as a young man in Sokolow in 1938/39 with a group of friends and his older brother Avrom. Beautiful young men, all nicely dressed in suits with white shirt and tie, all looking at the camera and Chayim with the characteristic smile. What wonderful times for these young men then facing what turned out to be more than an uncertain future that would fling them far in the prevailing winds and storm that was coming.

Another picture from even earlier, 1937, Chayim with two lovely young girls on his arm, taken while Chayim had visited Warsaw.

Chayim told us the story of what happened to him during the war and of returning at war's end to Sokolow, as my father had done, looking for survivors. Two pictures of his tell the story of what he found. The first shows rubble in fields, buildings decimated from shell bombardments, several men, including him wandering around looking to find those they'd lost, and in the middle of a field, a long ditch. In the second photograph, four men can be seen in what looks like a state of shock, overlooking the long winding ditch. In it, Chayim stands at the edge of the ditch, forlornly looking into it. As I now know the story well, during the war on September 21st, 1942, the ghetto holding massive numbers of Jews, Jews herded from the town and Jews assembled from surrounding towns, was emptied. Those who resisted were shot, some shot in their beds and homes they refused to vacate. The rest were summarily loaded onto railroad cars and shipped north a short distance to Treblinka where they were immediately killed. That ditch in the photograph contained the remains of those killed in the town that day.

Abandoning the town, exactly as my father had done, Chayim eventually found his way into a displaced persons camp as I had, as my surviving family had. He moved, as we did from one DP camp to another and several of his pictures were taken there. It was during this time that he met and married Rose. As I had done with all the other pictures I found, recovered photographs of the past, I preserved the names of those in his pictures for posterity. One picture particularly is wonderful, a photograph of Chayim after the war standing next to a bicycle, his young son Aharon sitting on the crossbars on an empty road with the picturesque hills of Austria serving as a backdrop for the father and son, happy and smiling to be together in the fresh air.

We spent some hours together, trying not to tire out our old couple and then parted reluctantly. The meeting, relatively short, brought threads from my life and my father's life together that had been waiting for what seemed like an eternity. From the time Chayim was a young boy playing in the streets of Poland with my father, until separated violently by the war, until miraculously they spied each other at wars end, both heading toward uncertain futures, the threads of their existence were meant to be somehow, sometime connected. Finding each other again in the United States, in Chicago of all places, bound their threads into a tapestry that, from then on, included me. And the story of their lives, the occasional re-connections they made and that I witnessed, haunted me forever and required me to find and document how they lived as friends and survived and thrived even as they were apart.

In less than a year after that emotional reunion, I got a message that Rose had quietly passed away. Chayim mourned her but joined her not long after. Two lives tested to the limits by fate, united, thrived, and forged a family to remember and continue after them.

After they passed away, I quietly asked Aaron if he and Pam would consider giving me the photographs he'd shared with me at the end to donate to the United States Holocaust Memorial Museum as a fitting memorial to their lives and a fitting resting place. They agreed. I received the photos, scanned them and documented them religiously, and once again contacted my friend at the Museum to ask whether she was interested in having the pictures.

It didn't take long for her response that they'd like both the photographs as well as the video recording on DVD of the interview, and the materials became available on the museum site for all to view. Another mission accomplished.

Slowly, bit by bit, my commitment to secure the memory of my extended family's past by finding and restoring photographs, identifying all who could be found, and recording the stories of their lives was being fulfilled. And even as I expanded my efforts to find others with similar connections and interests to my ancestral town, I maintained an ever closer communication with my friend Kasia from Sokolow.

Return to Poland

In early September 2011, I learned that Kasia had decided to hold a memorial service on September 22nd, the day that the Sokolow ghetto had been emptied of its Jews and the Jews were forced into railroad cars to be murdered in Treblinka. Many who resisted were shot. Many that couldn't face the horrors awaiting them didn't leave their houses and were killed in their beds.

Kasia invited any of our internet Sokolow community, our *havurah* to join us in Sokolow for that memorial service. She had also invited the Chief Rabbi of Poland to attend, as well as the Israeli ambassador to Poland, but had not received a response.

It was impossible for me not to go, and my wife agreed to accompany me.

We decided we'd go for two weeks and looked for help with travel logistics in Poland and help with interpreters. After a great deal of difficulty finding resources in such a short time, I was able to arrange for a driver/interpreter from Warsaw who would accompany us for the first several days. That was all the time our interpreter had available, and we rearranged our itinerary accordingly.

Besides visiting Sokolow I also wanted to do more research on my family, my family tree, and any other information or documentation I could get on the information I'd gotten from my father, and, as much as anything, I wanted to walk the streets that my parents had walked as young people in their hometown before the devastating war that changed so much.

We were committed to going. Now we had flight tickets and an itinerary, and we told Kasia we would be there to support what she was doing. Another of our on-line community, Shoshi Shatit from Israel, also had decided to go. As far as we knew, we were the only ones.

It was my first return to Poland in 65 years!

As we packed and readied to leave, I planned to keep a diary of our trip and our experiences.

Day 1: Wednesday, September 14th, 2011

Flew last night from Boston to Frankfurt. 5-hour layover. Already tired.

Flew into Warsaw and were met by Kris Klosinski, a young translator and driver we had hired who took us to our Sheraton Hotel. Kris is a nice guy, has good knowledge of Polish history, and is a former English Professor at the University of Warsaw. Now works in a bookstore besides guiding tourists around Poland looking for connections to family and Jewish history. We're looking for more than connections. We're looking for our past.

We went to the Jewish Historical Institute and met with Yale Reisner, who is the head of the Jewish Genealogy Center here. We spent about two hours with him going over the information we already have on our family history while he looked through his own records. No hints yet, but he gave us suggestions on our search for the next days. We'll cycle back to him at the end of this trip to review our findings and set our next steps.

We had an early dinner at the Pierogarnia Restaurant not far from the hotel. Delicious pierogies of all kinds; not at all what you get in the U.S.

Checked and sent off emails. Worried that there's nothing from Kasia in my email about our meetings. Is the town going to cooperate? Tomorrow, Kris will meet us after breakfast and go with us to the regional record archive in Siedlce that was a depository for Sokolow records for our first major search for family history and connections. High hopes, but low expectations.

Day 2: Thursday, September 15th, 2011

We left our two large suitcases at the hotel check-in in Warsaw until we'd return to the hotel on Sunday night. Kris picked us up at the hotel in his car, and we were off to Siedlce that was a drive of about an hour and a half. It felt strange to be in Poland, a country I'd only been in when I was four years old as my parents found their way back after the war and a country that I had a lot of trepidation about.

We found the Siedlce archive, and asked to see Anna Jaworek, archivist, whom Kris had spoken with before on our behalf. We met her, and she told us, in excellent English, that she'd been successful in finding references to some of our relatives. Far beyond that, she had compiled a two-page list and tree of what she'd found. She amazed us that she had been able to go back two generations earlier on the Felman family tree than any information that I had previously from my father. She gave that to us with page references to where documents could be found. She explained to Kris that, providing we were doing more than a limited family search but were doing broader community research, she could give us carte blanche access to all the records including the right to photograph whatever we wanted – all free of charge! She got us started by bringing the original old archive ledger books, year by year, to our table to let us start exploring on our own. Fantastic! Amazing! Far beyond any expectations that I'd had.

We settled in and started to do research. As a starting point, we transcribed Anna's written information into a spreadsheet to record the data, track it, and to cross- reference the names that she had (and the numbers we assigned to them) to the prior spreadsheet of names that I had compiled and provided to the Archive. That took some time, and then we proceeded to look for specific detail with Kris doing the reading of the ledgers for us.

The ledgers were all written in script, beautiful script. Some looked like they'd been written using a quill and ink. Some ledgers were very old, almost falling apart, and all were carefully maintained by the Archive. Some ledgers were written in Polish, some in old Russian (all script). Kris could easily read the Polish, although the script was a challenge. He could also read Russian, but the script was very difficult, and he could only read some with difficulty. We kept track of the documents and what we'd want to follow up with Anna for a later date.

We summarized our findings for that day as we tracked all we did in a small bound notebook that we'd brought along. As we continued, we photographed each page, and we got better at taking pictures of the important pages that we found. How much and how long I'd wanted to do this.

The Archive had opened at 11:30 am that morning when we got there, and we stayed until 6 pm when it closed. We packed all the records in a big briefcase and checked into the hotel.

Off to bed we went, and, unfortunately, I had a lot of trouble falling asleep. Too much excitement/jet lag? But a fantastic day!

Day 3: Friday, September 16th, 2011

After a nice breakfast we decided we needed to find a cash machine to have enough zlotys for this phase of the trip. That turned out to be easy and we pre-paid Kris for the two and a half days he was staying with us including the use of the car. His schedule was so booked, that was all we could get. We went back together to the Archive, which opened at 8:30 am on Fridays and went back to work.

We worked until about 2 pm; the Archive closed on Fridays at 3 pm.

We spoke with Anna, thanked her profusely for all she'd done. She maintained it had only taken her an hour to find all that she'd given us! I would never have found that information any other way than visiting her. We asked to continue to work with her after the trip, to which she agreed that it was officially possible. Their rate for additional research was about 60 zlotis an hour ($20 an hour) and she'd be sending us information on how to transfer payment for additional work to the Archive.

I had sent her my family tree information that I'd accumulated from my father the week before we'd left, including information on my grandmother's father, Yisroel Hersch Rosenbaum. I knew that he had been married twice but had conflicting information on the first wife. I knew that my grandmother, my mother's mother, was born from the second marriage. Of the information Anna was able to find, she found Yisroel Hersch Rosenbaum's first wife, Ruchla Leja Stolarz, their son David Rosenbaum, and some generations earlier including wives, dates of birth and ledger references. Wow, in one short visit I found family that I would never have been able to find another way. I was learning more and more about my family before the Holocaust.

She had been unable to find Yisroel Hersch Rosenbaum's second wife in the records, though, nor all the children from the marriages. She had looked somewhat and didn't know how hard it would be to find all that or even if we had enough information to make that possible, but she was willing to look further later after we left.

We left Siedlce and headed toward Sokolow Podlaski. I told Kris I wanted to trace my parents' path out of Sokolow when they left in September 1939. I knew that one of the first things they did was to cross the Bug River and go to a small town called Drohiczyn that was then in the Russian zone. We followed that path, and I took photos as we went. Most of the houses that we passed were of modern vintage, but every so often, we saw vestiges of the old buildings that must have been in place in 1939. The countryside was flat, pretty, with meadows with cows and lots of trees, bucolic today. Ironically, I couldn't avoid imagining in my mind's eye Jews hiding in these forests, or trying to, in later times when the Nazis occupied Sokolow and the beatings and killings began.

We got to the Bug River. It now has a very large and modern bridge crossing it. We crossed over, and I walked back and took photographs of it and the areas around it. While it took us only about 20 minutes to get there from Sokolow, it probably took several hours getting to the same point in 1939 when my parents left in a horse and buggy in that perilous time. Not much traffic today. An occasional bicycle going along. It was in this town that my father stopped and where his boyhood friend, Hyman Kawer, took a bicycle back into Sokolow to try for the last time, unsuccessfully, to convince my father's mother, brothers, and sisters to also flee. How many families face the same existential question, "Is it time to leave everything we've know?"

Kris suggested exploring Drohiczyn a little, and we drove around the town. It's a peaceful little town with at least three large churches and many nice little houses, all well groomed, with many flower gardens and sunflowers adorning them. Who knows what it was like back then. Probably the same and probably occupied by people who wanted to be left alone and not involved in the insane war. How did they deal with any Jews they encountered who were fleeing the war action?

We left the town and drove back westward toward Sokolow. By now it was about 4 pm and Kris offered to drive us north from Sokolow toward Treblinka, which is only about 15 kilometers away along a small road. It was almost as though Kris could read my mind. We went north, with trepidation and considerable anxiety on my part. As we drove along, we passed through many small towns, some not more than poor clusters of houses huddling together. And we saw railroad tracks heading north in the same direction we were going, tracks that had once led to Treblinka and dead ends. We stopped at one crossing, and I got out to look at those damning tracks. Overgrown with grass and weeds, almost gone, but still visible in both directions, back toward Sokolow, north toward Treblinka, the evidence of the tracks refusing to be wiped away. I got more and more quiet as the journey progressed.

Kris was very knowledgeable of the history of that time and of what had transpired here. He spoke quietly of those times and of what happened to the Jews as they went along, as they arrived at Treblinka, and as to how they were "processed." At one point, I couldn't stand to hear any more and asked him not to tell me more about what was happening, what had happened, and the tragedies underway. I knew all about that, and I couldn't bear it.

Even as we got close, there were still small communities around and very near, and it was impossible that they didn't see, didn't know, couldn't know, couldn't smell what was going on. And Kris was very honest with it all, admitting that they couldn't possibly have been unaware.

He told us that he himself had asked people, old people in these areas, didn't they know, and they said, yes, they knew. They could see. They could smell. But what could they do against the Nazi machine? Any collaborator, not only one who offered lodging, but one who offered a piece of bread to a Jew would be shot in place and all his family would be shot at the same time also. Impossible to understand how humans could do that. The terror was all around. The Jews died, but the people surrounding, most of them anyway, were also in terror of what was going on and wanted to be outside of it. And so they were bystanders. What a terrible thing to be a bystander and helpless. What would even our neighbors today do in circumstances like this? Die? Watch their own children die? To help the other? Impossible questions. Impossible dilemma. No way out. For the Jews, only to die...

We got to Treblinka. Kris had made this trip many times before. He told us that he had decided long ago that he didn't want to become a regular tour guide, that he never wanted this trip and this story to become a tour stop, to become routine, and for him to become immune to the horror that this place represented!

Kris told us that the train stopped a little north of Treblinka. There was a switching yard to take care of the many trains that arrived. He brought us there, and he and we were surprised to now see only overgrown fields surrounding peaceful trees and only hints of former tracks in the grass. Time was erasing that it had been party to this unspeakable place. Right nearby were newer houses; couldn't have been here in that time. But also nearby was an old farmhouse, and it had to have been here at the time. Kris said he'd spoken with the occupants, and they said, yes, they had seen what was happening, but what could they do? There were no choices to be made. Only to watch genocide going on before their eyes.

We left that place and went back toward the death camp itself. Outside a sign: Sokolow in one direction, Treblinka in the other. A stone memorial sign at the entrance to the camp; the camp itself, had been destroyed by the Germans at the end of the war as they saw they were going to lose. They wanted to erase and leave no traces of the horrors they had committed, and so they forced the inmates to dig up the mass graves and built mass pyres of the bodies they burned. The smoke and smell must have been unimaginable! They razed it all. Even the Germans understood that the war crimes they committed would be damning.

When the Polish government after the war built a memorial here, what it left was a path to the killing place with large stones marking the borders of the death camp, where was once barbed wire. Large flat stones were laid on the ground in a pattern representing the train tracks to an elevated platform where the victims were unloaded. They lasted only hours at most before they were gassed in the "showers." And now there are only broken stones, shards standing to represent the small villages they had come from, surrounding one massive stone representing the death camp and with the face of the massive stone figure at the top writhing in agony and despair. All along the base of that one stone are Yahrzeit (memorial) candles, some still lit, left by those like us who had come in the last day or so to witness the unspeakable site.

And surrounding that site were even larger shards representing the destroyed communities from Eastern Europe that fed the machine. We found Sokolow Podlaski and stood there, trying to choke out the memorial prayer, the Kaddish, for those of my family and other families that had been murdered there. I could only get out some words between the tears.

Surrounding that place were tall beautiful trees, sparkling in the setting sun and blue sky, witnesses to what took place and themselves a memorial to those souls, providing a serene scene for those souls that can never be at rest above that place. Death cannot be understandable there; peaceful beautiful forests surrounding it. How could it be? And how can we understand what man could do to other men?

We left and drove back to Sokolow, most of the way in silence. Part of the way we talked about that history and the history of antisemitism in the generations, almost millennia, preceding.

We found our hotel in Sokolow, stopping several times for Kris to get directions. Friendly helpful people. Incongruity! Warped space and time!

When we had decided to go to Poland, deciding whether to stay in Sokolow itself or in Warsaw was one of our big questions. We had been advised by one of our other survivor friends, Aharon Elster, whose parents were killed by the Germans as he watched while hidden in an attic in the town, not to stay there, since antisemitism was still a problem.

"Stay in Warsaw and take a bus back and forth," he said. But that would have added hours of travel time. Kasia advised us that there was a new hotel in town where we would be safe, and so we booked our stay there. She'd meet us there.

Kris helped us check in and made sure with the staff that everything was being taken care of and appropriate. He left us his personal cell phone number so we could contact him under any circumstance when we might need information or help with connections. He arranged with his girl friend in Warsaw to come and get us in Sokolow if it turned out we couldn't make planned connections or needed any other support. And he offered for the following Monday morning to meet us at our hotel in Warsaw and personally take us to the train station and platform to take our train onwards to Krakow, so we wouldn't be confused by the multiplicity of choices and miss our train. What a person!

Had God looked down on me and said, "For Fred to go back to Sokolow to see where his parents and ancestors grew up and for him to go to see the tragedy of Treblinka, I need to personally get him the best person to take him there," he would have picked Kris and told him, "Get him there and take care of him for me."

What a day!

Day 4: Saturday, September 17th, 2011

Couldn't sleep most of the night. Did I get any sleep? Tossed and turned; thinking back to those terrible times; worried about our safety, even now? Got up after 8 am, had breakfast, then came back to the room to take a shower and catch up on my diary. Amazingly, Kris called the hotel, and they brought me their phone. He already had choices for our Monday train travel to Krakow and would meet us at the hotel in Warsaw at 7:30 am to get us there.

Kasia sent me an email that morning, saying her son was sick. She would meet us at the hotel at noon to show us Sokolow.

We met Kasia at noon for the first time. Since her son was still sick, we only have a couple hours with her, but that apparently was not enough for her to show us everything. We walk from the hotel to the center of the city.

Nice houses on the way, some look upscale. Occasionally though, we see what looks like an old building from a bygone era. We pass something on the left that claims to be a museum with an iron fence around it. It's a big and very unusual windmill structure we find in front of the main house and all kinds of things around it. Kasia tells us this is the "tomb-stone museum," meaning this is where the man lives who has collected (rescued?) Jewish tombstones that were left after the war. We knew about this. The Nazis ransacked the cemeteries in Sokolow (and throughout Europe), destroying them and taking the tombstones, breaking them up and using them for building materials, inserting them into roads, walls, buildings, etc., to destroy all evidence that the Jewish people ever existed. To wipe out all memories of our existence and our past. This man recovered some of these from around Sokolow and has them displayed as a kind of museum. This is part of what I wanted to visit and Kasia tells me we can see this later.

We finally get near the center and see what looks like a small park with trees and benches, surrounded by small shops. This is what is left of what was before the *Grosser Markt* (Large Market). I have some old pictures of this, and this is where my grandmother once earned money by bringing geese that she'd bought from a farmer to the market to sell. This is where she earned enough money to live and when she and her two daughters, Leah and Freyde (my mother) came back to Sokolow from Warsaw to live with her relatives after my grandmother's husband Avram died and his flower factory was sold. I could tell Kasia a lot about that, but not here and not now. I took lots of pictures of that space.

We walk a little further, and less than a block away is an even smaller square. This is where the *Kleiner Markt* (Small Market) was. My mother lived not far from here on the same street. Today, this looks something like a small space between rows of shops. No sign of what it once was.

Kasia points and explains to me that one area of the shops used to be an area where shoes were plied and repaired. I can visualize Velvul Lopata working here. It feels very emotional to be in this space and feel that the spirits of those who once lived and worked here are around me – wrapping themselves around me. A very few managed to escape to life and better lives and some were never able to get away, who had lived wonderful Jewish lives all around here, but were trapped in the Hitler war machine and perished savagely. It's hard to talk while we walk around here.

We continue. Kasia shows us where the old synagogue used to be and where the structure still stands, but is now incorporated into a larger business building, the exterior spruced up, fresh stucco applied, painted, but I can see the soul of what once was still shining through. Nearby is the old *Beth Medrash* (House of Study) where students and their rabbis worked and studied. In my mind's eye, I can see those *bocher* (students) and their rebbe's sitting and studying, debating and working together with old yellow Yiddish books piled up and books all around in bookcases. How much was lost!

I don't know why, but Kasia is very reverential as she tells us about what was here. She shows us what was here, and what was there. She says with some deep feeling, "This was once a synagogue. Today there are no Jews in Sokolow, so it doesn't need a synagogue."

The "March of Time" and with the bustling shops all around: the "March of Progress."

We continue. The town has grown; the old houses have mostly disappeared although you can see many "hiding" under new exteriors. It's interesting when you look for traces of the old with the new. I took a lot of pictures! It felt strange that, somehow, it was a beautiful day to walk around. We visited the old cemetery, now a park, with only trees left to be witnesses to the souls who are still wandering around. It's a peaceful place. We visited the new cemetery, some distance from the town, with no trace of it at all anymore. Only mournful weeds. Time left it to forget.

We come back into the town, and Kasia takes us to a house with a yard that has some unusual feature around it. She tells us that this is where the last Jews were buried. They were forced to dispose of the last Jews in the town, told they would be allowed to live but, when they were done, they themselves were taken to this place, shot and buried in a mass grave. Today this is a kind of memorial to them; a small tree planted here, some circular plots for flowers to mark this place. No flowers there; only overgrown weeds. The memory of this will be allowed to disappear. Maybe only Kasia is here to make the town reconcile with its past and keep the memories alive.

I hadn't much noticed until now, but Kasia wears a necklace with the Hebrew letter "Chi", which means life. We ask about that, and she smiles and says a friend gave it to her. She walks around with a bag covered with lettering in Hebrew – Yerushalayim. We ask and get the same answer. A friend gave it to her. We ask if the citizenry doesn't object to these displays of Jewish content, and if they don't bother her. She only says no. Along our walk, Kasia tells us about what once was and what now is but is somewhat subdued. She doesn't talk much beyond this. It can't be easy being the only one here who's dedicated to our memories when the town itself would rather forget.

Kasia goes back to her sick child, and we walk around some more. Rhoda's tired, and stays in a quiet shaded park reading while I go back to walk around the streets some more. More pictures. Now alone, I look and try to see inside what is around me. I can now see buildings with modern facades, fresh paint, fresh stucco, but when I look higher I can see old wooden windows, peeling paint, places on the walls where the stucco has fallen off, and the old walls shine through. Old red bricks; old painted wood. Second stories that look like they once were, before the building was renovated. Many of the old houses are still standing, ghosts of the past, but in new clothes but serving new purposes. And as I walk around and as we walk back to the hotel later, I see many signs of these. I take pictures and pictures. Sad that they weren't preserved; happy to see they're even still there, even though underneath it all. I realize that it's not realistic that the past stays as it was, forever to keep the memory alive for anyone who comes back, in Sokolow or in some old city in America. Time marches on. The needs of the present and the future take over keeping the memories of the past.

But the past here is different. It's tragic, and from the past to the present, when there is such a past, there must be a transition; a reconciliation with what ripped the past apart. And even though that has happened in many places, in Apartheid South Africa, in the American West, in the American South, in Krakow in Poland, it hasn't happened here, and the ghosts still circle. The town here, the mayor continues to try to ignore that once a thriving civilization was here, a community of good souls, and that not only the Nazis, but also some in the town played a role in its savage destruction. Forgiveness may be impossible, but reconciliation, repentance, *Teshuva* is always possible. And until that happens here, the ghosts remain and continue to look for peace, just as the town and its memories, whether today or in the future, will always have those ghosts in its past.

Maybe that's part of what drives Kasia. She wasn't born in Sokolow but grew up here. Neither she nor her parents were part of this dreadful past, but she lives here as a Sokolower, and maybe is the only one who knows that the past must be dealt with, certainly for the sake of the Jews, but also for the sake of the people of Sokolow.

I take many pictures to seal my memories. Sadness at the terrible ending. Profound appreciation to be walking the same streets my parents and ancestors walked. Some happiness to still see pieces of our past.

Walking back to the hotel, we see again the "Gravestone Cemetery." It's about 4:30 pm and it closes at 5 pm according to the sign. The gate is open. We go in. Around the edge of the yard, we see *mazevoth*, head-stones with Hebrew/Yiddish script. Some very worn and clearly old. Some so faded that they're barely readable. Some intact, some only remnants, fittingly as the Jews have been many times remnants. We see maybe six or eight of these. Pictures and pictures. Are these all there are? We continue toward the back and find more. Pictures. Pictures. And we continue all around the house and find even more. More pictures.

Recording names and people to be resurrected later from their anonymity. As we seem to have exhausted what we are looking at, we start to leave, but I want to thank the man who preserved these. Rhoda is reluctant, "Maybe he's just a crazy old guy. Let's leave."

"I can't do that."

I find the door to the house and ring the bell. No answer. I wait for a while and eventually an old man opens the door. I've clearly interrupted his supper. I can't speak Polish, and he can't speak English. I only know one Polish word: *Jenkuye*, thank you. I point around at the headstones and say "Jenkuye." I give him a hundred zlotis for his efforts. I point to some and beckon him to come with me. Some are upside down I want to tell him. He points back that he has to go inside and motions for me to wait. We wait. He comes back out with me, and I motion to the ones that are upside down. He recognizes what I mean. He responds that they're upside down because they're broken. They stand that way. He's clearly involved with us. He wants to show us more. He takes us to the back where there's a small locked hut with many locks and chains. He unlocks them and beckons us in.

Do we dare go in? Is it safe to do that? We go in. Inside, all kinds of war memorabilia, knives, and guns. All kinds of stuff. What is here for us to see anyway? We're not interested in war souvenirs. He takes us to a corner and takes out old, yellowed, newspapers in Yiddish print and shows them to us from the early 1930s. I can only read part of them. Pictures. Pictures. He shows us pictures of his mother and father and tells us they were trapped in the ghetto also.

"Jewish?"

"No."

He shows us an old Jewish coin. He brings us to another corner and takes out a book – looks like a fairly new book. He opens it and shows us a section that seems to describe what happened in the ghetto and has pictures. Skimming through the pictures, I take a photo of the cover and of the ISBN number in case I can get a copy somewhere, even though it's in Polish. I look at the author on the cover. It has his last name on it, and then I understand. He is the author of this! He's written this because of his parents who were trapped in the ghetto with the Jews. His preserving the tombstones is also part of preserving his memory of the time his parents also were treated as though they were Jews in the ghetto. I look at the back cover of the book. It's a picture of him as a younger man, and then I see more books next to this that he's also written.

We get ready to go as his wife comes out of the house, a pleasant older woman. We shake hands again and repeat "Jenkuye." We take pictures of us all, and then we leave.

Again, as many times on family treasure hunts before, at the end of a day, at the end of a story, we find TREASURE.

Back to our hotel. Rest. Dinner at the hotel. They couldn't be nicer to us. Why were we worried?

There's no question about the old calamities, the horrors, the disasters that occurred throughout the Shoah and that will forever be a ghost for these places and for me, but before that there was Jewish life for generations, and it was worthwhile for me to connect with some of those threads.

Sunday, September 18th, 2011

Woke up early. Finished packing. Nice breakfast. Took taxi to Sokolow bus station to take a bus to Warsaw. Big terminal with lots of signs in Polish about buses and directions. Multiple buses to Warsaw. One bus to Warsaw central station. Kasia met us to make sure we got on the right bus. It was more like a minibus. Not many people on it, and no place to put luggage, so I used the chairs.

Very bumpy busride with lots of potholes. Bus went through every little town on the way and picked up passengers at a number of these. The bus became crowded, and I had to move the suitcases off the seats.

Arrived at the big bus terminal in Warsaw. Couldn't find a taxi to go to hotel, so had to walk two kilometers with our suitcases. Coming back to Sheraton was great.

Picked up our big suitcases that we'd left behind in storage to swap clothes for the next leg – Krakow by train. We were going to Krakow because it was still too early to be in Sokolow for the memorial service on September 22nd.

Monday, September 19th, 2011

Kris met us outside the Sheraton at 7:15 am to go with us by taxi to the train station so we wouldn't wind up on the wrong train. He takes good care of us; we didn't even ask for any of this.

At the train station, Kris educated us on traveling by train in Poland. Went with us to the tracks, and we talked about the history of Jewish development in Poland and the east. He's so knowledgeable. He could give a lecture on the history and development of Jewish Communities in Eastern Europe.

Kris got us on the train to Kracow, and we said goodbye to him. We'll keep in touch for more research together.

It's hard as we ride not to look at the passing scenery this September and not remember that this September 69 years ago, the Jews of Eastern Europe were facing their end. Trying to find someplace to hide. To survive. Through bleary eyes, I see Jews running among the trees, trying to find a haystack to hide in, a small hut to get out of sight. Must have looked just like this many years ago. What a placid countryside today. What a different world. Fitting that it's grey and cloudy.

Arrival in Kracow about 10:30 am and take a taxi to the Cracowdays Hotel. Old building. Ring bell. Walk up three flights of what seem like age-worn steps to what is called the first floor. They buzz us in. Two nice young ladies to register us. They show us the room with the double bed, the kitchen area for breakfast, and they have a new computer with free Internet access to use. All nice and very reasonably priced. We leave our things, put on our rain gear, take an umbrella and head out to explore. We get one-day passes to their electric tram system and head for the old town. We just want to wander, to take in the buildings, the people, the sites, to get a feel for the city. Nice to walk around. Wonderful picture taking of people with umbrellas; rain shining through on city streets, beautiful old buildings. We find the old city square with crowds; beautiful horses all dressed up with buggies for rides in the huge square. An immense church that chimes beautifully at noon. A bugler that plays something sounding almost like taps. Little cafes all around. A large set of stalls with shops one after the other inside. We wander some more, and I find a little shop devoted entirely to chess sets hand carved in Poland with beautiful boards to hold each piece in place. So many to choose from. We buy a large and wonderfully carved large set for David. It will last lifetimes. A memento of our being in Poland.

We drop off our packages and then head back out again and take the tram to Kazimierz to see the old Jewish city. We find the ancient synagogue, never bombed during the war, but used by the Nazis for stables now fully restored to its former beauty. Today it's really only a museum, no religious services, but has wonderful displays of Jewish life, religion, and culture over the ages. Central to the exhibit, in the middle of the hall is a Torah scroll. How sad to see the Torah isolated in a cage and separated from its people. Here it serves to explain to non-Jews how the Jews studied the Torah and worshipped. If only the interest had been there before!

Interesting but sad. The Jews have gone and in this part of Poland there's a massive interest in their civilization and the culture they have lost. Lots of crowds, reading with real interest all about us. But hardly any Jews.

Kazimierz was where there was once a large Jewish life and a number of synagogues. We see a "tourist group," a bunch of Israeli kids, come by. Their leader talks to them about what existed here while a "guard" stands quietly on the side making sure all is well. The guide speaks to them of the greatness of the Jewish community that was here. It serves, for them, as a reminder of the importance of keeping Israel, their homeland, secure so that what happened here, to the communities and culture that thrived here, never happens again. In a nearby tiny park, we see a memorial plaque recognizing the horror that was perpetrated here.

There are six synagogues in this area now, with one, a Progressive Synagogue (Reform) fully active. We'll visit that one tomorrow. The others are mostly museums for historic interests. We visit one of the old ones on the square – the Ramu Synagogue – a small old one that was very active before the war. There is a *Shamash* (churchwarden/beadle) to sell admission, let people in, and have them don a *kippah* (skullcap). The old benches are still in place; the ark on the far wall with the Ten Commandments and the *Ner Tamid* (the eternal light), the *Bima* (podium for reading the Torah) in the middle according to old Sephardic tradition and "walled off" by an ornate fence with beautifully carved gates for entry for reading from the Torah. Beautiful!

The Ramu is directly adjacent to the old cemetery, and we enter to look around. There are many visitors, including Israeli youth tour-groups, Black Hat Chassidim, us. We learn later that the Germans pillaged and destroyed this cemetery as well, but that after the war, the town found many *mazevoth*, restored them and the graves the best they could. They found many that been broken apart, many used for paving stones or walls, and they reclaimed these as well and incorporated them into a memorial wall surrounding the cemetery. The wall is called the Wall of Tears. Seeing that grabs at your heart.

We see a cluster of Chassidim praying fervently at one gravesite and speak to them after they're done. They're from New York and traveled on this pilgrimage just to visit this site and pray at this *Zaddik's* (righteous, saintly man's) grave. They will stay three days, then fly back. Constant visitors here. Dedicated to their strongly held beliefs. Respect for someone who earned it by his deeds during his lifetime centuries ago. Something to think about.

We walk by and recognize a famous restaurant, "Ariel," and try to get dinner tickets to their Yiddish show afterwards tonight. Sold out. Come back tomorrow. Amazing to see that there is so much interest in what was decimated. We reserve seats for Tuesday night. We find another restaurant not much further on that also advertises dinner with a Yiddish program afterwards called *Vilde Felder* (Wild Fields). We make a reservation for dinner that we return to later, a wonderful restaurant with a nice choice of menus. We have dinner and a male singer with guitar and his female partner with fiddle play for us. She's fantastic not only the fiddle but also what looks like a balalaika. He sings Yiddish melodies. Most of them I know. When they take a break, a CD player continues with more Yiddish melodies. We ask them for some of our favorites.

"No can do." They haven't learned nor rehearsed them with the music he says. They're wonderful, but we're disappointed that they can only do the melodies they've memorized. It makes it seem more like canned music. Had they been Jewish musicians, they wouldn't have had to resort to memorization.

We finish, take the tram back to the hotel, and collapse exhausted from the day, but happy.

Tuesday, September 20th, 20III

The day starts cool and rainy. We leave our hotel and head toward the center of Krakow to walk around and see what the city was like. Lots of interesting old buildings and people with their umbrellas on their way to school and work. Our main reason for visiting Krakow was to visit Kazimierz, which had a long Jewish history since the 15th century, a good time for Jews here. We walk around the town heading toward the main market square, to acquaint ourselves with the city.

Lots of people are out, even with the rainy weather, enjoying each other's company at an outdoor restaurant. We see many interesting old buildings with amazing facades on their front. A huge one even had life-size statues in varied poses along its upper stories. The blend of the old structures and the new construction create an interesting contrast.

Although it's rainy and many, including us, are armed with umbrellas, the wonderful street scenes in the rain remind me of impressionist paintings.

Ronnie and I separate, she to explore the many shops, me to take pictures. It's a rainy day with many tourists, raincoats and umbrellas, kids running around, and many opportunities for interesting pictures. Even with the rain everyone is out and doing their business or just hanging out.

We have lunch in an underground restaurant, with a beautiful carved roof and amazing lighting, and afterwards, we walk around for some more exploring the city before returning to the hotel.

In the evening, we take one of the trams and return to the Kazimierz area to go to the Ariel Restaurant, but their program is delayed. We pick a different restaurant featuring music, this time music played by a group of three gypsies. Very relaxing and pleasant! Lots of pictures and video of the playing before heading back to the hotel. A break from our delving into history and the sadness of he Holocaust.

A good ending to the day!

Wednesday, September 21ˢᵗ, 2011

We start out early the next day in Krakow signing up for a tour of Jewish Krakow and its history: Jewish Heritage Sites. There are several bus tour choices and many buses and tourists opted for a daylong tour of Auschwitz/Birkenau. After having already been to Treblinka, seeing Auschwitz was something we just can't handle in the same trip.

We see several buildings with a Jewish heritage with old Hebrew lettering around their peeling second stories now undergoing repair for the interest of the current tourists.

Before WWII, Krakow had at least 90 synagogues serving a Jewish community of 60-80,000. Decimated by the Holocaust, today the Jewish population is under 1,000 but there are still multiple synagogues in this little area. We'd explored some of them on our own the day before: the Stara (now a museum), the Remu, but also the Izaaka, the Kupa, the Wolf Popper as well as the Progressive Synagogue. The Popper Synagogue was founded in 1620 and was once a splendid house of prayer but is today a youth community centre with a strong accent on programs and work-shops exploring the coexistence of Polish and Jewish cultures. I still have to ask if they can coexist.

We wander with the group. We can see that many of the buildings have undergone extensive renovation with new stucco and paint jobs, but when you look closer at the walls and at the roofing, you can see the old buildings revealed underneath all the new clothing. With many build-ings that hadn't undergone extensive renovations, much old brickwork can be easily seen, as well as peeling stucco and moss and vines growing on the buildings.

We see a very small plaque in three languages, Polish, English, Hebrew, proclaiming: "Place of meditation upon the martyrdom of 65,000 Polish citizens of Jewish nationality from Kracow and environs killed by the Nazis during WWII." In contrast we see signs on cafes and cabarets advertising Jewish cuisine and klezmer music. We wind up again at the Remu Synagogue with one of the signs proclaiming:

"In memory of the Jewish martyrs of Kracow who were annihilated by the German Nazis in the terrible period 1939-1945. EARTH DO NOT COVER THEIR BLOOD."

We walk again through the Remu Synagogue with extensive renovation under way. The Bema is beautiful in the center with magnificent ironwork surrounding the entrance to it; beautifully bound old Hebrew/Yiddish prayer books grace the bookcases in the room.

Immediately outside the chapel we see a whole wall of names with *Yahrzeit* (Memorial) plaques and many beautiful things.

We walk again through the adjacent cemetery and this time look more closely at the "Wall of Tears," with thousands of broken tombstones cemented together to make the wall, the tombstones having been recovered from the cemetery after the war and too broken to be put back in place. Sad.

While we walk around the cemetery, several Israeli youth groups also come through and stop at the grave of Rabbi Moses Isserles, a famous rabbi. The gravesite is enclosed in an iron grating to keep visitors away, but still there were stones of memory placed on top of the tombstone and little slips of paper inserted all around for good wishes. It's an eerie experience to walk around this area.

From there we go to a memorial of the Warsaw Ghetto. It's surprising to see that all that's left is a large memorial square with empty chairs signifying those who are no longer there. It's chilling to see this strange site surrounded by buildings and normal life in the city, the square empty, the chairs.

We drive a little outside the city to the site of the former concentration camp, Plaszow, built by the Nazi SS. It was a work camp, and many who were too weak to work were sent to Auschwitz.

Some 8,000 deaths also took place outside the camp's fences with prisoners trucked in three to four times weekly. The covered trucks from Krakow used to arrive in the morning. The condemned were walked into a trench of the hillside and shot, bodies then covered with dirt layer on layer. In early 1944 all corpses were exhumed and burned in a heap to hide the evidence. Witnesses later attested that 17 truckloads of human ashes were removed from the burning site and scattered over the area. When the Nazis realized that the Soviets were already approaching Krakow, they completely dismantled the camp, leaving an empty field in its place. The area which held the camp now consists of sparsely wooded hills and fields with one large memorial statue marking where the camp once stood, with an additional small plaque with only Hebrew writing located near the opposite end of the site.

The site today has a huge monument of six figures on top of a hill with their faces pointing down, their arms hanging down, and their bodies broken, with a path leading up to them with stones marking the path on the way to the top. It's a chilling site and difficult to imagine the misery and sorrow that surrounded this place. The spirits of the dead must still be circling the hill.

The German industrialist Oskar Schindler established an enamelware factory in Krakow, adjacent to Plaszow. He attempted to protect his Jewish workers, some 900 people, from abuse in Plaszow and from deportation to extermination camps. When he moved the factory and his Jewish work force to the Sudetenland (an area formerly in Czechoslovakia) in 1944, he prevented the deportation of more than 1,000 Jews.

From this horrible site, we go to the new Schindler's Factory Museum located in the administration building of the old enamelware factory.

The museum opened in June 2010 and tells the story of the Nazi occupation of Krakow in 1939-45. It combines photographs, artifacts and other traditional objects with interactive components, sound, set-piece reconstructions and film and photo projections that put you into the middle of everything that was going on.

Wonderful images of Jewish life before the war are portrayed, but nothing the same after. Documentation swirls all around us creating a vortex of the increasing persecution of the Jewish community leading eventually to horrible physical abuse, deportation and death.

In one section, film videos can be seen of executions by hanging of ordinary Polish citizens with the executioners being Jews who were forced to hang them so as to increase hatred amongst the population toward the Jews of the city. It's impossible to imagine the horrors of those who were trapped in this space and time and impossible to imagine a people who would force others to carry out such savagery on other human beings.

A labyrinthine route leads through exhibit sections based on chronology, specific themes, and the experiences of individuals. Personal testimony and interviews assault the senses throughout the exhibit. The choices people had to make in order to survive also form part of the story, including the efforts of one man, Oscar Schindler, whose humanity saved many, but in most instances there's only collaboration and betrayal. In the section devoted to Oscar Schindler, a list of lives saved and pictures of those who survived and went on after the war to have families to remember and persevere was a welcome relief.

I take many photographs and videos of the stark exhibits. The museum leaves us with chills but constitutes a necessary reminder of the horrible history of the time. We know this is not just a place for Jews; it's a place for Poles to see the devastation forced on the Jews and a place for all people, no matter what race or country, to be reminded of what they must guard against from ever happening again. We leave the museum and escape to the outside. It's an awesome and somber ending to the tour. It feels good to be back surrounded by normal life once again.

From here, we return to the hotel, collect our luggage, and take the train back to Warsaw arriving there late at night. We arrive back at the Sheraton Hotel in Warsaw, go to sleep or try to. Tomorrow is going to be the important day.

Thursday, September 22nd, 2011

Took a taxi from the hotel to the bus station. We were lucky to get a driver from the hotel who spoke English and who helped us find the exact bus for Sokolow at the station. Not only that, but we got there just in time to take the earlier bus than we had planned, and we left Warsaw at 9:30 am.

The bus was packed. It was a small minibus, and we were lucky that we were able to put our two suitcases in the back, because there was very little room inside. We got the last two seats with Rhoda sitting right over the rear wheel well. Pretty uncomfortable and we already knew that the road between Warsaw and Sokolow was full of ruts. We were surprised that there was a demand for a full bus, even a minibus, between these two cities.

The bus picked up speed. We figured it was going to be a quick ride. Amazingly, the bus picked up more passengers on the way, and they didn't have any place to sit. They stood in the aisle between seats while the bus jiggled and lurched its way down the road. It settled into its own routine and gave me time to look through the windows and reflect again on my own thoughts that were impossible for me to escape.

Today, 69 years ago, Jews were pulled from their homes, in Sokolow as well as surrounding towns. After being pushed more and more into a crowded Sokolow ghetto, they finally were forced out even from that refuge. As part of the horrible Nazi death machine, some were shot if they rebelled. Some stayed in bed waiting to be shot rather than be taken to Treblinka for unknown tortures and un-imaginable deaths. Others ran, looking for refuge in the unforgiving countryside. When rumors spread, when rampages of hideous and often drunken soldiers started their terror, some had tried to hide the night before. Where could they escape to? Where to hide?

Some stood like scarecrows inside haystacks in the fields, more like ghosts than humans, hoping they wouldn't be found and dragged away. Others even hid lying down in the cornfields, cornfields just like I saw outside my window today, pushing themselves into the ground, aiming to become part of the earth rather than people so as not to be found. All these horrors and more are described in the journal that I'd found, kept, and published later, *The March to Treblink(sp)a*, a horror itself to be read.

Riding the bus to Sokolow, I felt like I was back there on this day in 1942, looking for places to hide.

"Stay away from the road; not too close to a farmer's house; beware barking dogs. Look for dense bushes; trees to climb; even holes to bury myself in."

Where in all this we passed could there have been sanctuary? If it were me out there then, could I have found where to go, how to survive? The horror of this day long ago now. And how to think of all those then... the soldiers who saw us as vermin, not people, the people themselves who were afraid to be involved. What would we find at the end of today, now 69 years later in that very square where Jews were dragged out, some killed, the rest dragged to rail cars, jammed in, men, women, children to be taken to Treblinka and murdered?

And what of my father's mother, Chinka, and her children? What was happening to them exactly on that very day?Something I didn't think I'd ever know for sure but would learn later. It was painful to even imagine that.

Besides me and Rhoda, would any from the town want to know or care? Would it be just us alone? As we left for the minibus, I got an email from Kasia. Both the Chief Rabbi of Poland and the Ambassador from Israel to Poland are coming to join us at the ceremony, to say Kaddish together! In this small town, with so few of us to remember, would anyone else care? When I asked Kasia before, how many she thought would come, she said maybe 40. I had a hard time believing that at all in this time and place. I thought, we'll be lucky to have 10.

Finally, the bus came into Sokolow, and we found our way to a taxi stand nearby. It was, somehow, incongruously, a nice and mild September day with some clouds in the sky. Hardly a day when slaughter could have occurred.

The driver is nice; doesn't speak English but takes us to the hotel and offers to come back whenever we need. Leaves us a card. We check in and read our emails. We need to meet Kasia and Shoshi and David at 3 pm at the local registrar to see if we can find any records we had inquired about. We take our map and start to walk there. Can't find it; it's not where the map says it should be. We ask passers-by for help. They all try to help, even though most don't speak English. Nice people though. We find a young lady with some English. She not only points where to go, she's going to walk with us to make sure we don't miss our way. Maybe things are different now?

We find the building. Kasia in front; Shoshi and David and David's cousins. We hug and embrace each other. All on the same search. We go inside. Kasia says we must hurry. Any found records must be paid for in 15 minutes because they're going to close. They found many records for me, whereas I expected none! Brothers and sisters of my father. We hurry to pay for the papers, take our receipt and stamp back to the clerks. They type out the documents for us. No, we can't have an exact copy of the document; no, we can't take a picture of it. Why? These records are less than 100 years old and are protected by Polish privacy laws. After 100 years, they go to Siedlce where they're considered then open and where they assume the people are no longer alive. We know, ironically, that most of these people perished long ago. There's nothing any longer to protect, and they're our flesh and blood. Doesn't matter. Rules are rules.

We finish and go outside to talk. David L. tells Kasia he plans to video record the ceremony tonight. She's aghast. Upset. Says no. He argues with her. She cries and her son that she's brought along, cries too. She says, "You can't do this. It's sensitive enough. If you try to record this, everyone will be worried what you are about. They will stay away. You'll ruin everything I've worked for to bring this together. No!" And she rushes away.

It's beyond belief what we've witnessed. David and his cousin try to explain that they should be able to record this. It's an important historical event. As relatives they should have a right. I try to explain to them why they're wrong in what they're doing. David records our conversation on video.

I explain to David how hard Kasia has worked to bring the town to reconcile with their history. To get them to understand the treasure of the lives that were lost. To get them to put themselves into the picture and to begin to want to restore the memories and history of the Jewish lives that were so long an important part of this town. What's important is not to have a video; what's important is to support Kasia in bringing understanding and humanity back into this setting. David says he understands and won't record.

It's still several hours away and we go back to the hotel. We have until 6 pm to meet at the little market square where the horrors of that night and day began.

Memories/Reconciliation

At 5 pm, we take a taxi to the square. We find Kasia. We find Shoshi. David and his cousins are there. The old buildings are still mostly there, painted up in their new cosmetics. Pictures again. Only a few people around. I'm not surprised. In front of one of the stores, two speakers and microphones set up. Very unusual for this square! Normally in this time, just a small shopping area and parking.

Kasia tells me the storeowner volunteered to let her use his electrical power to attach this setup, but he doesn't want to be acknowledged. Still afraid?

6 pm now. More people arrive. Chief Rabbi and Israeli Ambassador to Poland not here yet. Kasia says they went to the mayor's office and are talking with him. Kasia says she's really nervous. I put my arm around her and tell her we're all there for her.

A boy scout troop dressed in full uniform marches in, very serious with boys of all ages. A girl scout troop is also there. A little girl, about five years old, dressed in pretty clothes, stands there already with flowers to give. Along one side of the square memorial candles are lit, in a row, on the street, ready to give witness. Parents with children are there to witness this. A police car comes patrolling, to make sure all is well? More people arrive. Now 6:30 pm. The Chief Rabbi and Ambassador arrive, and we're ready to start. We notice now that the Mayor has also come. This was very unexpected.

There are at least 100 people around us. All are serious. All waiting to be part of this history. The houses are all around, to be witnesses to the horror exactly 69 years ago. They're witnesses to a new generation trying to come to grips with their history. Kasia begins by introducing us and explains why we're all here tonight.

The ceremony starts and the Ambassador goes first. He speaks to the crowd very extensively in Polish, emotionally and emphasizing his words with very strong gestures. Kasia tells me that he's explaining exactly what happened here. He's using very strong, brutal language, matching the brutality of that time. In my mind, I can still hear the screaming of the parents and the crying of the children as they're being dragged out of their homes to go to their deaths. Very hard to take.

It's our turn after the Ambassador. We introduce ourselves to talk about my parents, their long history in this town, and the generations that lived here in peace until that night and day. We show them pictures of what they looked like, normal people trying to live normal lives. We say to them and Kasia translates,

My name is Fred Feldman, and my wife's name is Rhoda. We came from New Hampshire in the U.S. We came here to remember and honor the names of those of our family who died during WWII. My father, and his father, and many generations of his family were born here. My mother was born in Warsaw but grew up in Sokolow. Her mother and her mother's parents were born in Sokolow, as were many generations of our families.

When Germany occupied Poland in 1939, my mother was attacked. My father took her, her sister, their mother and the sister's fiancée and they escaped across the Bug River to the Russian zone. My father wanted to take his mother, two brothers, and sister but they refused to leave. They said, "How bad will it be here? You have nowhere to go. We can survive here." He sadly left them behind and spent the war running ahead of the German army. First, they fled all the way north and east to the Ural Mountains, 1,000 miles away, then 1,000 miles south to Crimea. When the German Army again approached, another 1,000 miles east to Azerbaijan where I was born in 1942. Along the way, their first son Abraham died as a baby in Makhachkala.

With the end of the war, my parents, my brother, and I returned to resettle-ment camps in southwestern Poland. We arrived in Kamienna Góra where we miraculously found my mother's sister and children who had gotten separated on their journey. My father returned to Sokolow to try to find his family. None had survived. All were murdered in Treblinka. If he and my mother had remained, none of us would have survived either.

We were put into DP camps in Austria and from there came to America in 1949. My mother worked in the home; my father worked for the railroad. My parents had five children: one who died during the war, me, a PhD scientist, my brother Irving, an accountant, my sister Charlotte, first a congressional aid and now working for women's rights in Africa, and my brother Boris, one of the top lawyers in the U.S. We brought pictures to show you our family, here in Sokolow and later.

1. *A photograph in Sokolow of my father with his mother, brother, and sisters*
2. *A wonderful photograph of my father's mother, Chinka, who my sister is named after*
3. *A photograph taken in Sokolow of my mother and two of her friends enjoying a beautiful day before the war*
4. *Two photographs of my mother and father here, sweethearts before the war*
5. *A beautiful photograph of my mother and her sister taken in Sokolow, two little sisters.*
6. *A photograph of my father's older brother Fischel who was an officer in the Polish army and later a picture of him and his wife Faiga. He and his wife and little boy, Ephrayim Yitzhak, named after his father, as I am, also were murdered in Treblinka.*
7. *A photograph of a Jewish youth group in Sokolow that my mother and father belonged to. All but three perished in Treblinka.*

I show you this, not to show you just who died, but to show you what life and love there was in this town before the war and the tragedy that took them away.

Last, I show you two pictures beyond this sadness. One is a picture of my parents, grown old with their children grown up, me and my brothers and sister. The last photograph is a picture of all those who came from my father and mother, by leaving, by surviving, by believing in a better future, and starting new lives in a new country.

The originals of these pictures (and more) are now in the Washington D.C. United States Holocaust Memorial Museum for the world to see.

We come today to grieve for other lives that never had a chance to fulfill their potential, to have children and grandchildren to make this a better world.

We take courage and are honored that you also came today to join us in this as we and you look for a world where hate is not accepted, and everyone looks to make a better life for himself and his neighbors in love.

When we finish, Shoshi talks about her family and finishes by reading a poem.

When this part of the ceremony is over, people come to us and want to look some more at the photographs. A lady and man come over to talk. She speaks some English and thanks us again and again for coming and showing all this, especially the pictures. She introduces the older man who's responsible for the Museum at Treblinka. He would like to make the pictures part of the exhibit at the Museum and wants to know if that is possible. I'm truly overwhelmed and honored and give him the pictures to take. Another woman comes over, a teacher who teaches the kids about the Holocaust also wants the pictures. It turns out that she was Kasia's teacher, and she also asked for these. I'm going to send them when I get back. She wants them for her school and their program. There are three more teachers there with their kids. They emphasize they want them to understand exactly what happened so they can tell their parents, so they can be part of making sure this never happens again.

We became so involved in talking with these people that it was hard to break away!

They wanted to keep talking and stay with us. In the meantime, the ceremony continues to the old cemetery where they take the lit memorial candles and where the Chief Rabbi chants El-*Mole Rachamim* (a Prayer of Mercy, a prayer for the soul of the departed). The little girl leaves the flowers there, and all go home.

What an overwhelming day.

Friday, September 23rd, 2011

I got up early and wrote a letter to Kasia before we left.

Dear Kasia,

We are so proud to be your friends. To say only congratulations for a successful ceremony is to not say enough. It's not just about bringing people together, from a time and place that was horrible, and where people couldn't be together. It's about sharing memories, so people could understand and could learn better to live together and respect each other. It's about learning how to live with the past and not ignore it so that the souls of the past and the souls of the living can be at rest.

There are few people in this world to be blessed to understand this and few who are then driven to act. To act, not to stand by and not to be silent is the lesson we learn from the past. And only in this way is the evil in the world defeated

I know and your friends know how difficult this challenge has been, and I hope it gets easier. The most important thing is to know that your real friends understand and appreciate you.

Personally, for me, I would never have come to Sokolow without you here, and how much I would have missed. Everywhere we go on our search for family, we find treasures. You are the treasure that is here.

Best personal regards, Fred

We figured everyone had already left. Had a late breakfast and finished the last of the packing to get ready to go to the bus station to head back to Warsaw for the weekend and the trip home.

We were surprised to see Shoshi and Kasia sitting downstairs at a table. Shoshi was going back on the same bus, and Kasia came to say good-bye. Kasia told us what a good response there had been to the ceremonies last night. She was going to collect what pictures she could from others who attended and share them with us. We told her that people asked us for copies of the photos we showed, and she said we could send them via her address. She also gave us the name of the man who took care of the Treblinka Museum and spoke highly of him. We committed to send pictures to her that she'll turn over to the school for their programs and courses on the Holocaust. It felt a lot like progress to both of us. Shoshi checked out and I took the opportunity to thank Kasia for all she had done for all of us and left her with some special thoughts for her to read later about what a unique person she is, not only for putting the memorial service together, but working to get people to understand each other and the wrongs of the past and to get them to learn how to live together and respect each other. We went into town to take the bus and leave Sokolow on the way to Warsaw.

As we drove on, I still couldn't help but to look at out the window at the countryside without thinking about that day after Yom Kippur 1942 as if it was now. I looked at every scene looking for where a Jew could hide, where he could escape to. It was hard to come back to the present day.

It was such a beautiful day outside, the countryside so bucolic. I passed well-manicured fields with cows chewing grass and making milk. Bales of hay waiting in the fields for winter food. Were those hiding places for Jews to be inside them back on that day? I passed beautiful forests, trees after trees, with little brush between them. Could Jews have hidden there? I saw many new houses, many brightly painted with modern windows and nice shutters and beautiful decoration. Near many of them, I saw little old homes that could have been a poor Jewish family's home. Many of these in disrepair; some almost falling. Many had been reclaimed and were still in use, with new lacy curtains in old windows, with new metal roofs to replace old tiles rotted away long ago, some even with satellite dishes to announce they belonged to this era, not the one 69 years ago that's so painful to remember.

We approached Warsaw, pulled into the bus station, and Shoshi headed for her hotel and we for ours. We decided together with Shoshi to meet later Friday evening for Kabbalah Shabbat services and a community dinner at the old Nozyk Synagogue where the Chief Rabbi presides. It's the only surviving prewar synagogue in Warsaw and was built in 1902 and restored after WWII. We had also gotten an invitation to the communal dinner that night.

We took a tram and got to the synagogue a little early and met Shoshi. The synagogue is huge, and it took us a while to see where to get in. Security. "We're a little early," I tell them.

The women go upstairs to the *mehitsa* (separation for women and men); I join the old guys downstairs. Not many there and there's a *tish* (table) set up down in front of us so I join them at the tish. I meet a fellow traveler. This one from Georgia. Georgia of the former USSR. He asks where I'm from and I tell him I'm from Azerbaijan. Double take! I don't look or talk like I'm from Azerbaijan. I'm now from New Hampshire. He's here on business. Sounds like Jewish life in Georgia is ok. More people dribble in. Will we have a minyan? Rabbi comes in, sees me, recognizes me and sits to talk. Very encouraged by the proceedings in Sokolow.

More people coming in, then an Israel Youth group. Many of them. Maybe 200. We'll have more than a minyan. They fill the pews; noise; laughter; boys downstairs; girls upstairs. The minyan starts and stops and starts and stops as the rabbi tries to keep the noise down. *Mincha* (afternoon service). Kabbalah Shabbat. Lines of dancing start and I join in. Young and old. Then *Maariv* (evening service). This is where my grandfather Avram Altman prayed before the war, my mother's father. Awesome to be in this time and place!

Service over; everyone mills around outside. We had arranged to join the regular community dinner, and we find our way to the community kitchen. More security. Rabbi comes and encircles his arm around us and ushers us through. We get to sit at his tish. Maybe around 30 of what look like regulars around us. A place of honor. I get to sit by him.

The evening over, we walked part way back, but I don't feel so well, chills. Rhoda and I say goodbye to Shoshi and take a taxi back to the hotel.

Saturday, September 24th, 2011

I hardly slept at all last night. I'm sick! We were going to go back to the synagogue for Shabbat morning services and were going to see Yale Reisner and his wife, Helice Lieberman there. Later that night, we were going to go to Selichot services at the reform temple. Cancelled everything and stayed in bed. Emailed our daughter-in-law Lauren for help. By afternoon, I had a fever of 100.5. Calling Lauren on the phone, she agreed with the medicines we're taking and advised us to be careful with eating. No city water; only purified bottled water. Ate nothing that day. Slept away most of it. Had to eat something. Nothing in the hotel compatible to eat. We finally got them to send up some dry toast and broth. Broth was almost only water; no salts; no spices. Toast thick and so dry, couldn't each much.

By evening, my temperature had risen to 103. Alarming. Called Lauren again. Took a Tylenol on top of the Aleve; 2 Cipro a day until I get better. I tried a sponge batch. Temperature still up. We stayed up more hours. Checked Temperature 101.5. Better. Went to sleep.

Sunday, September 25th, 2011

Up multiple times at night; not much sleep. Sick. Little breakfast to celebrate temperature coming down. Not interested in much at this point. Sleep.

By afternoon, felt a little better. We took a bus to the old city. Had to see something in Warsaw! Walked about two hours. Saw sights, old neat buildings. Kids playing. Couples walking in the sun. Felt lousy again; worse. Bus back to hotel. Sent Yale and Helice a note that we wouldn't be able to meet them Monday morning at the Jewish Historical Institute to review our trip.

By evening, still hadn't eaten anything. Nothing in the hotel. No restaurant open anyway on Sunday night and Room Service menu incompatible with what I had. Hotel desk had a number for ordering in. We ordered Chinese! I took some plain white rice.

Monday, September 26th, 2011

Back to normal. By afternoon decided to go out and walk around a little. Found a couple large parks nearby. Really nice park with lake and ducks, a stream, trees, and nice little bridge. Very peaceful. Just what I needed.

Packed and got ready to leave for the airport at 7 am.

Didn't get to see much of Warsaw. Some old buildings were neat with all kinds of sculptured figures on them, larger than life size, some holding up the buildings. Many old ugly buildings from the long brutish Soviet occupation of Poland after the war. Lots of churches. Really saw little Jewish content here. Felt like a stranger in a strange land. But then, we didn't give it a chance to find that little treasure that we always find at the end of a day of exploration.

When I think back on this trip, it wasn't just a trip, it was a journey. A journey from my parents' time to mine; a journey to find and to understand; to appreciate a world that doesn't exist anymore; a journey to connect my roots firmly with their tree; a journey to find those who without the searching would disappear forever; a journey to mourn their end; and a journey to exult in the richness of culture and family that they had. A journey of a lifetime to show to, and explain to, those without one foot in the past and another in the present, by one born in the one and propelled into the other so that they too can come to appreciate where they came from, what they're missing, and what has to be preserved for the future.

The 36 Righteous

We got back to the United States just in time for the High Holidays (Rosh Hashanah and Yom Kippur), and our schedule came back to normal. Normal in a new sense though. Now retired from my job that I'd held for over 30 years, I could really focus on achieving those personal goals that I'd had for all that time. I had already completed the detailed history and very personal discussions with my father of his perilous journey before the family got to America. I had transcribed every interview I'd conducted with him and my mother. Even more, I had finished that very moving video documentary of their lives that would serve as a testament to what they had endured. And beyond that, now I had visited their home village, had walked the streets that they'd walked as children, as sweethearts. I'd personally seen where their lives had unfolded and where many of their closest relatives, my relatives, had perished.

Now I could finally contribute personal service to the synagogues we belonged to, to teach of the history that my family and I had lived through and could delve in more detail into the family history, even further back than my father had known.

In short order, I scheduled a performance, a reading, for a Kristallnacht service of a very moving play called "Nightwords: A Midrash on the Holocaust" by David Roskies. Nightwords is a liturgical reading on the Holocaust. It requires 36 participants to take part in roles with selected poetic, philosophical, and biblical readings in Hebrew, Yiddish, and English that emphasize the discussion, debate, and rage felt in attempting to understand the Shoah or the absence of God's interventions, the chasms of emptiness during the Holocaust.

The play is based on a millennium old legend from the Jewish Talmud that tells us that there are 36 hidden righteous people who live ordinary and obscure lives, but the existence of the universe depends on each and every one of them. If a single one of them, the *Lamed-Vav* as they're called, did not exist, God would, in effect, lose interest in the world and all of what we consider to be reality would immediately disappear.

As soon as a Lamed-Vav dies, another one is immediately born. No Lamed-Vav knows who the others are. In fact, they often do not know that they themselves are a Lamed-Vav. They lead challenging lives, taking upon themselves the sorrows of the world. When they are needed, they perform acts of kindness, charity, bravery, and then immediately return to their ordinary lives, with never the realization that they have just accomplished an act that has caused the Divine to manifest in the world.

The 36 participants represent ordinary people such as a historian, poet, storyteller, clerk, teacher, soldier, prophet, clown, and others. In the play all stand in a circle while reciting their parts. Throughout the play there is a challenging interplay with God, trying to understand emptiness felt during the challenges and failures of history. In one very moving scene that dramatizes the death camps, each member tattoos a number (with a pen) on their neighbor. Each is a victim receiving the number; each is a perpetrator on their neighbor. Watching the silent progression of the receiving and giving of the numbers, I could see the realization of the horror of the act in every face present. Young inflicting the old; husband to wife to child to parent; religious or secular, everyone grasped and understood fully what they might only have read or heard about before.

Everyone was emotionally affected, and it was a momentous feeling to know that we were able to bring that understanding to our community. We repeated this again in later years with a more expanded community in an inter-religious setting during a Holocaust Memorial ceremony at a Catholic University with Jesus looking down on us from high on a wall seeming to ask, "How can man do this to man?" All my research, all my studies of the Holocaust could be summed up in this question.

This play helped make real to those today, so separated from those events, the horror and the questions and the dilemma of retaining faith against devastation like that and to never let history be forgotten.

There was still much more to do to find my family, my family from long before the horrors of the Holocaust. I turned even more to exploring the avenues and access points of genealogy and joined the Jewish Genealogy Society of Greater Boston. It became a major resource of learning and a significant help in getting documents translated that I'd discovered while in Poland.

When I learned that the International Association of Jewish Genealogy Societies (IAJGS) existed and that the next international meeting was scheduled for Boston in August 2013, I registered for it. With Rhoda also now intensely interested in exploring family histories, hers and mine, I gave her that registration as her birthday present. It catalyzed the exploration of her history even more and gave us both more tools and methods for searching and documenting our discoveries.

During the program, I suddenly got a message that someone else was exploring connections to the same ancestor as I, to my great grandfather Yisroel Hersch Rosenbaum. This was a descendant who originated from the brother of my great grandfather. I had not even known of that brother's existence. This link was a validation of the family tree that I had already documented. Additionally, it doubled the size of the tree and provided me with access to others who were exploring the same roots as I. How exciting that in my lifetime I could be finding and exploring my heritage with relatives I had not known, those who had lived more than 150 years ago. My father would have been astonished. Even with all that, so much more to understand, so much more to do.

Despite my best intentions to keep going, to keep learning, I got a telephone call asking me to provide consulting help to a pharmaceutical company having problems in product development. It was painful to split myself again between my two interests, but I responded, and travel and science again intervened. I was diverted from my main love of family history for another eight months but finally stopped and tried to return to my mission. No matter how much you plan though, fate has a way of interfering. There is an old Yiddish saying, *"Man tracht un Got lacht,"* which translates loosely to, "People can plan as much as they want to, but God laughs at their meager planning."

A Tragic Loss – Brother-in-Law David

My brother-in-law, David Jacobs, beloved husband of my sister Charlotte, unexpectedly passed away in early 2014, and darkness came down on our family. Rhoda and I spent a week mourning with Charlotte and David's brother Johnnie at Charlotte's home. David had apparently known – although we didn't – that he had a dangerous condition that could take him at any time and that was inoperable, yet he lived his life to the fullest helping others in his mission as a doctor. At his funeral, we came to know and recognize many he had helped and saved, ordinary folks, diplomats, and scientists in the highest tiers of government. We had never known this. Throughout this entire phase of our life, we came to understand the importance of appreciating those who were close to us, but with whom we might never get to spend enough time to really appreciate them.

It was during this time that we really got to know David's brother as well, Johnnie Jacobs, who in his mourning very much wanted to know all those from his tree from which he and his brother had arisen. We helped him research and assemble the family tree of his and his brother's family while we helped each other deal with the trauma of loss.

IAJGS AND Family History Library / Moving Forward

Later that year, we had another opportunity to gain more tools in our search for family. The IAJGS was having their next annual meeting in July of 2014, and this one was going to be in Salt Lake City, Utah. We knew that Salt Lake City was the home of the Mormon Family History Library, the most famous family history library in the world. It's run by members of the Mormon Church whose mission includes scouring the world for records of family, birth records, marriage records, and death records and recording them on microfilm for world-wide access. I had already explored access to their records in a local Mormon family history library ten minutes from my house, had found records in Polish and obtained the microfilms to study the citations. This meeting would not only expand my learning on doing genealogy research, it would give me direct access to the full research capabilities at the library. And all research there was free, a phenomenal opportunity.

While there were many new ideas and approaches to conducting research presented at the meeting, I found two treasures that propelled everything I would do for the next several years. One was a tool. It was a scanner the size of a paperback book that would enable me to scan and copy hundreds of photographs in a short time. No longer would I need to drag a big machine with me for future interviews. Little did I know it would be a tool that would help me solve one of my oldest mysteries, that of my father's sister running away from home to Israel before the war.

The second treasure was a speaker, David Laskin, the lead plenary speaker of the entire conference who spoke on writing a book, *The Family: A Journey into the Heart of the Twentieth Century*. The book combined his research on his family, his genealogy, but also blended his discoveries into a memoir of his family. It clarified everything that had been burning inside me and set my direction for the next years.

The conference provided me with one set of treasures, but the Family History Library afforded me another set. We brought all our history research, files, notebooks, and computer, and spent a week following up questions we had from our prior research searching their microfilms. While we had translations of many of the documents we'd copied in Poland, we didn't have translations of many others we'd found from there and subsequently online. A major resource we found at the library was Mrs. Maria Eppich.

Mrs. Maria Eppich was the library's expert on Poland. Whenever visitors had questions on a record, a search, involving Poland, they were referred to her. It didn't take me long to find her, and I showed her my briefcase brimming with files of Polish ancestors, documents and lines and maps of relationships. On top of that, I had my computer always open to my Ancestry.com family history tree and files. What I looked for initially was her help in translating the records that I'd brought back from my visit to the Siedlce, Poland regional archive. Those records I'd printed and brought for help.

She was happy to help with translating and show me how to use the library's resources. I learned how to search using the massive banks of microfilm readers, to print and save even more documents and kept coming back to her with more work to do.

The translations started, but she was just one person, and there were many demands on her time. Coming back to her, day after day, she was able to finish translating the photos that I'd come with and, ultimately, we ran out of microfilms the library had scanned on the records in Sokolow. Some were just not there, but there had to be more records in Poland. If I'd only known to ask the Siedlce archivist, Anna Jaworek, about them while I was there!

Maria Eppich by now was fully engrossed in my project and also wanted to know what else we could find and said, "I'll call Anna in Poland. I'll explain what we're doing and ask her to do another search." I was amazed. I was nothing to either of these people and now one expert in Utah and another in Poland were going to collaborate to bring old dusty records back to life for me.

The next morning some more records showed up. Anna offered to help more but was leaving for the United States to do research for her doctoral program. But, she offered, I could continue to correspond with her for future needs. Maria Eppich also offered to continue to help through email even after I returned home. And, as a parting present, she showed me how to conduct more direct research into documents in Poland without ever leaving my computer from home and access not only references to people, but to the original documents themselves.

More and more I was able to expand my knowledge of those of my family who had lived so long before me, those in good times and in bad.

What resources I'd been able to uncover! In my search for family, for answers to potentially unanswerable questions in the vastness of history, I'd gained resources of people like Kasia, Katarzyna Markusz, a direct and vibrant link to the town and its Jewish life, someone with a passion for knowing what happened during the darkness of the Shoah. I'd found people like Anna Jaworek, keeper of the musty, but precious, tomes of records of long ago with the precious data of births, marriages, and deaths of those relatives I'd never known. And I'd found people at the

Mormon library like Maria Eppich, master of access and translation to those Polish documents and a willing contributor to my findings. I'd also found resources to the mountains of information, resources like Jewish-Gen.org with hundreds of databases and links to others immersed in searches like mine; resources like JRI-Poland (Jewish Records Indexing) and holdings of the Polish State Archives. Enough resources to engage me for a lifetime.

Part of the new information from these meetings landed on a close branch of my family tree, that of Aharon Schwarzbard, my paternal first cousin and one of the three children of my father's sister, Shoshana. Shoshana Felman (originally named Rojza Felman) was the one who had run away from home, from Sokolow Podlaski, to Israel, then called Palestine, in 1936 in one of the mysteries I struggled with and hadn't been able to solve. I was even more desperate to know what the circumstances were of her leaving her family? How did she get to Israel and what happened to her?

Aharon was always someone who maintained close ties to our family. He was always present at celebrations, never missing the chance to be present when we were mourning losses or tragedies. Aharon was a constant. He and his wife Lea could always be counted on to be with us whenever we needed them. And now a rare opportunity presented itself for us to be present at one of their celebrations, a wedding shower for the youngest of their family, Limor.

We drove to their house in the spring of 2016 before the shower armed with our new genealogy tools to also take advantage of the opportunity to spend a week with Aharon and Lea to get them involved in tracing their pieces of family history and help them get started. Little did I know of the connections and results that would bring.

Always looking for historic pictures of the family, I started with that. "Aharon, do you have any old pictures from your mother or father that go back to when they were in Poland?" That was a question I'd asked him and his siblings many times before but never gotten an answer that led me anywhere.

"Sure, I have many," he said. "Over a hundred! Do you want to see them? What do you want to do?"

"Well, first, we're going to work on your family tree and fill in whatever information, names, dates, and stories you have that I don't already have on the tree I started for you. Then we're going to scan your pictures and put them on my genealogy web site to make sure they're protected from ever getting lost."

I already had much of Aharon's family incorporated in my family tree, even five generations back from his father and four generations back from his mother. Aharon had never seen the information on those generations and as we spoke of his ancestors, the stories of his generations came forth.

When his wife, Lea, saw what we had done, she said plaintively, "Wait a minute. What about me? I have pictures. I have family. Do the same thing for me," and she brought forth a large envelope full of photos for scanning and started to talk about her family. We started doing research to fill in a family tree for her, one that no one on her side of the family had ever started. We found people and names going back from both her father, Moniek Nissenbaum, and mother, Faiga Malach going back three generations on her father's side and two generations on her mother's. But Lea had over 300 photographs to scan of her family, and that took all the rest of the time we had with them. I posted all the scans of their original photographs on separate genealogy galleries on the Internet for them for their use and for posterity. The family history/genealogy bug had bitten them too, especially Lea, and she started her own research. After Limor's shower, we left planning to join with them again to separately identify all those in the photographs and, especially, mine the stories of their family to preserve them as well. Ultimately, time and fate intervened, and greater priorities and concerns prevented that.

PART IV

CONNECTING THE THREADS

13

STARTING TO FIND ANSWERS

What Happened to Chinka?

So much accomplished. So many people interviewed. So much history unearthed. So many relatives reclaimed. But still strong and urgent questions continued to drive me. What had finally happened to my father's mother, Chinka, after he left home, and she'd been forced into a degenerating and devastating ghetto? What had motivated his sister, Shoshana, before that, to run away from home? How had she finally been able to get to Israel/Palestine and what happened to her there while wars raged everywhere? Had time been successful in finally burying all answers to those or was there still any hope to find out?

Beyond any expectation, one answer would come in a few months; the other would take much more effort but would come also in a short few years.

The Thunderbolt

It came in the middle of the night. I was thunderstruck when I opened an email from Kasia. I don't know and never found out what motivated her, but she'd gone to the archive in Siedlce and done research on what happened in Sokolow on that terrible night of September 22nd, 1942. Was it even possible that anything at all could be found?

I already knew much of the history of that night and the days and nights leading up to it from my father and from reading the description by Simcha Poliakevitch who wrote *The March to Treblink(sp)a*, that I found in the Memorial Book to Sokolow published in 1946.

The ghetto had been filled far beyond its capacity. More and more captives of surrounding towns had been torn from their homes and thrown bewildered, confused, and distraught into the Sokolow ghetto, uncertain what fate ultimately had in store for them. And on September 22nd, 1942 the ghetto had been forcibly emptied, the Jews who resisted killed, and the rest sent to and murdered in Treblinka.

My father came to know that the family he'd left behind had been murdered. He had discovered that when he finally made his way back to Sokolow after the war, but he never knew exactly what happened to his mother Chinka. Neither did I. Not until I got the email from Kasia in 2014. I was astounded. It was a simple message.

"Dear Fred, I found in Siedlce Archive two court cases that might be interesting for you. I rewrote what is written there. Maybe you can translate it with Google translate. It's all attached here and in 2nd email.

Kasia

The second email immediately followed, and she summarized:

The first case started on June 22nd, 1946 and it says Szmul-Mendel Felman lived at the time in Sokolow at 42 Dluga Street. His lawyer was Stanislaw Lewartowski. Chinka (yes, in Polish it means Chinese woman) was married to Froim. Her parents were Boruch and Rojza Szwarcbart. She died on September 22nd, 1942 in Sokolow.

Witness Jan Michalski (pic number 007) and Wiktor Telenczuk (008) said that he had seen how Germans (sp) shot her.

2nd case is about Helena-Rozalia Felman, wife of Hercko Felman. She was born in Siedlce in 1901. Her father was Ajzyk Felman and mother Sora Grynberg.

Apparently, and unbeknownst to me in all the research that I had done, when my father returned to Sokolow in June 1946, he hired a lawyer in Sokolow, Stanislaw Lewartowski, to petition the court to find out what happened to his mother in 1942. The court found two witnesses to those horrific events, and they testified that they knew her and had seen how the Germans had shot her. She died in Sokolow while others were being dispatched to Treblinka. Additionally, the testimony showed that my father's uncle's wife, Helena Rozalia, was also shot during that time. Amongst the victims were many family members.

Attached to the emails were 16 original court documents including a document hiring the attorney with my father's signature and papers on every aspect of the testimony and court proceedings including finally a death certificate.

Finally, more than 60 years later, more than 10 years after my father died, I was able to find the truth to what happened to his mother. Did he ever know? There was never an indication that he had learned that the lawyer had indeed taken his plea to court, had found and forced witnesses to testify, and demanded the truth. The many times I interviewed my father and we discussed what happened to his family, when he pleaded that they leave also, when we talked about what he saw when he returned, he never responded that he knew. And he had never disclosed to me that he had been so bold as to hire a lawyer in that lawless time nor that he'd been notified at any time afterwards.

How could they have told him that the truth had been uncovered? When he left the town after much distress, he had no idea where he and the family would wind up. The lawyer must have been paid in advance. It is a testament to him that he proceeded with the case, that he didn't just pocket the money. It couldn't have been a popular thing for him to do in that town in 1946 when so many had been either bystanders or perpetrators to that inhuman action or simply profited from the remains of what had been left behind by those who had been murdered.

As I'd already experienced many times, at the end of a long interview, of discussions, of photographing documents, of seeking truth, a treasure finally reveals itself. Who could have known that after years of asking questions about what finally happened on that fateful night, that such a truth could have been revealed? Too late for my father to know, but for me it allowed me to finally put an end to that question, a sad ending, but at least a truth.

Joy in Cancun but Puzzle

Limor, beloved daughter of my first cousin Aharon and his wife Lea, was a single mother and she and her young daughter, Madison, were going to get married to Jeremy Eill in 2015. It wasn't only a marriage for the mom. The love between Madison and her new dad shone brighter than the sun that day on the beach and lit up all the faces that had come for the destination wedding in Cancun. Relatives and friends came from all over; even Israeli relatives had arrived for the event. It was a wonderful opportunity as well for a mini-vacation of sun and beach, especially in February, and Rhoda and I came and extended our stay, not only to enjoy the climate, the pool, the beach, but also to spend time with my first cousin Bat-Ami from Israel. Bat-Ami, the youngest child of my father's sister, Shoshana, had come for the wedding as had her husband Meier. She, especially, wanted to spend time with her brother Aharon and sister-in-law Lea. Their older brother Ephrayim had been unable to come, something that unfortunately caused a family rift.

It was inevitable that the conversation would turn to our common interest in our family history. It surprised no one when I started that conversation.

"You know I've been trying to find out for years if your mother and father had any old pictures from when they were growing up in Poland. You already know that I worked for years with interviewing my father about his experiences in Poland before and during the war. Did you ever talk with your mother and your father about that?"

Bat-Ami said, "Sure, we asked a lot of times, but Shoshana really didn't want to talk a lot about that. Her early life in Israel was tough, there were wars, and she had all she could do after she got married to raise her family. After a while, she did tell us what it was like growing up in Poland and how she came to Israel. All of us, me, Aharon, and Ephrayim were together as young children when she finally talked about it. And, yes, we do have a lot of pictures from her as well as her passport that she used to get to Israel."

I couldn't contain myself and announced, "There's a genealogy conference next summer in Israel. It's the conference we've been going to for the last few years. It's the annual conference of the IAJGS (International Association of Jewish Genealogy Societies) and this summer, it's going to be in Jerusalem. If we go, can we spend time with you scanning your pictures and hearing the stories from your mother? It's been too long since we were last in Israel. I'd especially love to see Shoshana's passport from Poland."

Bat-Ami and Meier were amazed. "Sure, we'd love you to come. We'll spend as much time with you as you'd like. Just let us know what you'd like to see. That would be fantastic. What do you have in mind?"

"Well, we'll register for the meetings. They'll take about a week and we'll be in Jerusalem for those. Maybe we could come a week before or stay a week or so after and go to Tel Aviv. It's a chance to do more genealogy research, to spend time with you and Ephrayim and finally do what I've wanted to do for years. I'll work up a schedule and get back to you."

"In the meantime, though, I want to tell you that one of the things I'll want to talk about is the time that your mother, ran away from home to go to Israel. I asked my father about that many times, and it's a puzzle to me what happened. That's one of the things I've been trying to understand for years. Did she ever talk about that? What my father told me was that when she ran away from home, his mother Chinka sent him after her to Warsaw and that he couldn't find her. He had to go back home and tell his mother. What did you hear from your mother?"

Bat-Ami was puzzled. "It's not at all what our mother told us. When she ran away her mother accused her of stealing money and sent police after her, but she put on a disguise and got away. It's completely different from what you told me. I don't understand. We'll have to talk about this much more."

"Now we have to go to Israel to figure that out! We'll spend time with you. We'll spend time with Ephrayim. Besides the pictures, I have to know what happened. This is the final piece of a mystery that I've been trying to understand for decades."

The time together was just too short. Blue cloudless skies, shimmering water, multiple pools to sit by and read, relax. It was wonderful, but too soon we parted, vowing to explore in much more detail the discrepancies that emerged from our brief discussion.

There wasn't much time for planning. As it turned out, we found out that my brother Boris and his family also had planned to be in Jerusalem for a week, a week before the time of the IAJGS conference. How could we go to Israel and miss my brother and his family by a week?

We, therefore, made plans for Rhoda and me to spend a month on our trip. We'd arrive the week before to spend time with Boris and his family in Jerusalem, then visit Bat-Ami and Ephrayim for a week in Tel Aviv, return to Jerusalem for a week of genealogy meetings, and return again to Tel Aviv for final family discussions and even a little rest and relaxation. Time to combine both research and family. What could be better?

14

JERUSALEM

The Old City

The week in Jerusalem with Boris and his family is wonderful. Our hotel is a short distance from Boris's and the Old City, and we walk everywhere. Boris has been many times to Jerusalem and knows the Old City well, including several of the Arab shopkeepers in the Old City's narrow streets. For me, it's an opportunity to really enjoy my surroundings for themselves, without forever being driven to search, to explore, to understand. Time for that later after Boris and his family return home.

Walking to the Old City, Rhoda and I pass through a marvel of an outdoor shopping center, Mamila Mall. It's the first time I've seen this, and I'm in awe of what's been created here. It's incredible with white marble walls and statues and art works lining the path from one end of the mall to its exit into the Old City. I love what I see spread out before us.

As soon as we enter the mall boulevard, we see a group of life-size statues of musicians, one playing a bass, one a guitar, one a violin and two playing horns, a trumpet and a trombone. They're portrayed so realistically, you can almost hear the music pouring out of them.

A few steps later, a bronze woman gymnast with her arm stretching to the sky. Congruously, a life-size wooden American Indian figure, then two bronze wrestlers locked in combat. Two huge rams rearing on their hind feet and horns clashing together, a lumberman precariously balancing himself on logs; a green bust of a woman rising out of waves, a young girl on a swing with the two ropes holding the swing and her descending out of the sky. All these works are apparently available to purchase. Spectacular art pieces by very talented people. Did the artists intend for their works to have deep underlying meaning? I don't care. I love them just as they are. These works must change regularly as buyers respond.

At the end of the boulevard, a cascade of steps leads up, and at the top we spill out with a spectacular view of the Old City walls with the Jaffa Gate welcoming us into the plaza. What a sight: Orthodox Jewish women in long black skirts with their hair hidden under caps and pushing baby buggies with other children clinging on; Arab men in traditional garb; cars careening down narrow streets; tourists everywhere; orthodox men in black hats and long black coats, bearded and with side locks swinging from their hair; Arab women in garb of all kinds, most with their hair completely covered, many wearing long, dark dresses, younger ones dressed in bright colors. We chose to exit the plaza and the careening cars and head down the age-worn steps into the narrow alleyways of the city where merchants of all types ply their wares from narrow stalls and cubbyholes. We're assaulted by a riot of colors and noise.

We see people walking in groups like us, merchants noisily hawking their wares, some in Arabic, some in Hebrew, some in English, all depending on how they assess who's passing in front of them, who might be entreated to stop and look and maybe buy. It's totally fascinating, not only to look at the exotic things for sale, but even to people-watch this enormous assemblage of humanity.

We can't help coming back again and again to these streets, these alleyways bustling with people. When we're here on Friday, these streets amass with people so that there's hardly room for movement. It's the end of Ramadan, the holy month for Islam and, fortuitously, it's coming to the hour when the Jewish Sabbath comes, a holy time for both religions. What's most amazing is that everyone seems to get along. How different from the constant screaming headlines of conflict and hate. The merchants don't seem to care to whom they sell, the Arabs and Jews apparently occupy the space amicably. Each goes about preparing for what's important to him and they seem to be able to coexist, at least for now. If only the governments could adopt this attitude. If only the world could behave in the same way. It's a joy to see. We feel no sense of apprehension or fear by being surrounded by this diversity.

On one of our visits to the Old City, Boris takes us with one of the Arab shopkeepers he knows on a special tour of the rooftops above the Old City split into four quarters: Jewish, Christian, Muslim, and Armenian. The bustle of the souks below can hardly be seen or heard from this vantage point. It's so calm and quiet and peaceful here, so different from the conflicts that we always hear about. It's such a pleasure to just enjoy the day.

It's a beautiful day even with the sun beating down mercilessly on us. The fleecy clouds drift sleepily across the bright blue sky and the white Jerusalem stone and the red-tiled roofs of the buildings that are a hallmark of this spectacular city. Looking around we see spires and minarets, churches and temples, the golden Dome of the Rock and, farther beyond, The Mount of Olives. Is there really not enough to share to make everyone happy?

It's marvellous exploring all this with family. We've never really had a chance to spend time together like this. Boris's kids climb over the rooftops, scale walls between the buildings, hurdle deep crevasses between buildings to get better views, much more daring than Rhoda and me. They cluster together to get their photos taken with the golden Dome as a backdrop. So do Rhoda and I. I even get a picture taken of Boris and me against that setting. In one of those, I get a big kiss on the face from what used to be my baby brother. I couldn't be happier. We come back many times to explore the Old City.

We meander down narrow alleyways, we follow the Way of the Cross, the Via Dolorosa, to the Church of the Holy Sepulchre where Jesus is said to have been buried and was resurrected. What a magnificent and awe-inspiring edifice with soaring arches, towering balconies, magnificent mosaics, and brilliant light spilling through the dramatic dome high above. Long lines of people in many forms of dress line up to view and give tribute to their religion.

We come back to the Old City another day, again going through the Mamila Mall on the way. We already see changes in the artwork and sculpture that lines the boulevard. Every piece of art appears to be for sale, and we see new things amongst what we saw before. We still see the four musicians inviting people into the mall, but this time, we see small children in their space, dancing to the silent music that they hear. They make the dead sculptures live. How appropriate! We see the wooden Indian again, but this time we notice that he's standing in front of a smoke shop. Again, how appropriate. Just like the old West. We see the bronze wrestlers again. Still locked together, neither has won yet.

Something new – we see a black iron crow standing atop a hollowed out grinning face. The crow screams at the crowd going by while the face, immobile, just grins. Further along, a man is perched on a high stool, dressed in jeans, tee shirt and cap. He has his oil palette in hand and is concentrating deeply in his painting. The painting rests on a wooden tripod and he's dabbing at the canvas with a small brush. Rhoda goes to stand behind him to see what he's painting. It's a clown. She admires his work, then realizes the painter isn't real. He and his work are a life-size statue now on the boulevard. It's so lifelike that it attracts the curious to watch him do his painting until they realize that it never changes and that he's just a statue.

Further down, more new things. A brilliantly colored chicken, red beak, yellow feathers, pink eyelids, green and brown tail feathers is drinking with a brown straw from a deep blue mug held in purple wing/hands. It's sitting on a high table and looks so smug and proud of itself. An egg appears to be dropping down from the table and down below is an egg that's already been opened and a tiny yellow chick, eyes wide open and bright orange beak is just emerging. Whimsical!

It isn't our intention to explore these works at all. We're only heading toward the Old City again, but it's impossible to merely walk by and not marvel at all the creativity. We meet another beautiful work looking like it was sculpted from wood. It looks like the trunk of a large tree with a nude woman figure kneeling on top, head down, with a massive cascade of braided hair, hanging all the way down the trunk. Climbing up the trunk is a smaller figure of a nude male, using the cabled hair to help him climb upward, and, at the bottom of the tree trunk is a small nude figure, possibly a child holding on to the trunk. Is it a variant of the story of how the world was populated by the original man and woman? Whatever the story, however it was interpreted, it is stunning.

We feel like figures in the Mussorgsky symphony "Pictures at an Exhibition," making our way from scene to scene. In the next promenading, we see a baby, sculpted from stone, in a small hammock-like blanket, one arm protruding, the other cradling the head in smiling sleep. The hammock-cradle-cloth is tied to what looks like a wooden branch suspended in the sky with no apparent connection to anything. What holds the entire sculpture up we wonder? A few steps ahead, another work, a young woman on a swing. She looks like she's ready to take off, the wind ruffling her short skirt, the tension in her legs ready to push off, her arms straining at the ropes of the swing. The ropes here also descend from the sky and there's no discerning what holds the whole display in place. Again wonderful. What beauty, what creativity these extraordinary artists display. How awesome, I think, what that world of immigrants to this country has contributed, has achieved.

Today we visit the museum of The Tower of David in the medieval citadel of the same name. It's near the Jaffa Gate where we entered after the Mamila Mall. The Museum displays the history of Jerusalem from the time that there was any evidence of the city throughout all its evolution and through it the impact of three religions that influenced it. The Tower itself is spectacular, and we have a breathtaking 360-degree view of the Old City and its four quarters, the new neighborhoods, the Mount of Olives, Mount Scopus, the Judean Desert and the Dead Sea in the distance.

The exhibits in the museum depict 4,000 years of Jerusalem's history, from its earliest beginnings as a Canaanite city to modern times. Using maps, video, holograms, and models, the exhibit rooms show Jerusalem under its various rulers. Standing here I could see how Palestine had been a bridge between cultures and empires; seeing all the rulers and religions that passed through this city makes me feel like I'm watching the march of time around me. It's truly inspiring and a place I could come back to time and time again.

We visit the Western Wall multiple times during this stay. I've been there before, but its awe inspiring every time to see it with its ancient stones crammed with letters of appeal to God stuck between them. Tourists of every stripe there, Jews of every conviction, many clothed in prayer shawls, praying intensively against the wall. On one side, only men allowed; on the other side of a tall fence, a place where the women can also pray in front of their section of the wall separated from the men. What a diversity of people here, but all drawn to this vestige from the second Temple.

While I watch, a small group of Israeli soldiers march through the plaza dressed in fatigues, each carrying a lot of gear, each with a deadly rifle. No one seems to pay any attention to them. So commonplace here for civilians and military, police and soldiers to mix everywhere. Whether a Jew or Arab, this is commonplace here. It's a fact of life and ordinary life goes on, but how wonderful if it were no longer necessary.

On one of the days, we go with Boris and his group to the Mahane Yehuda, called the *shuk* (market) to get something to eat. It's only about a 10-minute walk from the city center and it contains a warren of small aisles where there are dozens of stands, stalls, shops and small restaurants. It makes you dizzy to wander through with crowds of people jostling each other, especially on Friday when the Sabbath is going to start. There's everything there from cleaning supplies to live still-wriggling fish. The best part, though, is the cornucopia of different foods, especially Israeli and Middle Eastern delicacies. We see stalls of piles of olives, spices of all colors and scents and flavors, huge blocks of *halvah* (a soft, fudge-like candy made out of sesame paste), fresh fruit, figs, nuts, and dried fruits. We see mountains of peppers, yellow, red or green, avocados, oranges, lemons, grapes, luscious cherries, giant watermelons, whole and split in half, a riot of red. The bakers offer an enormous array of breads, roles, and challah breads braided in all shapes, fresh smelling and straight out of the ovens. Pastries tease us as we go by. "Buy me, buy me," everything screams.

We find a restaurant amidst the mass of humanity and eat an Israeli lunch of all kinds of salads and wonderful breads. I'm on overload, sensory and otherwise. I don't eat much and later discover I'm sick.

At night in my room, I develop a fever and severe gastric symptoms. I can't sleep, and we eventually call a doctor who comes to the room. We've brought us with antibiotics and gastro-intestinal medicines that he approves and recommends rest and fluids. Boris and family leave a day later to return to the U.S. while we, nevertheless, continue to our next destination in Tel Aviv. I'm still sick and can't wait to get to our lodging, a BNB apartment we rented in central Tel Aviv. We call our relatives, Bat-Ami and Meier and they recommend that I go to a clinic to be checked out. We also call our friend Jay who made *aliyah* (citizenship application) to Israel the year before, and he meets us and helps us get to the clinic. They tell me that besides the GI infection that I have that I'm severely dehydrated. Everyone kept telling me to drink lots of water. "The sun will dehydrate you." I did. I just didn't understand how much and that it meant constantly! They give me IV fluids to restore my fluid balance.

We stock up with lots of big bottles of water. I keep taking my medication. I still don't feel well. My head is hot, and my face is flushed, but there's no way I'm staying back. We're going to take a taxi and go on. How can I take it easy?

This is what I've been waiting for. This is really the core of what brought me on the trip. Not to be a tourist, although I loved it. Not to attend the Genealogy Conference, although I love those. No! To be with my cousins, Bat-Ami and Ephrayim. To finally try to answer my last puzzle. To get as much as I can of the history of their mother and any pictures that she might have left behind; to find out, if at all possible, what happened to their mother when she ran away from home. To find out how she managed to get to Israel. To find out what Shoshana knew about what was happening back home, with her mother Chinka, with her brother, my father, with the other siblings that had stayed behind. Everything else was secondary, and I hoped I might be able to find answers this time, especially with all the contradictions I'd heard when we were together in Cancun just months before. I wasn't going to let being sick stop me now.

The Interview – Bat Ami

It took about an hour for the cab to get to Bat Ami and her husband Meier's home. We sit around her big oval dining room table and Rhoda is again acting as cameraman, recording everything we're doing just as she has many times before. Bat Ami pulls out what pictures she has to show to us. And while she does that, she talks about when her mother Shoshana first came to Israel.

As she talks, I listen and open my laptop and go online to Ancestry.com to open my genealogy tree to track what we know about Shoshana's family history.

Bat Ami has a lot of pictures. I wince. They're not at all organized. They're random! And while we're starting to look and sort pictures, I show Bat Ami what I already know about her family using my Ancestry files.

Meier brings more documents. I'm blown away. He has both Bat Ami's father Rachmil and Shoshana's passport.

I can't believe it. "Wow. This is incredible!"

They had told me that they had Shoshana's passport. I didn't know that they had her husband's as well. I stop looking at the pile of pictures in front of me and flip through Shoshana's passport. It's her Polish passport, a timeworn blue cloth cover emblazoned with "Paszport and Rzecz-pospolita Polska" on the front. Inside the front cover is a sticker of a ship with Polish Palestine Line written (in English, no less) above a ship and an imprint of the name of the ship "Polonia" with the number 316 stamped on it. How can it be? It's apparently the ship that carried her to Palestine from wherever she boarded it.

I'm amazed that the pages of the passport are completely intact. There are many pages with writing, clear and legible, and stamps from official agencies and border crossings, a treasure-trove of historic importance for me.

The first page shows the passport owner, Felman, Rojza, Soshana's birth name (Rose Felman, but in its original Yiddish and in the Polish script). It's an emigration passport with a Polish stamp and it shows the owner's destination stamped: Palestine. The following pages show documentation and signatures. Rojza's date of birth, 1914, her town, Sokolow, and other information in Polish I don't understand. The next page is where the photograph once was pasted. Sadly, it's gone now. Underneath is her signature boldly written, and the page bears a Sokolow stamp. Following pages show documentation of Sokolow Podlaski and a date, July 6th, 1936 that must be a date of application for the visa and permission for a single trip abroad. This page goes back to when she was still home and apparently getting ready to leave. The passport showed an expiration date of July 6th, 1937, so if Rojza was going to change her mind about leaving, she had until that date.

To get to Palestine, she had to get British permission and there is a page covered with green and red stamps from the British Control Office, the governing body from their Warsaw office on July 10th, 1936 for a visa that gives her permission for entry to Palestine.

As I leaf forward, I see a page stamped in Warsaw on July 13th, 1936 by the Inspector for Emigration, which must be the date that she left, documenting a fact I didn't know before.

Some stamps in the book aren't in chronological order, not too surprising since some stamps came into the book wherever blank pages were available. But I can clearly track her journey.

It's amazing but the passport looks like it has all the information from when she left Poland until she arrived in Israel. I never imagined that I'd ever be able to see this. Original documentation! More information and more stories to keep!

Leaving Poland, she comes to a town called Sniatyn, a rail border crossing between Poland and Romania. The passport was stamped there on July 14th, 1936. By July 15th, she receives a visa and a stamp by the port police of Constanta, Romania on the Black Sea that is likely where she boards the ship. The ship presumably sails past Istanbul, Turkey through the Bosphorus Strait that ultimately separates Europe and Asia.

Her journey by ship takes four days, and she arrives in the port of Haifa on July 19th, 1936. Her passport is stamped by the Government of Palestine, Department of Immigration, and now allows her to remain permanently in Palestine as an immigrant. She's reached her destination!

My objective was to unearth my father's sister's journey and to learn and preserve as much of her story as I could. I had met her husband, Rachmil Schwarzbard on my trips to Israel and knew that he also originated from Poland, but I never knew much about him or how he had gotten to Palestine as well. It is totally unexpected that I get to see his passport also and learning of his trek is suddenly tantalizing. I never expected I would get that opportunity, yet here is his passport in front of me.

Rachmil was born in 1909, five years before Rojza. He was born in Ostrow Mazowiecka, a town not far from her (about 35 miles). Earlier than Rojza, he had reached the conclusion that he had to leave Poland for Palestine. His passport shows a passport application for Palestine on March 30th, 1933. Five years older than Rojza, it was evident to him even in 1933 that Europe was not safe for the Jews. He applied to get a British visa. It was issued on the 26th of June in 1933 in Warsaw for a single entry to Palestine. Two days later, he got a visa, also in Warsaw, for a single entry into Austria, and two days later, he secured a visa in Warsaw for a single entry into Czechoslovakia. He had planned a different route to Palestine than Roja eventually took. By July 1st, he got his emigration passport issued in Warsaw, and he was ready to leave. On his trip, the passport shows a stamp on July 31st, 1933 from a town by the name of Zebrzydowicach as well as a Visa stamp from Zebrzydowicach (on the border with Czechoslovakia).

A day later, August 1st, 1933, it's stamped in Breslow, another town on the border of Czechoslovakia and Austria). On August 1st, he enters Italy. He's there through August 30th when his passport shows an Italian Visa Stamp in Trieste, Italy.

The path he took to Palestine is clear now. From Warsaw, he headed southwest through Poland, entered Czechoslovakia and traveled through it into Austria then Italy where he headed to the port town of Trieste on the Adriatic Sea. From there, it was possible to catch a ship going from the Adriatic Sea through the Ionian Sea around Greece into the Mediterranean and head straight for Palestine, although it apparently took him a month to make those arrangements. He arrived in Haifa three years earlier than Rojza. Until I saw all this, I knew nothing of Rachmil's story, his passage out of Poland and into Palestine where he eventually encounters and marries Rojza, who changes her name and becomes Shoshana.

Ninety years after all of that time, I could finally see and document their journeys from Poland to Palestine! Incredible! Wonderful!

I go back to sorting the pictures. "They're a real jumble," I mutter.

While I'm working, Guy Joseph Levinger, one of Bat Ami and Meier's grandchildren is there and listening closely. He's 16 years old. While most youngsters of his age would have little interest in this history and these stories, Guy is very different. He's a very bright young man who's interested in all of this and who stays attentively throughout the entire time I'm there. My discussions with him later become fascinating especially as they relate to his great grandmother Shoshana's early life.

It's not my intent to scan every picture that Bat Ami has. I only want to scan the pictures from Poland or those of early life in Palestine/Israel. I also want to know a lot more still about Shoshana's leaving and her arrival in Palestine, but I have to do a lot of picture sorting first.

We multi-task. I sort while relating the genealogy I've uncovered of Bat Ami's family history that goes back to her great great grandparents. There's a lot that I found that she didn't know, about her grandparents or even about her mother Shoshana, my father's sister. She didn't know that her grandmother (her mother's mother) Chinka had a sister that had come to the U.S. in 1911 and that an entire branch of that family had grown up in New York and spread to other parts of the country. And in the telling, we weave the threads and stories of our histories and lives together.

While I relate Bat Ami's genealogy, Bat Ami speaks of what happened when Rojza arrived in Palestine. First, she acquired a new name, Shoshana. Shoshana knew almost no one in Palestine other than the few who had also left Poland as she did. But she knew Rachmil Schwarzbard. He was a cousin that she'd known from back home.

Our discussions veer back to Rojza's early life in Poland and the period of 1925-1935. Bat Ami talks about how the Jews from Palestine marshaled efforts to convince Jews in Europe to leave and emigrate. Those Jewish emissaries were called halutzim (pioneers), and their mission was to open the eyes of their fellows in Europe to the dangers they saw them facing and get them ready for a life in Palestine which they envisioned as an eventual Jewish state. Many of them went to small Jewish towns in Poland like Sokolow Podlaski or Ostrow and started Zionist youth groups. In those groups, they infused a love for Israel while teaching of the dangers brewing in the countries around them. I learn from both Bat Ami and, later, Ephrayim that Rojza joined those groups as a teenager and came to know more and more about the dangers starting in Germany, Austria, and countries around her.

As I separate out the pictures of Shoshana's early life in Poland, I'm astonished to find photographs relating to her interaction with the halutzim and pictures of her as a young woman with friends who shared her interests and concerns. While trying to sort out different piles of pictures, I come across several of Rojza as a young child in a schoolroom with other children and a teacher. So hard to put the puzzle of her early life and later life into a coherent whole, and Bat Ami's story drifts back and forth across time.

We come back to Rojza's first encounter with Rachmil. Rachmil had come to her town as a student living in her house while he studied. That was his first encounter with her. He was five years the senior and met her when she was about 15. Over the next years, and until he left for Palestine, he became very fond of her. Even after he immigrated to Palestine, he continued to correspond with her and, ultimately, when Rojza arrived in Haifa in 1936, he met her at the port and helped her get settled early on. He fell in love with her, but in their early encounters, she wasn't very responsive to his gestures of affection.

I'm still looking to bind several threads of story with the pictures that I can now see, and I'm deeply driven by several questions that I've never been able to get answered. What were the circumstances around Rojza/Shoshana's running away from home? What was the relationship between my father and his sister and how did they react when my father came to Israel, almost 50 years after he'd last seen her?

When I was with Bat Ami and Engel in Cancun five months before, I already knew that they had a different version of Shoshana's leaving Poland than I had from my father. Now I wanted to get their details and find why we had such different stories. The story that Bat Ami had was the same story I'd heard from her brother Aharon when we visited him in New York. And now, I heard that same story repeated by Bat Ami's grandson Guy who must have heard it also many times before.

Rojza had been brought up in a very religious home, but she had little interest in the rigidity. She was interested in what was going on around the world, especially in Europe. She was interested in Israel. And so, she took every opportunity to immerse herself in the activities of the youth group. She attended many of their meetings, sometimes, early on, leaving home for a night or two. She even attended programs, training sessions for a week at a time or more in other cities. She wanted to go to Israel. Her mother Chinka, her older brother Fischel didn't support her interests. They wanted her to stay home according to their traditions.

I'm still trying to sort and scan the old pictures and not really ready yet to discuss what happened when Rojza left home. Bat Ami and Guy can't wait though and now unroll their story to me and say, "Her brother Fischel and her mother Chinka didn't want Shoshana to go to Israel. On the day that she had decided to leave, the halutz movement knew that when she'd leave her mother would try to stop her. So, in anticipation of that, they told her, that to leave, she'd have to put on a disguise, so they wouldn't recognize her if they came after her. Chinka and Fischel learned that Shoshana had gone, contacted the police and told them that Shoshana stole things to motivate the police to go after her. In the meantime, Shoshana had dressed as a boy, wore a hat, sunglasses, and gone to the train. Once the train had started to leave and she couldn't be stopped, she took off her hat and disguise and waved back at her mother and Fischel who were at the train station saying, "Good-bye. I have to go."

This is so different than anything I've heard before about Shoshana's leaving home. I have a critical question and ask, "They were at the train? At the train station in Warsaw?"

They're all fully and dramatically engaged in this discussion now. Bat Ami and Guy are surprised at the question, but it's a critical question.

"No. No. The train station in Sokolow!"

"Her mother and brother and father are at the train station?"

Guy nods., "Yes."

Bat Ami contradicts him. "No. Not the father. The mother and the brother."

I ask, "When Shoshana told you this, how did she know that they called the police since she was already out of the house?"

The answers are vague. "No, she didn't know but she saw the police at the station. The families came to know exactly when the group was leaving. The halutz had told all the kids to dress up the same in disguise because they expected the parents would try to stop them."

I say to them, "You heard this story later in Israel long after the fact."

Bat Ami and Guy say that they heard the same story from Shoshana's friend that left with her and who also saw the police.

But I repeat my question, "How would the friend know that they'd called the police on her since she'd already also left?"

They answer, "Because the friend also saw the police at the station."

A lot of debate in Hebrew goes on for minutes back and forth between Bat Ami and Guy that they don't translate.

"I have two other stories about this to tell you that are important," I say, but they're not listening. They're still engaged in heavy debate with each other.

Then Guy says, "I might have missed some detail before that I just now got." And he relates more "evidence." "While Shoshana was waiting at the train station, there was an announcement on the loudspeaker that the police were looking for Rojza Felman and that if anyone saw her that they should stop her."

"Where does that part of the story come from?"

Guy says, "From Shoshana."

Bat Ami adds, "And from her friend."

I still hadn't even finished with sorting the pictures, but this discussion captured me, and I had to stop what I was doing and get completely involved now.

I say again, "I have two other stories about this to tell you," and they start to listen. One story is from my father. The other story is from your mother."

They're listening closely now.

"The story from my father I heard many times from him including the year before he died. The story from your mother is when I visited you at your house. The story from my father is that your mother ran away from home. They found out she had gone, and she had run away to Warsaw."

Bat Ami asks, "Why Warsaw?"

"To connect with a group to go to Israel. Chinka found that Shoshana had run away and told Mendel to go and find her and bring her back home."

Bat Ami, "Why?"

"Because she didn't want her to go to Palestine." I continue. "My father said, 'I went to the train station in Warsaw to find her and bring her back home, and I couldn't find her. And I went back home and said to Chinka, she's gone. I couldn't find her.' That's **story number 1** from my father. Many times, repeated! From your mother when I was here, I said to her, 'Here's the story I heard.' And I repeated all of that exactly. And she said, 'No, that's wrong!!' And I was shocked! She said 'Yes, I ran away from home. Yes, Chinka sent Mendel after me to bring me back. HE FOUND ME!'" And I can't go on. I hold my face in my hands and break down weeping silently.

Bat Ami and Guy are shocked. Rhoda tries to answer, but Guy stops her.

Still emotional, I recover enough to say, "Shoshana told me that my father found her in the train station in Warsaw, and he said to her 'You have to come back home.'"

I point at Bat Ami and say, "This is your mother talking to me! Your mother said again to me, 'It's true that I ran away from home, and

Chinka sent Mendel to find me. But it's not true that he didn't find me. He found me in a station in Warsaw and tried to convince me to go back home, and I said to him, 'No, I have to go! I'm going to Israel. I'm not coming back with you.' And he went back home and told his mother what my father later related to me many times, 'I couldn't find her. I couldn't bring her back home with me.' He couldn't tell Chinka that he'd found her and that she'd refused to return home.'"

Throughout all this, Bat Ami is looking closely at me, obviously distraught as I relate this story, and Guy is pensively listening, chewing on his thumb while he hears something new, something very different from what he's heard before.

I look at Bat Ami again and say, "Your mother told me that story! And my father never said to me that they accused her of stealing things. He never said anything about that. They wanted her home because they loved her. Your story is that Fischel went to look for her, not my father."

Bat Ami says, "I remember Fischel and Chinka."

"Your mother never said anything about that to me. Nothing about Fischel."

Bat Ami is very puzzled. "I remember Fischel and Chinka." She doesn't understand how these stories can be reconciled. "I don't understand, but what is the difference if Fischel went to get her or Mendel?"

I keep saying, "It's your mother who told me this story. When was this, what was the year that I was in Israel when Shoshana told me this?"

Bat Ami asks, "Was Shoshana good then? Was she fine?"

I say, "Yes, she was fine." (Was Bat Ami concerned that her mother was having problems with memory?)

They try to pin down the year when Shoshana told me that. It turns out that it was the year that our son David had his Bar Mitzvah in Israel. We had sat in Bat Ami's house. They recall that David had sat with Ephrayim's son and they'd played chess. David was 13 in December 1990. It was the summer of 1991 when we'd been there, and Shoshana had told me about her leaving. It was in 1991.

I turn back to Bat Ami. "I interviewed my father last in 2002. During that time, I said to him when we were talking about this again, 'You told me that you didn't find Shoshana. Shoshana told me that you had found her.' My father said, 'Yes. That's true.'"

"But Fred, does it matter? What's the difference?"

"The difference is that they never accused her of stealing. He was sent after her. He found her. That's my father's story. That's your mother's story. Both stories are the same."

Bat Ami still persists, "What's the difference?"

"Mendel stayed behind and was home after she left for years after that. The difference is that I never heard the story that she was accused of stealing. He would have told me that."

"Tomorrow you're going to visit Ephrayim. Ask him. He has the same story. What difference does it make?"

I laugh, "I guarantee you that tomorrow we're going to have the exact same discussion."

Bat Ami laughs also.

But I stop and say, "No. There's one more thing. If my father had convinced Shoshana to come home, she wouldn't have been a survivor."

And with that, there's an awed expression on Bat Ami's face as she realizes the impact of that one-time very fateful moment. And with that, also, I again can no longer control myself and again weep silently.

Bat Ami reaches out a hand to my shoulder and, with a smile, lovingly comforts me.

And Bat Ami nods her head in agreement, "That's true! That's true."

The intense moment is over. I pick up yet another of the pictures, show it to Guy, and ask him whether he knows the picture of two very young bedraggled boys. Guy has never seen it before.

I point at one of them and say to Guy, "This was my brother who died just a few years ago. And this is me."

It's one of the pictures that are very dear to my heart (**Photo 5**). It's a picture of the two of us, me four years old, Irving two years old from 1946 when we were going to a displaced person's camp in Austria. Both of us are dressed in dark, heavy winter coats complete with mittens and white scarves around our necks. Both of us wear heavy shoes. Our pants are too short, not really reaching the tops of our shoes. I have a grey hooligan-style wool hat on. I'm looking straight at the camera and smiling. Irving has a grey stretch cotton beanie type hat on that covers his whole head and stretches down covering his ears and tying under his neck. Strands of hair peek out in front from it. He has a forlorn expression on his face. He's never had much reason to be happy in his short life. We're standing close to each other. From the picture, though, you can tell right away that we're close. Brothers.

Bat Ami remembers when Irving was in Israel and visited them, and her memories come back to her. "He was just nineteen years old and on a short leave from the Army. He'd been stationed in Germany and took a little time off with one of his army friends to hop over and visit Israel in 1964." Bat Ami remembers him smiling. "Very very nice guy. He was here a couple days. Aharon and I picked him up when he was here, and we went to Tel Aviv with him, to clubs, dancing, and singing and had fun together."

She has such a warm and happy expression in her eyes and on her face remembering those good times. I had never heard that story. Reflecting wistfully on my brother's life I say, "That's wonderful!"

Ever since Irving's death, I've been sad about what a hard life he'd been dealt, but I'm cheered that at this part of his life he'd found some joy.

Throughout that whole day, throughout all those discussions, Guy has stayed with us, engaged a great deal of time. Sometimes he bolstered Bat Ami by helping with translating; sometimes he added bits of knowledge that he, himself, knew of. Sometimes he just walked around the tight group, listening, watching.

As I look back on that day, on that sharing of minds, of memories, of stories, of disagreement, of sharing difficult emotions, of coming together, it was also a time of handing all of that from our generation, of my generation and Bat Ami's generation to the generation of grandchildren, to make sure that those memories and stories would be preserved and shared further down the chain of generations.

I turn over the picture we've been looking at. "There's writing on the back of this. Is it Hebrew?"

Bat Ami says it is Yiddish. "Mendel sent this to Shoshana. It reads, 'These are our children, Yisrolek and Ephrayim (Irving and Fred), dear sister and brother in-law.'"

I explain what I know of the origins of this picture. "I was born in Azerbaijan, Irving in Crimea. Crimea is in Ukraine now and so much in the news."

Bat Ami knows that story, that history, from other writings of mine that she's read. Bat Ami looks again at me, puts her arm on her forehead and says, "I just thought again what you said. If my mother had gone back home, she wouldn't have survived."

And both Bat Ami and I share the pain of that memory, of how close to more tragedy those two were and the realization of how much history could have changed. None of Bat Ami's family would exist and I wouldn't be sitting at their table sharing memories with them. Sadness, near tears, is close to overwhelming us at that thought.

"She was very strong you know," she says. "When she came to Israel, there was only rock, hardly anything." And memories of her youth flood out.

With that, with a very long day, we left and went back to Tel Aviv. Tomorrow, our goal was to visit my cousin Ephrayim and his wonderful wife Tamar, see what pictures he had of his mother's early times, ask the same questions and see what answers and understanding would come from them.

The Interview – Ephrayim

Rhoda and I get up early and take a taxi to Ephrayim and Tamar's apartment.

We start at the table, Ephrayim and I, with Tamar watching. As I did for Bat Ami, I had prepared a book printing out all Ephrayim's ancestry information, a graphic of his descendants and dates, a graphic of ancestors going back generations, and printouts of all the documents that I'd found connected to him, something for him to keep, something for him to pass on to the next generations so nothing would be lost in the stream of time.

We started by working on the family history book I put together for Ephrayim and gave to him. Going over the lineage of the genealogy, Ephrayim is very excited to trace this with me and translates constantly to Tamar.

He asks me where all the information came from, and I told him about how I accumulated everything, our trip to Poland, the translations from the Mormon family history library, and the transfer of dollars to zlotys in Poland to pay for more record copying. I told him the book I prepared was for him, his children, and grandchildren. He was very moved.

As we talk, the stories start to come out. He tells me how his mother, Shoshana, had sent my father a box of cigarettes from Israel to the displaced persons camp in Austria to give him something to sell. I knew the story of my father selling cigarettes. I hadn't remembered they came from Shoshana. He told me that my father wanted to come to Israel. He asked if I knew. Yes, I knew. He said that Shoshana told him to come to Israel, but Mendel said he couldn't come. Ephrayim wanted to know why not. I was surprised to have to explain that it was because he could find no way to come in 1947 because the British had an embargo on immigrating to Israel.

I showed him the galleries of pictures I put on my Smugmug internet photo site and showed him the picture of my father in 1947 in the Wels displaced persons camp where he sold the cigarettes he received.

Ephrayim asks me, "What does your son think of all this. Does he think you're crazy to do this?"

"No, he thinks it's interesting. He doesn't have time for things like this. It's the same problem with all our children. They're busy. Jobs. Work. No time for things like this."

Ephrayim nods his head in understanding.

The conversation turns momentarily to grandchildren when Tamar brings her phone over to show off one of her granddaughters. We pull out our phone and show pictures of Ellie. Ephrayim looks at mine; I look at his. Two old grandfather farts exchanging their pride. Wonderful!

He interrupts, "You know, Shoshana wrote a letter from Israel to Chinka in 1938? It says: 'Take your children and come to Israel.'"

It took me by surprise. Just one year before disaster struck. If only Chinka had taken her family and come. How much family history would have been changed.

"Did she get an answer?"

"No."

Sadly, we continue, "Now let's look at your pictures."

Ephrayim shows me copies of all the passport cards my father sent him from the Holocaust Museum in Washington. Father gave those to all of us also. He shows me more pictures, but they're new pictures of his kids and grandchildren.

"Do you have any old pictures from Poland?"

"No."

"You have no others?"

"No, maybe in another box."

"How big is the box?"

"Big."

Disappointed! He hasn't gone through it at all. We go through the stack of pictures he pulled together. He pulls out a stamp-sized picture with writing on the back from Poland. I scan it. Also, another one and another one with me and Irving on a hill with Yiddish on the back. Writing on the back in Yiddish: "Pictures of my children, Ephrayim and Yisroel from Wels." I have that one also.

I finished looking at his pictures. Tamar serves us a beautiful lunch. She knows I'm still sick and is doing everything she can to help and make me comfortable.

We start again with Ephrayim wanting to know more about Ephrayim Yitzhak Felman, Shoshana and Mendel's father. I was surprised he knew nothing of him from his mother and repeat the story I know so well now.

"Shoshana and Mendel's father was a very ill man who was once attacked brutally by a Polish man. The man had owed taxes on his house and the government had taken it over and sold it on auction to Ephrayim Yitzhak Felman's mother, Ruchele Fischel Bloch (Ephrayim Yitzhak's father was Fiszel Jerychem Felman). Ruchele gave it to her son Ephrayim. The man was very angry, came over to what had been his house that they now occupied, took an iron bar, and hit Ruchele's son Ephrayim in the head with it. Epharayim Yitzhak survived but was never the same and was unable from then on to do much work. That was why Chinka had to work so hard after that. And Ephrayim died young, probably from that injury."

Ephrayim, "I never heard that before. Shoshana never told me about that."

"So that's the background to Shoshana's growing up. She has a father who can't work, who can't help with the store. I don't know what kind of relationship she had with her father. Did Shoshana ever tell you anything about her brother Fischel?"

Ephrayim says, "Fischel was the oldest. He was in the army, an officer, smart. He married. He didn't have children."

"No, he had one. He had a little boy. Guess his name."

"I don't know."

"Guess. His name was Ephrayim Yitzhak, after Fischel's father."

"I don't know. Shoshana never talked about this."

I say to him, "While Shoshana was growing up, the family was too religious for her. Is that what you understand too?"

"Yes."

"Did she know what was happening in the world?"

"Yes," Ephrayim says, "because of the halutzim."

I ask Ephrayim what I really came for, "What stories do you remember about your mother's growing up?"

"Shoshana was living in a religious home. It was too religious for her. From time to time, she'd go to a halutz meeting, a group of men from Israel who'd speak with young people in Poland. She was maybe about 16. The halutz group was in the town of Lodz, not very close to Sokolow. She went by herself. She didn't much want to speak about this time. She never told me about her father or mother or children. I know her mother Chinka was working in the home. Chinka bought grain from the farmer, and she put it in the cellar in the summer. In the winter, she processed it and sold it."

"Do you know how big Solokow was?"

"No. She didn't want to talk about it."

"Did you know that Sokolow had a *Bet Midrash* (house of study)?"

"Yes. She told me that her father sat in the Bet Midrash the whole time and he didn't do anything."

Now Ephrayim and I start to cover some of the same history that I did the day before with Bat Ami. Some of it is identical to what my father had told me, and I summarize. "Fischel went into the army in 1932. He was an officer in the cavalry. He was 21 years old, tall, big, strong. Shoshana was born in 1914, June 16th. When she was 16 years old, she joined the halutz group in 1930. She was with halutz for six years. She was 22 when she went to Israel."

I already know the history of what was transpiring during that time in Europe with Hitler coming to power and the rise of Nazism, the burning of Jewish books, the increasing exclusion of Jews from all forms of public life and professions and more and more restrictions on Jewish life or even travel. From 1934 onwards, illegal immigration to Israel had already started to organize by the halutz movement who could already see the writing on the wall for the fate of the Jews. They increased their efforts to organize the Jewish youth of Europe to immigrate to Palestine, and Shoshana, more and more, joined their meetings and training programs.

While Ephrayim talks, I continue to look for information on the Internet for the history of development of antisemitism during this time and the history that may have influenced Shoshana. It results in long gaps of time while I'm doing this, and Ephrayim is incredibly patient with me.

So, as Ephrayim tells me, the effect on Shoshana is that even if she's 16 years old, she hears all this, and she gets increasingly involved with halutzim. When she's home, instead of being religious, she joins her friends. She goes with them, and then comes home. Shoshana is hearing more and more from the halutzim that Jews should leave Europe. I understand that her parents aren't happy with this. She's probably hearing more about what's going on in Germany than her parents who aren't reading newspapers or hearing from halutzim. By 1934-35 everything that's happening in Germany is being seen in newspapers, and Shoshana hears this from the halutzim. Chinka probably isn't reading newspapers. She's busy working, taking care of the store, and taking care of the children.

Ephrayim continuing, "The halutzim say to Shoshana, 'We're going to take you to Palestine. Fischel knew about that. He would have gone too.'"

Ephrayim again tries to get into the story of how Shoshana ran away from home to Israel. I again say I'm not ready for that.

But I start, "1936 comes and the halutzim convince Shoshana and her friends that now was the time, that they prepared everything for them to leave Poland and go to Palestine."

Ephrayim says, "Maybe she told Fischel or Chinka or both of them."

"Or nobody. Now there are two stories about what happened. One is your story and Bat Ami's story. The second is my father's story. You tell me your story. Then I'll tell you mine."

Ephrayim starts, "Fischel went to find her."

"No, please start earlier with 'one day Shoshana's gone.'"

Ephrayim tells me the same story that Bat Ami told me but with more detail. "She left home. Many times, she'd been gone before. But this time, she doesn't come back and Fischel can't find her. He can't go to the camp where the halutzim might be. He didn't know where it was. He went to the police and told them that this woman took some things from the home, that she was a thief. That he wanted to find her. Then a poster was put together. He had that poster with her picture. And that poster with her picture was posted in different places. The halutzim saw that and said to Shoshana, 'Be careful. The police will find you. You have to leave now.' Shoshana left and went to the train."

"Where? Where did she go? Warsaw, Sokolow?"

Ephrayim, "I don't know. Maybe could be Lodz? That's where a lot of meetings had been. She went to the train station, changed her clothes to men's clothes so she wouldn't be found. Fischel was at the train station. He didn't see her. Shoshana got on the train to leave. When the train closed the doors, Shoshana saw Fischel, took off her disguise, and said 'I'm here and I'm going.' And he couldn't do anything and that was the last time he saw her."

"Ok, that's the story as you know it. The story you told me is the same story that Bat Ami told me. Almost. So, here's what you told me. Shoshana is ready to leave home and to go away to Palestine. She runs away from home. When she runs away, Fischel realizes that she's run away from home, but this time he doesn't think she's coming back. He goes to the police and tells them there's a woman who's run away. 'She's a thief and you have to find her.' The police put out a warrant. The halutzim see the warrant and tell Shoshana she has to leave now. Then Fischel goes to look for her and finds her at the train station. Shoshana already is at the train station. Fischel is outside. The doors to the train close; she's dressed as a boy. When the train starts to leave, she sees Fischel outside the train, takes off her hat so Fischel can recognize her and Shoshana says, 'I'm here. I must leave. I can't come back.'"

"One more question and then I'm going to tell you a different story. My question to you is when did you hear this from your mother? How old were you? Were you five, ten, twenty?"

"I don't know maybe 30. Around 1969."

"How old was Bat Ami?"

"About 21."

"How old was your mother? About 55 years old when she's telling you this? This is important. Here's the other story I heard from two people."

"This story is from my father who told me about this. My father is in Sokolow in 1936. Shoshana runs away from home. This piece is the same. She runs away from home because she's a Zionist and wants to go to Israel. Chinka sees that she's gone and doesn't think she's coming home. She sees she's run away. Chinka sends Mendel to find her, not Fischel. This story is from Mendel to me in 2002. Mendel goes to Warsaw to find her at the train station. My father says to me 'I didn't find her.' My father goes back home and says to Chinka, 'I tried to find her and didn't find her. She's gone.' No story about they accused her of stealing and went to the police. Nothing. What I told you was my father's story to me, and I'm not young when he tells it to me. I remember every word exactly as he told it.

"The second story comes from your mother, Shoshana. She told me 25 years ago. It's when we came with our son, and we're sitting together. We're talking, and I say to Shoshana, 'My father told me the story of how you ran away to come to Palestine. I want to tell you his story.'" And I told her what I just told you. My father said, 'I tried to find her and couldn't find her.' Upon which she said, 'It's not true!'"

Ephrayim, astounded, echoes, "It's not true!"

"She said, 'Yes, it's true that I ran away from home. Yes, it's true that I went to the train station. Yes, it's true that Mendel went to find me. No, it's not true that he didn't find me!' She says to me, 'He found me at the train!' She said to my father, 'I'm not coming back.'" (I'm again very emotional with this and start to cry; Ephrayim also is emotional with this.) "She says, 'I have to go. I'm going to Palestine. I can't come back home. He left and went home.' She didn't see him again until after the war when he came to Israel. She told me this story. Shoshana said nothing about Fischel. She said nothing about the police or about being accused of stealing. My father in his story never said anything different. Even when he was running from the Germans, he was writing to his sister. And when he was finally in the United States, he wrote letters to your mother."

Ephrayim, emotionally, "Now I know that your father tried to find my mother. He told Chinka he didn't find her. Why?"

"He didn't want Chinka to know he found her and that she didn't want to come home."

Ephrayim confused, "The second time he found her."

"There was no second time." And I repeat the story.

Ephrayim is still confused. "We know in our story it was Fischel who found her."

"I never heard any story from my father about Fischel and Shoshana. I heard the story about Fischel the first time from you, Bat Ami and Aharon."

"Maybe my mother didn't want to speak about your father, because I don't know how the two stories can be so different."

"It's possible both stories are true. Rhoda came up with this. One possibility is that there was a train in Sokolow. I saw the train and the tracks in Sokolow. The train doesn't run anymore now, and the tracks run north and south. I can show you pictures. It's possible that Shoshana ran away from home and Fischel went to look for her in Sokolow and didn't find her. And Chinka said to Mendel, 'You have to go find her,' and Mendel went to Warsaw and he found her. Two people, Mendel and Shoshana, tell me that Mendel went to look for her."

Ephrayim, "Why did she change the name from the brother that went to find her? Why?"

"Maybe she told you the story of when Fischel looked for her in Sokolow and she didn't tell you the story of when Mendel looked for her in Warsaw. In Warsaw, she was leaving the country. I believe Mendel's story that he went to find her. I believe Shoshana's story that he found her. Now there's something very important."

Ephrayim, "What is important?"

It's so hard for me to say this. "What's important is if Mendel had convinced her to come home, she would not have been a survivor. There would be no Shoshana, no Ephrayim, no Bat Ami."

And with that, both Ephrayim and I break down, grab each other and hug, and both cry.

I want to continue and see what else I can learn. "So, I want to know more about Shoshana's early life in Palestine. In 1936, Shoshana leaves Poland. How did she come to Palestine?"

Ephrayim didn't know. "The ship arrived in Haifa."

"When the ship arrived in Haifa, where did she go?"

Ephrayim didn't know.

Asked what was life like there.

He didn't know.

Ephrayim, "She was working with the men. She was at the train station working to make money on the railroad tracks to keep them working."

I'm amazed at this, something I hadn't heard from Bat Ami or Aharon. "Funny, that was my father's job. Just like this." I tell Ephrayim what his work life was like, leaving during the week, working on a machine during the day summer and winter, being called from home to work at night to shovel snow.

"His life wasn't easy."

"Indeed, his life was never easy."

Rhoda interjects, "I have a question about Shoshana arriving in Palestine. I heard a story from Bat Ami that Rachmil was a *yeshiva bücher* (religious student) who sometime stayed at Chinka's house while she was growing up. After Rachmil immigrated to Palestine, he corresponded back with Rojza. When Shoshana arrived in Palestine, he met her when she arrived."

Ephrayim says, "Yes. He met her when she arrived in Haifa. She still remembered him as the pious religious student he was in Poland. She wasn't interested in a romantic relationship with Rachmil after she arrived in Israel. But he had changed a lot. He was working outdoors. He was bronzed. Rachmil arrived in Palestine in 1933. Shoshana arrived three years later. She wasn't much interested in Rachmil, but they got to know each other and fell in love."

Rachmil in Poland was religious, even while working in a tailor shop.

Ephrayim relates a story he heard from his parents about an experience of Rachmil's in Poland. "Not long before leaving Poland, he saw once a German beating a Jew. Rachmil was a young man. He couldn't stand by. He took a piece of wood and hit the German to keep him from attacking the Jew. The people from the community said to Rachmil, 'They're going to find and capture you. You have to go to Palestine now.' He ran away from Poland, came to the Port of Trieste, in Italy where he took a ship with 300 other Jews and many Arabs and Germans. The captain was a German. When they were underway on the sea, one of the Germans went to the Arabs and said to them, 'These Jews want to take your place in Palestine. They're going to take everything away from you.' The German was stirring up trouble, and there was fear that a riot or worse would start. The Jews went to the captain and said to him, 'You have to do something. We fear for our lives. If you don't, we'll have to take things into our own hands, and we'll throw this German and the Arabs into the sea.' The captain realized the danger they were all in, and he put the German and the Arabs into the brig until they reached Haifa."

While I've been surprised that there were many things that Eprayim didn't know about his parents' lives, I now can see that many of their stories were passed on to him.

"So, you got a lot from your father, but your mother didn't tell you about any of this."

"No, this was only late in his life."

"I want to know more about Rachmil's early life in Palestine."

Ephrayim finally opens up, starting to talk about his parents and what life was like in Israel during treacherous times while he's growing up.

Back in Palestine in 1936, Shoshana arrives in Haifa, and it is Rachmil who's waiting for her. He helps her adjust to her new surroundings and, with time, they get close. The first place they work is in Kibbutz Rachel. At that time, Rachmil is working at the north at the Dead Sea in a factory that made tires. It was near Jericho. He was working at the same time with Arabs. They worked side by side. He became very tanned from the sun. Shoshana and Rachmil fall in love and marry in Jerusalem on November 15th, 1937.

Ephrayim is the first-born, born on the first of September in 1939. More memories now surface from those early times as he relates them to me. Ephrayim recalls increasingly underlying tensions growing with the British who controlled the country as well as more battles with Arabs. Rachmil joins the Haganah (the Jewish paramilitary organization in the British Mandate of Palestine 1921–48, which became the core of the Israel Defense Forces (IDF) about 1942-43. The British drastically try to control weapons and fighting. The British come to know that Rachmil is in Haganah and they go searching for guns. Rachmil and Shoshana live in a small apartment. Rachmil is gone when the British soldiers come looking for guns. One soldier suspects that guns were hidden in a quilt and takes his knife to cut open the quilt. Shoshana tries to stop him and puts her hand in the way and is stabbed, bleeding badly. Ephrayim at age four (1943) cries bitterly, afraid his mother is going to die.

This was around 1945, the time of a major attack on Etzel, the radio station in Jerusalem. It was a tumultuous time for the family. Aharon was born in 1944, Bat Ami in 1947. Rachmil left Jerusalem in 1946 for Tel Aviv; he went to work in construction.

Ephrayim talks about increasing terrorist activity between Arabs and Jews in 1947-1948. At one time a British officer came to the house looking for Rachmil because he was in the Haganah. Rachmil had a gun with him. Rachmil climbed a ladder to hide in the attic of the roof. The officer couldn't find him. This was right before Bat Ami was born.

We now get to 1948. Ephrayim is nine, Aharon is four, and Bat Ami is one year old. The war starts.

"What do you remember?"

"We're at home. We hear the UN vote for Israel, and everyone went to the street to dance and celebrate, but it doesn't take long for war to start."

I look at Ephrayim and tell him, "You gave me a lot. You're the only one who could do this, not Bat Ami, not Aharon. I scanned a lot of pictures for Aharon and Lea, last October. But no stories. Aharon promised to come to my house to tell me the stories. Not yet though. I scanned a lot of pictures from Bat Ami, but no stories yet. I still have to do that. From you I got stories, that's what I need."

The Second Interview with Bat Ami

It doesn't take long when we visit with Bat Ami again that Guy returns to hear more. He wants to know what Ephrayim told us about Shoshana leaving Poland. We tell him what we said back to Ephrayim.

"What Ephrayim said was exactly what Bat Ami told me. I could see Ephrayim's face while he told me the story. I could see his face and he's thinking, 'What can I do with the difference in this story?' I've reached my own conclusion. In both your stories, it's Fischel who looks for Shoshana, not my father."

Bat Ami, "Yes, Aharon says the same thing. It can't be Mendel because he was so young. Aharon said that is was not Mendel, but Fischel."

"How many years was there between both?" I summarize what I already know about their ages. "Fischel was six years older than Mendel; Fischel was born in 1911; Mendel was born in 1917; Shoshana in 1914. So, in 1936, Fischel was 25, Mendel was 19, and Shoshana was 22."

Bat Ami, "So it makes sense that it's Fischel. He's the oldest."

"We're talking about 1936. Fischel was 25 and Mendel was 19. Mendel's old enough to be sent to find his sister!"

Bat Ami, "Why did my mother say she sent Fischel?"

"But you were young, and it was long after all of this happened. The biggest difference in all of this is, I talked to your mother! I will accept everything if you can explain what your mother said to me. You know she gave me the same picture you have of Fischel and his wife? You were right there. Some of my father's pictures came from Shoshana. My father said, 'My mother sent me to look for Shoshana and to bring her home. I came back home and told Chinka I couldn't find her, and she's gone.' I told this story to Shoshana and she could have said, 'This is wrong. It wasn't Mendel.' Instead she said, 'Your father told you wrong. He found me, and I told him I couldn't go back!' She could have said, 'Your father told you wrong. It wasn't him; it was Fischel.' If you explain what your mother said to me, then I'll believe the rest of the story you have."

Guy is present during all this, listening intently.

Bat Ami says, "So why did she tell me and Ephrayim the story we have? Why did she need to tell me a story?"

"How many stories did she tell you?"

Bat Ami, "Not many."

Closing the Thread

"I think that's part of it. She didn't tell you all the stories, because it was a very confusing time. Here's what I believe really happened. Rhoda came up with this resolution. "That time in 1936 was very complicated. Shoshana was 22 years old. She started going to halutzim meetings when she was 16, six years before. What Ephrayim told me was that she lived in a very religious home, that she was not happy at home, and she didn't want to be involved so much in religion. I also know that things weren't good for Jews at the time. There were many restrictions on Jews; Germany was getting worse and worse for them. Chinka was busy with her life. She didn't have time to see what was going on in the world outside of Sokolow. But Shoshana was involved in things. The halutzim were involved in bringing young Jews to Palestine. Shoshana was one of those. At halutzim meetings, they talked about the Herzl idea, about why she shouldn't stay and why she should leave for Israel. It's a big decision to leave your family, to leave all behind though."

Bat Ami, "But how did she know what was going on, that things weren't going to be good for Jews in Europe?"

"Exactly, that's what she heard at the halutzim meetings. There's a word for this. The word is indoctrination."

Bat Ami doesn't understand what I mean. Guy comes back in, and I try to explain what the word indoctrination means. "On one side of the word is 'teaching.' On the other side of the word is 'brain washing.' Indoctrination is in the middle. Indoctrination is to teach and convince. The purpose of the halutzim in Poland was to bring young Jews to Palestine. They believed that ultimately things would be bad in Europe. Their purpose was to convince young people to believe, that they had to leave their parents, their homes, and go to Israel to start a new life there even under very hard conditions. And the halutzim knew that very bad things were already happening in Europe! That's the core of the halutzim. There were millions of Jews in Poland. They wanted them to survive, to be pioneers."

I turn to Guy, who has been listening intently to all of this and ask, "Guy, how old are you?"

He's taken aback by the question. "Sixteen."

"Let's try this. Let's say that you're living a nice life in Israel and things are good. They're perfect. It's safe. Your mother and father are taking care of you. No problems anywhere. A stranger comes to you, let's say from China, for example, and says to you. 'You need to leave this place. Things are going to be very bad here. You need to leave your mother and father. You need to come to us. You need to farm. There will be mosquitoes, malaria. It won't be easy, but you need to leave now.' Then you start to read newspapers and you see that in states around you, things are getting bad, very bad. Things are bad for Jews. And your mother and father say to you, 'Stay. Things have been bad for Jews before. There were wars. We survived. Stay.' Who do you believe? What do you do? You have to decide to leave everything. What do you do?"

Guy looks me straight in the face and announces with no hesitation, "I would stay here and die!"

We're all greatly shocked.

In the midst of the stories of the past, of the difficulties of deciding to stay or to leave, there comes to a stunning realization. Even today, the decision to stay or go could be tragic. Along with the stories of Bat Ami's memory and Ephrayim's memory comes the distressing conclusion that even the great grandchildren could come to such an impasse. From the past to the present, the cycle of despair repeats itself!

Bat Ami talks to him in Hebrew.

He repeats what he said.

She's shocked and says, "Then my mother was very clever."

I counter, "No, that's the wrong word. Yes, she was clever, but that's not the word for this. The word is 'brave.'" And I show them the Hebrew word for brave off the Internet.

They agree, "Yes, she was brave."

And Bat Ami says with a sorrowful smile and a quiver in her voice, "Yes, she was brave. Otherwise, she would..."

Answers

"OK, and now before I leave, yes, she was brave, but Shoshana left at a time of relative peace. When my mother and father left in 1939, especially when my mother left, she already saw German soldiers in the street tearing hair out of beards of Jews and worse, and Chinka said to my father the same thing she told Shoshana, 'Mendel don't go. The Germans were in Sokolow before. Where will you go? Where will you live, what will you eat? Don't go.' So Chinka, the mother of Shoshana and Mendel, said the same thing to both of them, once in 1936, again in 1939, 'We've been here for generations. We survived. How bad can it be? Stay.' And if he'd listened and stayed and not left, just as it was with Shoshana and with him, none of my family would have survived.

"My mother and father, my brothers and sister, me. None of us would have survived. We've walked around the big question, though. What really happened on that day? I want to tell you what I believe. Shoshana left many times from home. She'd go for a day, a month, but she'd come home. Now she's 22 years old and the halutzim show her newspapers where she sees what's happening to Jews in Germany, where they're taking away citizenship and arresting them and more. She sees what's she's been told, and she believes. And this time she leaves, and she doesn't come back home. Separately, to add encouragement to leaving, she's been getting letters from Rachmil that says she should come to Israel. Now this time when she leaves the house in Sokolow, she's not coming back. She's not taking a big suitcase. She doesn't say goodbye to Chinka, to Fischel or to Mendel. All of them would have tried to stop her. So, she leaves. Fischel finds out she's gone. Fischel goes to look for her.

"Sokolow has a train station. We were there not so long ago. We saw the tracks. The tracks don't go to Warsaw! They go north and south. South to a town called Siedlce. North the tracks go to Treblinka! I confirmed as well that in 1936 the tracks didn't go to Warsaw. My belief is that she went to the Sokolow train station and went south to Siedlce, which is a big city, and from Siedlce there's a big train line and from there she could go to Warsaw. My belief is that Fischel saw her in the train station in Sokolow."

Bat Ami listens intently, her hands holding up her face, listening, listening.

"From that point, I take your story. Fischel found that Rojza had gone; he went to the police, told them, 'You have to help me find her, she's gone.' (Bat Ami smiles and nods her head yes). "He goes to the trains, she takes off her hat, he sees her, the doors are shut, and she leaves."

Bat Ami says, "Yes. Yes."

"Shoshana goes to Siedlce. There's no train or ship from Siedlce to Palestine. She's gone. No way to catch her. But she had to go to Warsaw. There's no place else to go to leave, and I see that from her passport that you showed me. Her mother's still frantic to try to stop her. Chinka sends Mendel, the other brother, to Warsaw to see if he can find her. The two stories together.

"My father never told me about Fischel. So, let's try to continue your story. Fischel comes home and says, 'Well she's gone.' What does Chinka do? Does she say, 'Well I guess that's it. Nothing we can do. Let's clean the store? No. Chinka is strong and stubborn just like Shoshana is – just like we all are. She says to Mendel, 19 years old, to go and find her and bring her home. No use to go to the train station in Sokolow. She's gone. So where would he go?

"In Warsaw she must be leaving the country. Maybe he can catch her there. So, he goes to Warsaw. There we have my story. The important part of the story to know is, she was found! In Fischel's story, he had no choice. The doors were closed. She was gone. In Mendel's story, he found her. He had a chance to change her mind. He could have grabbed her and said, 'You're not going. You're coming back with me, big sister.' But he didn't, and she convinced him she couldn't come back. Mendel, too, was in the halutzim movement. He heard the stories. He wanted to go to Palestine, too."

"Why didn't he? Why didn't he go with her?"

I say sorrowfully, "Because he's 19 years old. His father died. He's helping his mother take care of the store and the children. He couldn't go. She could go, but he couldn't. He had another little brother and a little sister still at home. He couldn't leave them. That was the first time he faced a choice. The second time was in 1939 when the war had already started, when Germans were in the streets, when Frieda, his sweetheart, had been raped and said to him, 'I can't stay, I won't stay, I'm leaving. You decide if you're coming with me.'"

Bat Ami smiles, happily. "I agree. I agree."

"I've been working on my book for three months. In the book, I'm in 1939. I'm almost at that story. That's why I had to come now. To sort out what happened. I heard your story last year from Aharon. I had to decide what to do with this, to decide what to write about this. Now we come to a different question. It's a hard question. Maybe not a friendly question," I say. "Why didn't your mother tell you all these stories while you were growing up?"

Bat Ami ponders. "She didn't want. You know when I asked? When I was 16 years old, like Guy. I said, why didn't you tell me about this, about the Shoah? My mother said, 'Look, I wasn't there. I was in Israel. It was so much later. I forget. It's bad days for me.' In all the years I was growing up, Israelis didn't want to talk about the Shoah. Maybe it was old Jews versus new Jews. The story about old Jews was that they didn't fight. They were victims. In Israel they fought, they developed a new image. The younger generation didn't want to hear the older generation's story."

Guy's again listening intently to this dialogue. He joins in and talks about the Eichmann story. "The trial was on the radio. Every day. 1960-62. It was the trial of the century. It was a closed wound that no one wanted to handle. The government didn't want to handle it. The families themselves kept to themselves. The people, who were not part of the Holocaust and also those who were, neither wanted to hear the stories or to tell the stories. It opened up an old wound. It also opened a discussion. What that trial changed was in the hearing part. They wanted to hear the stories from the Holocaust. Part of Israel still doesn't want to hear it."

Lots of big discussion in Hebrew between Guy and Bat Ami.

"Since then," he says, "Yom Hashoah has a big impact in Israel. Before the trial, you needed witnesses to testify. They collapsed on the stand. Lots of publicity. Newspapers. Radio. The trial was live broadcast. It was a closed wound that no one wanted to handle before this. Israelis that weren't part of the story didn't want to hear about it; those that were part of it didn't want to talk."

I complain though, "Where does this fit in? The question we're discussing is why Shoshana didn't tell Bat Ami and her children more about her stories? One answer that I accept is that in the 1950s she was busy. She was taking care of her children. She was sick. Stories? This was old stuff. She didn't want to deal with this. Now we come to the 60s and later. The Eichman trial. Why didn't she want to talk about her stories?"

Guy, says, "For this, I have to get my grandfather."

"Why do you want Meier to come?"

Guy, "One year ago, in memory of the Holocaust, we met with Shoshi and members of the Sokolow community and went with members of that community to someone's house. When we talked, my grandfather, who has nothing to do with that community, whose father was from Hungary, also didn't talk about the Shoah. We don't know anything from him about that time either. I just wanted to show that it was not something unusual for people to hold back from talking about their stories. Even in school, we didn't study about the Holocaust. After the Eichmann trial we did. You can connect how that was. Now before kids go into the army, they send them to Poland, so they can know what happened. We're being taught in the 8th grade and 11th grade what happened in WWII. It's a difficult thing. And you hear heavy, heavy stories from families."

Guy chokes up telling this, but continues, "You hear things you could never imagine. How people could do this. They teach us about numbers, the numbers don't matter, they teach us about communities" Guy is very emotional here, face contorting, arms flailing, hard to keep from crying at the memory of what he learned.

It's just Guy and me now, and it's about transferring the "stories," the history from my generation to his, jumping three generations, keeping the stories, the knowledge, going.

Guy talks more about what it's like during Yom HaShoah, the documents, the films they're shown. I tell him about a film he's seen called *The Nasty Girl* about a German girl in modern times who wants to know more about what happened during the Holocaust and how the town wants her to stop and how they rebel against her. I tie that into the history of the town of Sokolow Podlaski, where, for generations, there was antisemitism against the town Jews. Always antisemitic. Russia, Poland, whatever.

I say, "Before the war 7,000 Jews in a town of 10,000. WWI happens. WWII. You know all the stuff that happened there. Then we come to 2011. For 20 years I'd been traveling back and forth between the U.S. and Germany. I had responsibilities for research groups in Germany. For over two years, I went at least once a month to Germany. It would have been easy to go to Sokolow. But I never did that. I didn't know what I'd do if I went there. My father would have gone; I didn't speak Polish. I didn't know anyone in the town. I started working with the Holocaust Museum in Washington. They told me about Katarzyna Markusz (Kasia; Guy met her). I started communicating with her. I formed a Sokolow global havurah, and we communicated a lot by email. She isn't Jewish. She's young enough; she wasn't there during the Holocaust. Sokolow is a half hour from Treblinka. The train from Sokolow goes north and south, south to Siedlce, north to Treblinka. Kaisia is a photojournalist. She's interested in what happened there during the Holocaust. There are books written by survivors, Yurzeit Bücher (Memorial books). The books have history, maps, stories and they're all in Yiddish. Kasia got one of these and she recognized some of what the town looked like. She takes pictures of places in the book, goes to places that she recognizes and takes pictures of what is there now and shows comparisons, the changes of time. She has a website with all of this now. The reason I'm telling you this is because the town didn't like what she was doing to bring memories back. Kasia decided to have a memorial service for the day that the ghetto was emptied, and the Jews shot or sent to Treblinka. Can you imagine, here's one girl in this town that's going to do this? So, we decided we had to go. The point is things changed! Now some people want to know. In that town, the children are being taught what happened in that town, which used to be Jewish, now Jewless. And Kasia is teaching the kids just what happened in the Holocaust in their town, where they had nothing to do with it and where some of their grandparents may have been involved. This is a very long detour from what we were talking about, which was why Shoshana didn't talk about her past, why others also didn't want to talk about their past. And that was a good learning and discussion. Back to other things. How long did Shoshana communicate with Chinka? Did Shoshana ever say if she got letters back from Chinka?"

Bat Ami, "Yes, she got letters back."

"Do you still have those letters?

"No."

"Where did the pictures you showed me come from?"

"From their home, after they died."

We go back and forth still trying to recover more information from the past, more history, more documentation, more stories to keep. Bat Ami keeps being pressed on how the letters didn't survive. I get nowhere. She's sure the letters are gone. I can't believe that Shoshana wouldn't have kept, wouldn't have preserved those letters. I keep going back and forth with Bat Ami and how they could have gotten lost or discarded. I get nowhere.

I change questions. "Bat Ami, do you know what Chinka wrote Shoshana?"

"No."

"I also heard from all three of you, Aharon, you, Ephrayim, that Shoshana wrote Chinka that she wanted her to come to Palestine."

Bat Ami, "Yes. Yes. But I don't know what she answered."

Shoshana was the only one who apparently could still communicate with Chinka during this terrible time. I really wanted to know what was being said. "Do you know when she wrote her that she wanted her to come?"

Bat Ami, "Every time."

For years, I'd tried to find out all these things, but nothing ever got told. Now finally, the stories come out. We go back and forth talking about what happened during the early part of the war, with families leaving, some not able to come back, some coming back and being trapped.

While we're doing this, Meier comes back to our table. He's stayed out of our discussion the whole time only listening in now and then., but he comes back now.

"You know, when I listen to all of you, you have a huge problem. You are trying to figure out what happened in the past, 70 years or more ago, trying to figure out what happened with the people. No one knows what happened on that day. Maybe your father didn't tell you everything that happened that day. Your father told you a lot. My father didn't talk about it at all, and all his family died in the Holocaust. He didn't talk about it at all. He didn't want to talk about it. You know part, Bat Ami knows part, but nobody knows all of it."

"I take everything you say. My response to it is that I'm not writing a book about the Holocaust."

Meier, "That's correct. You're writing about the family. But the family also told us something. That's their way of viewing what happened. And Rachmil also had some memories, he told us the same. Each person had a view. It doesn't say that view was correct. In my family, most of them died in the Holocaust. His sisters and brother they came to Israel and parents came to Israel. I'm not involved in this, but I'm listening to this. It's very hard to reach a full story from the parts. Nobody kept letters. After some time, most of the things you want, you'll lose. When you move, pictures, papers get lost."

Bat Ami says, "You know my mother had a book from Sokolow."

I can't believe what I'm hearing. Could this be another find, a treasure, completely unexpected? Excited I ask, "You have it!?"

"It was written in Yiddish. It was annotated on the side."

I'm afraid to ask, "Where is the book?"

Bat Ami, "I can't find it. I put it someplace. I can't find it. Why did you decide you wanted to write this book? How did you decide how you were going to do it?"

"I didn't want to write it as another book about the Holocaust. What I saw in collecting and saving all the stories for future generations was that it was a book about hope, about making difficult decisions and hoping that a better world could still come, a book about taking chances and living as though they could survive to a better place and a better time. I have a lot of research. I have a lot of genealogy. Some of it is about before the war, during the war. The thread of it all is family. And I know a lot about my family. Like you say, they're images of my family. Pieces, fragments of my family. Some are from your mother. But it's not going to be about the Holocaust. It's going to be about survival and hope, and that doesn't matter if I have every detail."

There's universal agreement to this from everybody here.

Meir says, "And not just about survival, it's like the story of the Phoenix. It's like the bird coming from the ashes. It's about rebirth. It's about not just those who survived, it's about the kids and grandkids that come next."

Bat Ami says, "My mother was victorious. With her way, she won. She had kids, she had grandchildren."

"That's what the book is about. So, one question. Who's my book for? Who's the audience?"

Meier, "The family. The Sokolow Podlaski group."

"No. I intend to publish it. I intend for it to have wider interest."

Meier, "Really? I don't think someone outside of the Sokolow Podlaski group will have interest."

"My book shouldn't be of interest to just people from Sokolow or even only to Jews. Just look at the world today. There are millions of people homeless and displaced today, suffering like many of those we know about during WWII. They have the same kinds of trauma and miseries and hopes."

Meier, "But they won't be interested in what happened to the Jews from Sokolow Podlaski."

I laugh, "Depends on how good a writer I am."

Meier, also laughing, "I hope you'll be great, and your book will be great and read all over the world."

I can't stop now. "What you've seen is the research, the pieces, the genealogy. Those are the threads. What is the challenge is putting them together into something that's a picture and understandable! Not just about the genealogy and the family that I have, or besides them, the Sokolow community or anyone from the war. The challenge is why anyone should care. I may fail at that. I don't know. What I have now are pieces. I don't know yet how I'm going to pull things together. So, I'm working on the threads. So, in the meantime, I have to capture all the pieces, all the stories, all of the threads that I can and see what that tells me and how I can represent that. Then I become a weaver!"

Bat Ami interrupts, "What does your son David know about this?"

"He knows a lot."

Bat Ami, "From where? From you? From the school?"

Rhoda, "No, nothing from the school."

Bat Ami, "He knows because he has Fred for a father."

I laugh.

She says, "I ask Aharon's kids."

Meier says, "How about Boris's kids. What do they know?"

Rhoda and I answer simultaneously, "His kids know a lot."

I say, "Boris is like me."

I ask Rhoda, "How would David describe my work, my involvement in this kind of work. If he had one word, what would he say?"

Rhoda says, "Obsessed."

I laugh and say, "Obsessed is the right word."

"What describes David, one word?"

I say, "Busy!"

Meier says, "That's what happens. But I think that when he retires, he'll continue to do something like this."

Meier now is so actively involved. "Everyone is busy. When I was working, I was busy! I didn't care about anything." His face is so dramatic, his hands up emphasizing his point, remembering himself. "You don't have the time. You get up in the morning, work. You come home and think about what you're going to do tomorrow on your projects. You don't have the time. David has a job, he travels, and he has a wife. His wife is pregnant. He can't think about any of these Feldman project histories. He doesn't have the time."

I say, "I agree. David, do you hear this? But I want to tell you a story. We're living in Illinois. David is around 12. Rhoda and I are busy, working. He says, 'I don't want to be like the two of you. I want an easier life. I want to be well rounded. I want to be like Boris.' He sees that Boris has a nice office, toys all around, and seems easy. 'I don't want to work all the time. I want a well-rounded life.' He didn't understand how hard Boris works."

Meier is laughing.

"Look at David now. Now he's 38. Now what you see is he pulls all-nighters. He works intently. He's involved deeply in his topics. He's not the well rounded he talked about at all. He never understood when he was young. Now he understands. But he is a wonderful father."

Meier agrees. "That's the way when you're young. When you grow up, you understand. There are things you want. You have to work for these. Then when you retire, you begin to think, 'I wasted so much time during work; I didn't make any life.'"

"And sometimes you ask, 'I wish I had asked my mother or father all these questions, and it's too late.' Now I ask again, 'Who did I write this for? Maybe for my son's grandchildren."

Meier, "It's for you. You want to do this."

Bat Ami says, "Not all children are the same. Guy has always wanted to know this. He's always gone with us to the Holocaust memorial."

Guy comes forward, and I ask him, "Why are you interested in this, Guy? Why have you been here with us for two days listening and participating in this? Why are you interested or why aren't you interested?"

Guy, hems and haws, a little embarrassed to be drawn directly into this, says, "There's a phrase that says, 'You should know your past before you know your future.'"

Bat Ami is surprised and pleased. "This is the first time you've told me this."

I say, "Those who fail to learn from history are condemned to repeat it.'"

I summarize the chronology of what I know to Bat Ami:

Sept 7th, 1939 - German airplanes bomb Sokolow.

3rd week of September - Germans leave; Russians come Sept 27th.

October 1939 - Germans return; severe abuse of the Jews ensues.

November 1939 - Germans take property away from the Jews. Chinka's store must have been taken away.

End of November 1939 - Germans form Judenrat in Sokolow.

End of November 1939 - Germans start a ghetto in Sokolow, but open.

Beginning 1940 - Chinka probably had to leave her building.

June 1940 - Jewish cemetery taken apart.

August 1940 - Took the two ghettos and made them one.

August 1940 - Built walls and barbed wire/broken glass around ghetto; Jews couldn't leave anymore.

September 1941 - 5,000 Jews in the ghetto.

November 1941 - Jews from other towns moved to the Sokolow ghetto; some taken out as forced labor; matzevoth taken from cemetery to make streets; cemeteries destroyed.

1941 - Typhus in ghetto. If Jews leave ghetto, they were shot.

June 1942 - Jews from Sokolow ghetto taken by train to help build Treblinka. None ever came home.

December 1942 - Jews in Sokolow ghetto started to worry if all going to Treblinka. Started making hiding places in houses.

August 1942 - Posters in town: no Jews can travel; some have to give their children to Christians.

September 22nd, 1942 - Yom Kippur. Germans and Ukranians and some Polish brought together to empty ghetto. Moved Jews out of ghetto and if didn't want to go, shot them. Moved the Jews to a train to Treblinka where they were killed immediately. 4,000-5,000 Jews taken to train. About 2,000 refused to come out. Many hid. 1,500-2,000 found and shot. 100-120 Jews picked and made to clean up. When they finished and everyone else gone, made to dig a hole and shot there.

Bat Ami asks, "What happened to the family?"

"Until this last year, I always thought that Chinka was on a train to Treblinka and died there. Kasia sent me a document last year that there was a court proceeding and a testimony that said she was one of the ones that was shot there."

Even with the last thread resolved, the story of what happened to Bat Ami's mother, they can't stop asking questions about what happened to the family after her mother left. The stories keep rolling.

Guy is so involved in the story of the family and what happened to them, that he couldn't help but ask, "What happened to Fischel?"

"Fischel started in the Polish army before the war. Later he was captured by the Germans and imprisoned. He was released and sent back to Sokolow and went through all of what I just showed you. He married and had a child. Sorrowfully, they all died in Treblinka. The documentation of what happened in the town comes from a friend of mine who is an archivist at the Holocaust Museum in Washington. I found the reference to this document from another source and asked her for this. She sent me this document a month ago. It's where I got all the details. I didn't know about this until then."

Bat Ami is still bothered why Mendel even went back to Sokolow later. "After the war, your father went to Sokolow? Why?"

"Because he didn't want to stay in Russia, and he wanted to find his family. He knew from a letter he got from Shoshana in 1940 where she said Chinka was put into a ghetto in Sokolow. Somehow, she knew that in 1940. My father's memory was totally sharp until the day he died, sharper than mine. Everything he related, he knew precisely the dates and days when things happened. I always wondered was he right? When I took the information he'd given me on the family to Poland, everything I checked at the archives was exactly right."

Since Bat Ami still wanted to know about Mendel returning to Sokolow after the war and what he found, I bring her full circle into everything I now know about our history.

"When the war finished, we returned to Poland in 1946. Jews who survived went to refugee collection centers. My parents returned to southwestern Poland to Kamienna Góra where my mother was miraculously reconnected with her sister. My father didn't know what happened to his mother, his brothers, his sister. He goes to Sokolow and finds out there aren't any Jews. He sees a big hole in the ground. He sees some Polish people who say to him, 'Mendel it's a shame you weren't killed also.' He goes back to the refugee collection center, and we're all sent on to DP camps. My father didn't want to stay in Russia or Poland. He wanted to go to Israel but couldn't get there in 1946."

"So that's why he went back to Sokolow. That's the question you asked me."

"A question I still have, that I've never been able to answer, is that my father last saw his sister in 1936. What happened when he finally saw his sister again 32 long years later when they went to Israel on a tour? The answers I got from him were: 'It was very hot. We were with a tour group,' etc. I got no answers that satisfied me. I wanted to know, when you don't see your sister for more than 30 years, when you've both survived and finally meet again, what's it like. I ask you, what was it like on your side? I expected emotion. What did you see?"

Bat Ami, "I was there at the airport when they met. They saw each other. My mother hugged him. He hugged her back, close. They didn't speak."

"Maybe they couldn't?"

"Yes, of course. They couldn't speak."

"She could recognize him? After more than 30 years?"

Bat Ami was adamant, "Of course she recognized him. He recognized her. Of course."

I'm almost crying. hearing of their final reunion together. "Then what?"

"Everybody hugged each other. We were all together. All the family was there. I remember. I was only 19 years old. I remember the meeting like it was yesterday. It was so exciting. Every time a letter came from your father, my father, Rachmil, would see it come and would call my mother. 'Shoshana, you have to come. You got a letter from your brother.' They were so excited. Maybe they couldn't speak the right words. Maybe they couldn't speak the right feelings."

I agreed with that, "My father could never express his feelings."

"The meeting was so exciting. And when they came to our home, my mother prepared everything. She didn't know what to do with him. And we found their friend Shayndel and Ruchel (her daughter), the friend they had in Sokolow when they were growing up. But you're writing about that meeting between Mendel and Shoshana. There was a lot of feeling, a lot of tears. From both of them. My mother was always a strong person. She didn't cry. She fought her whole life. But when Mendel came, that was the first time I saw her emotional."

"I never saw my father emotional."

Bat Ami is thinking deeply back to the meeting between her mother and my father and how different her mother seemed to her at that time. Bat Ami again talks about my father's coming to Israel. She can't understand why he didn't stay longer to talk more with Shoshana. She says that Shoshana wrote him that after his tour he should stay with her for a week to spend time with her. She can't understand why the tour was so important to him, and why he wouldn't stay longer.

I try to tell Bat Ami how my father traveled so much during the war in the worst circumstances and how, once he was in the U.S., he didn't travel anymore. He worked. He traveled while he worked, but mostly he wasn't a traveler anymore. I emphasized that she's a modern. I'm a modern, but my father never became a modern. He was a railroad worker who never made much money, and even going to Israel was a major change in his life. His trip to Israel covered a tour and travel. He had no idea and maybe couldn't change his itinerary to stay longer.

He couldn't imagine that he had choices with his travel and by that time, he was weary. Bat Ami and I are world travelers. My father never was. He was a displaced person traveling during the war.

It's been an exhausting and exhilarating experience exploring the threads of times now long gone and the memories that arose from them to generate the stories that lived on. In each family, a fundamental life event spawned ripples that swept across time and generations that would have faded forever without exploration and would have shed all meaning. The key event in Shoshana's life was making the decision to leave her home forever and to strike out not knowing if it led to disaster or to a future and a better place for her. So many today around the world face the same uncertain decision – to stay or to go. For my father, it was also a seismic event. He caught her and might have turned her back, but she convinced him, and deep in his heart, he agreed that she'd made the right decision. How frightful it is for us to know, and for him to realize, that had he succeeded, her future and all her future generations would have ceased. How close they both came to that disaster. They both must have come to know that, and neither wanted their future generations to know how close that came.

But so many other answers bloomed as the wounds of time were gently uncovered. Exactly the bitter dilemma that Shoshana faced did my mother and father face just a short three years later when the shards of war already hit them. They also had to face, "do I stay, or do I go," and again that fateful decision was made that allowed future generations to flourish.

Those who survive share instincts that enable them to ultimately weave a rich future for themselves and their families. They persevere even when the odds say it's hopeless. They never give up but maintain hope that even in the worst circumstances an answer will come, that they will have a home and a future again. And while looking for that path, they continue to live as though there is no doubt that they will find their way.

After so many years, I had shed all the conflicts that had for so long prevented me from searching and seeing what had been given to me by my forebears and populated the treasures of my life. Bits of facts collected over decades, stories found and told and retold, pictures jealously collected and secured, names and faces resurrected, documented, validated, all those gems that coalesced into lives that could be seen and understood and cherished and kept forever.

15

FULL CIRCLE. JUNE 2016

"I had the feeling that I owed the world something."

Less than a year after those interviews so much had changed; so much had stayed the same, as it always has. The world was in shambles. Once again, tens of millions of displaced peoples on the march, seeking shelter from war and chaos, trying to keep their families together, trying to keep their families safe, looking again for a place to call home.

Christine Brinck, war-weary reporter from the German daily, *Der Taggesspiegel* (The Daily Mirror) found Talya Feldman in Berlin. Talya, a Jewish American, recent Yale graduate who, before her commitment to a career in Psychology, devoted herself for a period of a month to help Syrian refugees on Lesbos and Idomeni in Greece. The reporter tried to understand. How? Why did this young, petite blonde find her way to a remote island in the Aegean Sea to help those fleeing from war? Why was this young Jewish woman seeking to help Arab displaced families, families desperate to leave Syria, to find any place to go, fleeing to Turkey where they were hardly wanted, mistreated, threatened, abused, risking at the threat of loss of life to board flimsy overcrowded rubber rafts, to make their way to Lesbos, a tiny island in Greece? What could possibly motivate her?

Talya, you worked with IsraAid in Greece. You aren't an Israeli. How did you decide to work with this specific NGO?

Talya: *I had determined to go to Greece to help refugees. My grandparents were the reason for that. After the Second World War, they lived as refugees in Displaced Persons Camps for years in Austria. I grew up with their stories. They had fled on foot through Europe before they eventually found that they could go to America.*

I didn't only grow up with the stories of their lives, but also those of the people who helped them while they were under way.

Everything I read about the refugee crisis in Greece struck me as being the same as the stories my grandparents told me about. I had the feeling that I owed the world something, that I have so much that I have to be thankful for, and I wanted to help.

Didn't your parents have any worries that it could be dangerous for a Jew to be there among Arab refugees?

Personally, I didn't have any concerns. Naturally I thought about it later, that I could be taking a considerable risk going with an Israeli organization. However, in Lesbos, it had no effect. We wore shirts that showed an Israeli flag and a Star of David. We never had problems with refugees. Occasionally we had problems with other NGO's.

Why?

Usually it was with smaller NGO's and volunteers who said they didn't want to have anything to do with Israel, never refugees, whom we were helping. Effectively, Israel is at war with Syria. There was one family whom I got to know better. I had organized their travel tickets; they had lost everything on the way and had no money. We had drunk tea together, and they said they had never seen an Israeli nor met a Jew, and they hated the Israeli government. They said to me, "This shows us that the government and people can be of all kinds." They were astonished and overjoyed that people throughout the world, Israelis included, wanted to help them.

Certainly, Palestinians and Israelis work together; also, Jews and Moslems. When I was there, it was such a mixture of the world. But the salient feature is that of Palestinians and Israelis working together.

How did you understand each other?

The team members were capable of speaking to almost all Arabs, Jews and Muslims. I could not, however. The psychological support was usually available in Arabic. We had team members who came from Iran who spoke Farsi, which was good for the Afghan refugees. When no one was available to translate, you could communicate well because a surprising number of refugees spoke enough English to translate for each other.

Enough, it means you could get through to them?

Partially, but what made IsraAID so special is that they have Arabic speakers so that they can provide psychological support in Arabic. I didn't do so much psychologic work in Lesbos but was on the beach when the boats arrived and helped there. In Idomeni where I was until the end of April, I myself have built a program.

Was there a difference?

Idomeni was completely different. There was no hope. We held daily a child session that went well enough to speak without the language. The children in Idomeni were terribly traumatized, totally confused and hard to control. The parents were also traumatized and just did not have the strength to take care of the children.

Did you ever feel helpless?

Sure, but in Lesbos I could see every day and experience what I achieved with our work, when you pulled the traumatized people from the boat when it was brought to safety, when supplying them with dry clothes, when you could calm them. In Idomeni I felt totally helpless because the help that the refugees needed of us, we could not give them. The only thing they wanted was the opportunity.

This event still took place before the Turkey-EU deal

Two nights specifically come to me. The last boat that came in before the deal had two deaths on board. They were drowned in the boat. The refugees knew the deal was coming and were desperately trying to get out before the deal so that the boat took about 80 people. Far too many, it was built for 20. The boat quickly filled with water, and the two drowned. Our team was immediately on the beach and in the boat, but for the two nothing more could be done.

The next day, the deal was now in force; the sunset was more beautiful than ever; a boat reached our island. The sea was calm, everything was fine, but the refugees were now like prisoners received from the police. Maybe we spent an hour with the people. I looked after the children and tried to calm them down. We examined the pregnant women, gave them fresh water and felt that we had got to know them well. And when the police came, we had to have the refugees line up like prisoners. Then women and children were taken to the bus and then (to) the registration center, what was tantamount to a prison. All the team of IsraAID, that had received and looked after hundreds of boats and thousands of refugees cried when these people were discharged as prisoners. "Yesterday we lost two people, today I have a feeling that they are all dead," lamented a teammate. Because with the new deal they sit one month in prison and then go back to Turkey. Overnight a sense of hopelessness for all of us was born.

So much had changed; so much had stayed the same.

In 1939 the world was at war again, a second war after the war to end all wars. Hatred spreading throughout the world and tens of millions killed, families displaced, looking for help and hope and never giving up hope that some might help, that someplace safety would be found, that once again they would find a place to call home.

More than 70 years after that war ended, the scourge of war again uproots families, and again many die, and many are displaced. But imbedded in the human spirit is the belief that some might help, someplace would be shelter, someplace again could be home to those displaced and their children.

From Mendel to Fred to David, from Mendel to Boris to Talya and his other children, from Mendel to Charlotte to her children, across generations, a spark was being passed, a belief that there might be a better place, that hope should prevail, that humanity should erase differences and demand that help be given and that the hope for a better day never be dimmed.

Mendel would have been very proud.

16

A SPARK HAS BEEN PASSED

Two years later, I look around me and look at the world. Around me, our son is now married, and we have three granddaughters, Ellie Rose, Sammy/Samantha Brooke, and Zoe Madison.

Ellie Rose also has a Hebrew name, Yael Shoshana. The first name reminds me of my brother Irving, Srul, Yisruelik who died ten lonesome years ago. The middle name Shoshana reminds me of my father's sister who ran away from home in Poland in 1936 before the Holocaust and made her way to Israel. Ellie's five now and just getting ready to go to first grade. She's a beautiful and smart and lively young child, very similar to what my wife Ronnie was like as a young girl.

Samantha also has a Hebrew name, Shuli Yita, named after her mother's father and her mother's fraternal grandmother, a survivor from Auschwitz. Sammy has a beautiful face with eyes that stare right at you and hair that's wild as the wind, as Sammy herself can be. Also, beautiful. Also, smart, and brooking nothing from anyone, even her sister. Sammy is almost three years old but with an awareness far beyond her young age.

And the youngest, just one month old, Zoe Madison, far too young to begin to know the challenges that my generation will leave for her to solve.

Our son David is a wonderful father, far exceeding what I ever was, also always busy, but never too busy for the girls. Even with that, he's an accomplished IT professional in high demand in his job and in his extended network, often being invited to present at conferences, here and abroad. He's everything we could have ever hoped he would be.

Rhoda/Ronnie, and I are both retired, but retired in a good way. Always busy and with not enough hours in the day to get everything accomplished which we've set ourselves to. And me? Since full retirement, checking off every box of what I'd wanted to do for decades, just as I describe in this book. My biggest goal after completing the video-documentary was to write and publish this book.

Looking beyond me at the world today, I'm alternatively filled with both despair and hope. Around the world, I see more conflict than ever. In country after country, the cries of hate burn brighter than before. The multitude of displaced peoples, the millions on the move looking for a place to finally stop and build a home and a future for themselves and their children, are in more distress than before. The tide of refugees from Syria and surrounding lands that finally reached Lesbos in Greece struggling to reach sanctuary in Europe have been stopped and, in many places, incarcerated, and have no place to go next.

The hatreds against the other, the persecution of the migrant, the immigrant, the Arab, the Muslim, the Mexican, the Christian, the Jew continues with voices louder and shriller than before. Once again "leaders" come forth to drive fear and sow chaos and gain political power for their own ends. And even the United States, that bastion of freedom, that last chance for hope for many in the world, has descended into the same maelstrom.

One day, my son called to tell me that his daughters chanced to hear the news on the morning programs while his wife was getting dressed. He heard Sammy ask, "Daddy, why are they taking away the children and the babies from the mommies?"

He heard his wife reply, "Because they're bad!" And he saw the shock on Sammy's face, as she said, "Are they going to kill them!?"

David said urgently, "No, Sammy. It's not the children that are bad. It's the government that's bad." To which he heard Ellie say, "Daddy, I know from listening to Grandpa Fred, from the stories he told me, that it wasn't like that when he and his family came to the United States! How can we make it better?"

From grandfather to child to grandchild, a spark has indeed been passed, a belief that there can be a better place, that no one should give up hope, that humanity erases differences, that it demands that help be given, that the hope for a better day will never be extinguished and that all of us do owe the world something.

In New York harbor a statue still stands with arm stretched resolutely into the sky holding a torch to never be quenched but, in looking closely now, the face looks sadder, and looking even closer, a tear might be seen in one eye. But, above all, one can still see in that countenance, in that determination ... hope!

POSTSCRIPT: "DON'T GO ALL WEEPY ON ME"

"Okay, guys, this is incredible. Don't go all weepy on me," the email said which we got from my brother, Boris, in February 2020.

Somehow, a fifth-grade teacher, Christa Post, from a small town called Cumming, Georgia managed to get in touch with him with astonishing news. The email was titled, "Mr. Feldman I had to reach out to you."

None of us knew anyone in Georgia. How could we be connected in any way to her, but what she wrote us made the hair stand up on the back of our heads.

She wrote, "*Good evening. This is probably going to sound like the craziest email ever, but I felt I had to find and email you. I am a 5th grade teacher in Georgia just north of Atlanta. I teach all subjects, but my favorite is history. We are in the middle of our World War 2 unit, which includes lessons about the Holocaust. I use story identification cards that I obtained from the Holocaust museum in Washington D.C. I pass out a card to each student randomly and have them read the story. Once they have finished taking notes on their story, I pair them up with another student in the room that also just finished. My first year (three years ago) doing this, a pair of my students excitedly came over to me and said they discovered that the cards they had happened to be husband and wife. Those cards belong to Mendel and Frieda Felman. It surprised me that any of the cards were related, and we agreed that it was very amazing.*

The main reason I am emailing you is that every year that I have done this lesson, your parent's cards inexplicably happen to "find" each other in the room. We did the lesson today and one of my girls had your father's card. Two of my boys tried to time it to where they finished at the same time so they could be partners. I split them up (because I wasn't born yesterday) and had one of them pair with my girl. Within two minutes, they came over to me excitedly to report their cards were husband and wife. It is something that is more than coincidence and moves me every year. I sat down at my desk this evening and wondered if I could find more information about them. That is how I found your name and information. My apologies if this email is out of sorts, but I had to tell you how much their story means to my classroom. My students walked to the buses to go home talking about Mr. and Mrs. Felman, and how amazing it was that the cards found each other. Bless your family and I hope that this finds you well."

The immediate responses I saw from our family, spread over the country, included shock and disbelief: "Unbelieveable! Just incredible! Gave me chills! Wow! I am certain that Bubbe and Papa would be kvelling (bursting with pride) at the many grandkids and great-grandkids carrying on their incredible legacy."

But the comment that got to me most came from my sister-in-law Robin, Boris's wife who wrote, "Oh, my goodness. Really did tear up. And coincidentally, I was reading last night about the halachic view (based on Hebrew oral or traditional law) that the bond between spouses is so strong that they continue to connect to each other, even when one has passed away.

I replied to Christa to learn more about this amazing occurrence and she wrote:

"Each year that I use the cards I truly am dumbfounded when your father and mother's cards find each other. I pass out the cards completely randomly with the covers closed and the students are paired (to compare and contrast the stories) randomly, simply based on who finishes their reading notes first. The two students who had their cards were SO excited to know that the tradition continued with them. This morning I was telling the class how I found you and your brother and how Boris had sent the wonderful links. My student who found your mother's card had their names and hometowns memorized. He

knew their story by heart and said he would never forget this. That is all I could ask/hope for."

And this was all that I could ask for. That the memory of them, and others like them, would never be forgotten and that hope could continue for all those who, today, suffer and strive for just a place they can call home and a place where they can raise their children in peace.

ACKNOWLEDGMENTS

There are many to whom I owe gratitude for enabling this book to be published. At the top of the list are my parents, Mendel and Frieda, who unlike many survivors, were always willing to tell me their history and stories without which so much that I know and have been able to write about would have been lost.

My father's memory and attention to details of exact time and space were astonishing even until the time of his passing. It was he that collected and somehow saved precious photographs that I inherited and deposited with the United States Holocaust Memorial Museum (USHMM) to remain testimony forever of what was before his family was engulfed.

There were many who helped me in tracing and documenting my family history and genealogy. The resources of JewishGen.org and JRI-Poland enabled me to search and make connections to tie my family's history together.

I am indebted to my friend Teresa Pollin of the United States Holocaust Memorial Museum who provided me with details of the history of my family's hometown of Sokolow Podlaski.

Likewise, I thank Ania Jaworek of the Polish State Archives in Siedlce, Poland for allowing me access to all the birth, marriage, and death records for Sokolow Podlaski and finding records of my family.

Along the same vein, the help provided to me by Sister Maria Eppich of the Family History Library in Salt Lake City, Utah was invaluable. By locating records and helping make translations she enabled me to greatly expand my family tree and enabled stories to be found and kept for future generations of my family.

The debt that I and others who are connected to the town of Sokolow Podlaski owe to Katarzyna Markusz (Kasia) is beyond payment. Without her, I would never have walked the streets that my parents had and never felt what it was like to have lived there for generations. I would never have seen and recorded the remnants of tombstones that were saved by Marian Pietrzak in his Muzeum-Skansen, the only remaining testaments of their lives. To both, I can only hold my hand on my heart and say *Jenkuye!* It is only Kasia's efforts in researching old Polish court records that I was finally able to learn how my father's mother was murdered on September 22, 1942. Without her, that story would have remained forever a mystery.

I had a great deal of help from my special "genealogy buddies," Judy Jankowski, Bonnie Hoover, Byra (Honey) Warner, and Myrna Millman who all contributed to tying my family linkages together.

A special thank you also goes to Don Halasz for identifying innumerable photographs with his mother Evelyn and to Don's brother Howard Halasz. I owe a lifelong debt to Howard for preserving and converting to digital format the only existing films of my family's first weeks in America that would have been otherwise lost forever. Never in my wildest dreams did I imagine that I could see those.

I'm very grateful to Barbara Hartman and Loretta Kotzin, sisters who travelled with me from our journey in Europe on the ship to America and who shared their own stories of survival and success with me.

To my father's sister's children, Ephrayim Schwarzbard, Aharon Schwarzbard, and Bat Ami Engel (nee Schwarzbard) who shared their mother's history with me along with precious saved documents and stories, I am especially grateful. They helped me solve the story that had been a mystery for over 75 years.

I spent a great deal of time with my dear friend and relative Dory Goldberg, a Holocaust survivor who shared her story with me of her parents who also originated from the town of Sokolow Podlaski but were trapped later in Paris and perished in Auschwitz. The photographs and history she saved and shared with me preserve the invaluable story of her own family.

My father's boyhood friend, Hyman Kawer, who also escaped Poland before the war but was found later in America provided a valuable direct link to that past. Finding him again with his son Aaron just a year before he died, Hyman gave me his photographs of life before the war that I was able to preserve forever at the USHMM.

Judy Faust of "Connect Your Stories Video Productions" provided invaluable help and guidance in my producing a family video-documentary, "From Generation to Generation". Her vision converted what would have been just an interview to a work of art and helped lay the foundations for writing this book.

Many helped in previewing and editing my drafts as I wrote the book. Sheldon Kotzin provided valuable insights into making this a book for wide-spread interest rather than just a book for family. Larry and Sherry Cann provided comprehensive and insightful comments on my final draft, and my wife Rhoda, read every draft and provided valuable inputs into making my manuscript readable.

Special thanks go to my brother Boris who believed in me and continually encouraged me to write the book. My sister Charlotte provided tremendous guidance in the final editing and even the selection of the book title.

While the research, photographs, and documentation of the book were accumulated over a 50-year timeline, reduction to the format that is now a book was only achieved during the last four years. During that time, I received great encouragement from the Writers Group in Exeter, New Hampshire. Special thanks go to Robin Lent for organizing our group and providing me with invaluable comments that guided me in my writing. Betsy Baker, June Fabre, Lisa Latimer, James J Freiburger, PhD., and Andrea Adams provided great encouragement from my start with the group and are excellent critical writers themselves.

Lastly and of great importance, my editor and publisher, Liesbeth Heenk of Amsterdam Publishers provided tremendous encouragement and insight from the beginning of our relationship. Without her, my manuscript would never have been converted to a book.

PLATES

Photo 1: Mendel and Freyda, Strolling arm-in-arm in Sokolow, 1937.

Photo 2: Yitka Vloss, Elka Rosenstein, and Freyda, 1938

Photo 3: Chinka Felman, Mendel Felman and brothers and sisters, 1935. Felman family portrait in Sokolow Podlaski, Poland circa 1935. **Seated from left:** *Mendel Felman, brother Moishe Velvel, sister Surah Rifka, mother Chinka Schwartzburt Felman, sister Rojza and brother Fischel Felman.*

Photo 4: Havurah (Youth Group) in Sokolow, before WWII, 1938. **Standing in the back row from left:** *David Shiedler, Mendel Felman, Shaindel Pfefferkranz Kneipper (leaning to the right), Yoseph Penzak, Frieda Altman Felman and Pesach Rubinstein.* **Front row from left:** *Avrom Dobszynski, Beryl Kosov, Zelig Leszcz, Aaron Tumer and Itka Wloss.*

Photo 5: Srul and Ephrayim (Irving and Fred), 1946

Photo 6: Steyer DP Camp, 1946

Photo 7: Steyer DP Camp – Camp "Policemen" 1947

Photo 8: Freyda and Mendel, before the war: 1936

Freyda and Mendel, after the war: 1948

*Photo 9: Joe and Anna visit the Wels DP Camp 1947. **Standing, back row from left**: Mendel Feldman, Eli Reich, Fred Feldman, Barbara Lopata, Wolf Lopata **Sitting from left**: Frieda Feldman, Anna Rosenbaum, Joseph Rosenbaum, Ida Altman, Leah Lopata **Front from left**: Loretta Lopata, Irving Feldman*

Photo 10: Bremerhaven. On the Way to a New Land. October 1949.
Left to right: *Irving Feldman, Frieda Feldman, Fred Feldman,*
Mendel Feldman.

Photo II: The New Immigrants. South Bend 1949. **Standing left to right:** *Joseph Rosenbaum, Anna Rosenbaum.* **Sitting left to right:** *Ida Altman, Leah Lopata, Loretta Lopata, Wolf Lopata, Frieda Feldman, Fred Feldman, Irving Feldman, Mendel Feldman.* **Front:** *Barbara Lopata.*

Photo 12: Chaya Altman, children, brother, sisters. Sokolow 1921.
Left to right standing: *Bernard Rosenbaum, Bernice Rosenbaum,
Sarah Rosenbaum.* **Front**: *Leah Lopata, Ida Altman, Frieda
Feldman, nee Altman.*

Photo 13: Mendel and Fred. San Gilgal. Austria 1946

Photo 14: Fischel Felman as a Polish Officer. 1933

*Photo 15: Paris-Dory (Dory Goldberg with her parents). Paris about 1940 **Left to right**: Jenta (Kierchenblatt) Cybulski, daughter Dora (Cybulski) Goldberg, Eli Cybulski*

Photo 16: Barbara Lopata and Fred Feldman. Austria 1948

Photo 17: from left to right: Irving Feldman, Mendel Feldman,
Charlotte Feldman Jacobs, Frieda Feldman, Fred Feldman, Boris
Feldman

Photo 18: **Front row, left to right**: Irving Feldman, Frieda Feldman, Talya Feldman, Ilana Feldman Jacobs, Natalie Feldman, Mendel Feldman, Robin Feldman with Eli Feldman, Rhoda Feldman. **Back row, left to right**: Amanda Feldman, Kimberly Feldman, Dan Feldman, Linda Feldman, Benjamin Jacobs, David Jacobs, Charlotte Feldman Jacobs, Aviva Jacobs, Boris Feldman, David Moses Feldman, Fred Feldman